Serfs, Peasants, and Socialists

Serfs, Peasants, and Socialists

A FORMER SERF VILLAGE IN THE REPUBLIC OF GUINEA

William Derman

WITH THE ASSISTANCE OF

Louise Derman

UNIVERSITY OF CALIFORNIA PRESS

BERKELEY · LOS ANGELES · LONDON

University of California Press
Berkeley and Los Angeles, California
University of California Press, Ltd.
London, England
Copyright © 1973, by
The Regents of the University of California
ISBN: 0-520-01728-5
Library of Congress Catalog Card Number: 78-117148
Printed in the United States of America

To David and Rosalind

2
14 — 43 — 57
3 — 119 — 121
17 — 173 — 192
38 — 192 — 230
15 — 237 — 252

89 | 2

45   4
5

245

Contents

TABLES AND FIGURES

Acknowledgments

To the government of the Republic of Guinea I owe a great debt for accepting me as a representative of the discipline of anthropology and thereby allowing my wife and I to live and study in their country. Anthropologists have not always deserved this trust, which assumes that the only purpose of ethnographic study is to contribute to mankind's knowledge as a whole and not to serve short-term national political interests. In particular I wish to thank Mr. Bounama Sy and Mr. Ray Autra, who served as directors of the National Institute of Research and Documentation of the Republic of Guinea during the time of this study, for their help in setting up and facilitating my work. I hope that my material will be of some use to the National Institute's historical and cultural studies of the people of Guinea. A special word of appreciation is also due Mrs. Fanny Lalande-Isnard, then librarian of the institute who went out of her way to see that a raw scholar learned the complexities of working in the Fouta-Djallon, and made available the resources of the library.

Ultimately, it is the villagers of Hollaande, who permitted my wife and me to live with them, who patiently tolerated our ignorance, and who shared their knowledge, experiences and feeling with us, to whom we owe the most. The friendship they gave us will never be forgotten even if the means of keeping that friendship fades with time.

To Alpha Oumar Diallo and Mamadu Baillo Diallo—friends, interpreters and assistants—I cannot find words to express adequately what they gave in terms of insight, patience, and constant comradeship.

Reverend and Mrs. Harry Watkins, missionaries formerly at Labe, greatly assisted our understanding and learning of Fulfulde by making available their outstanding unpublished work on the language of the Fulbe. They gave generously of their time and hospitality. Their aid will be long and warmly remembered.

For the many favors done and hospitality offered by Mr. and Mrs. Walter Girdner, Naomi Chamberlain, Karen Doering and Henry Norman go many thanks. To Walter, particularly, much appreciation is due for his interest in my work and the considerable pains he took to help make it successful. Special thanks also go to Larry Busch and Bill Reiss for their invaluable support during inevitable times of discouragement.

To my teachers at the University of Michigan, and especially Marshall Sahlins, Elman Service and Eric Wolf, I owe the debt of a student. To Dr. Iwao Ishino I express thanks for helping me see the manuscript through to completion. Professor Jean Suret-Canale was kind enough to critically read the manuscript and made several helpful comments and corrections. Albertha Brown and Jane O'Neill set aside much time from other work and did an excellent job of typing the manuscript.

This book is a joint effort. Louise and I shared the experience of living and working in Guinea. Together we worked out many problems. Louise gathered information about the Fulbe economy, and the Fulbe women and children. Also she edited one version of the manuscript, thus contributing throughout to the study and this book. Therefore, acknowledgment needs to be greater than a dedication.

The study was made possible by a fellowship and research grant from the National Institute of Mental Health and by a dissertation grant from the National Science Foundation.

I ask forgiveness of my Guinean friends and colleagues for my mistakes and errors of interpretation. The responsibility is mine and mine alone. I regard this study as a beginning step toward exploring the rich and significant life of the Fouta-Djallon and the Republic of Guinea.

W.D.

Serfs, Peasants, and Socialists

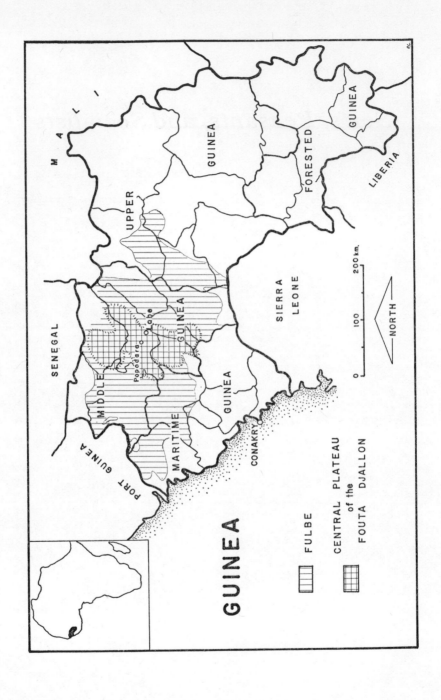

GUINEA

FULBE

CENTRAL PLATEAU
of the
FOUTA DJALLON

One

Introduction

The inhabitants of the Fouta-Djallon in the Republic of Guinea are overwhelmingly Fulfulde speakers. Fulfulde speakers refer to themselves as Fulbe, a usage I shall follow despite the extensive literature that refers to them as Fulani or Peul. The Fulbe of the Fouta-Djallon are linked historically, culturally, and linguistically with the other Fulfulde speakers of West Africa.[1]

Fulbe society in Guinea has undergone a series of profound transformations as a result of French colonial rule and recent independence. The crucial impact of these two periods is evidenced by the fundamental change in the role and position of serfs. The institution of serfdom is now legally abolished. Despite the widespread distribution of hereditarily subordinate populations in precolonial Africa there has been little discussion of the effects of colonial rule on their status. In examining the past relations of former serfs to their Fulbe masters in the Fouta-Djallon, the key economic, social, and ideological institutions of the Fouta-Djallon, and the great changes they have undergone will be discussed. In

---

1. For an introduction to the Fulbe the reader is referred to Stenning (1959), still the most complete summary available of the distribution and characteristics of the Fulbe. Of more recent interest, and unfortunately too late to be incorporated in this study, is M. Dupire's (1970) study of the social organization of several Fulbe groups.

this context, an ethnographic account of contemporary life in Hollaande, a village of former serfs, will be presented.

Before the coming of the French at the turn of the century the Fouta-Djallon was a confederation of provinces under the *almamy* (from the Arabic *imam*) of the Fouta-Djallon. There existed a relatively developed territorial organization based upon an Islamic model, but it did not supersede the kin organization which was based on maximal, major, and minimal patrilineages. Four major social strata cut across the territorial and kin organizations. These were the chiefs and their patrilineal kinsmen, the free Fulbe, the Fulbe of the bush, and the serfs. We might speculate that had the French not intervened, the Fulbe socio-political organization might have evolved toward a pyramidal "feudal" organization with chiefs as lords, the free Fulbe as vassals, the Fulbe of the bush as freemen, and the "serfs" as serfs. However, French colonial rule abruptly halted indigenous trends. The features of colonial rule that undermined serfdom also undermined the position of the other strata and led to the creation of a peasantry.

The political changes induced during the colonial period resulted in the alienation of political power from the underlying population. We need not underestimate the power of political leaders during the precolonial era in order to emphasize the far greater power of the French and their Fulbe representatives, the *chefs de canton*. The legitimacy and the reciprocal nature of chieftainship was ended. The generosity of chiefs toward the population decreased as the exactions demanded from them increased. A clear separation of interests between the developing peasantry and their new colonial overlords was created. As a result all Fulbe and serfs came to view the "state" (the colonial rulers and the *chefs de canton*) as separate and distinct from themselves. Admittedly this is a question of judgment as well as an analysis of the relation of chiefs to other Fulbe during precolonial and colonial times. In the precolonial period the chiefs ruled in conjunction with the elders and religious leaders of the

2

nonchiefly, maximal lineages. In contrast, the French did not seek the consensus, agreement, or support of the Fulbe in the selection of the *chefs de canton,* as the most important criterion for office became loyalty to the French.

Another political consequence of colonial rule was the decline in significance of the maximal patrilineages. The abolition of the chiefs' right to tribute from the Fulbe of the bush led to a decline in the importance of the distinction between them and the free Fulbe. Even the chiefly lineages declined greatly in political importance for during the 1920s the French began selecting the *chefs de canton* and village chiefs from the other nonchiefly maximal patrilineages. Moreover, the separation of all strata from the new French rulers deemphasized earlier distinctions and led to a merging of the strata.

The economic consequences of colonial rule were as great as the political effects. We shall consider the results of the imposition of taxation, the introduction of money and markets, and the competition for the labor of serfs as significant processes leading to the decline of serfdom. The beginning of the end of serfdom appears to have been the breakdown of the reciprocal relations of serfs and master, as serfs had to assume the payment of their own taxes to the French. However, taxation affected all strata of Fulbe society. The new taxes will be viewed as the fund of rent that the new rulers took from the population. Once payment in money became a necessity no strata of society was free from the new demands of the colonial authorities. Because taxation was imposed on all sectors of Fulbe society it had the effect of forcing most of the population, at least in part, into a money economy.

The particular form the economy took was greatly influenced by the ecology of the Fouta-Djallon. The ecology has, at least until the present, mitigated against large-scale cash cropping, inhibited the formation of plantations, and provided no mineral resources of significance. This has meant that there have been no sources

3

of large scale employment within the Fouta. In order to earn money, many Fulbe have had to seek sources of employment outside their natal area. Although small cash-crop gardens were introduced and a few state farms were established by the French, these provided only limited employment opportunities relative to the need for cash. The consequence was that many Fulbe left the Fouta for work on the peanut farms in Senegal, the pineapple and banana growing areas of Guinea, and the cities of Guinea, Senegal, Sierra Leone, and of the Ivory Coast. In short, the dominant commodity the Fouta could supply was labor.

Unlike most other commodities, land did not greatly enter the money sector of the economy. Some land was sold during the colonial era, but in the land-short area around Hollaande—and I suspect this to be true of most areas—the amount sold was small. This was due in part to the inalienability of land from the major patrilineages. Some serfs became landed proprietors by buying land, but the small extent to which land entered the market impeded the merging of the Fulbe-serf strata. The vast majority of serfs did not become land proprietors, and therefore, despite the gradual ending of their labor obligations, significant social and economic differences remain between serfs and Fulbe.

The introduction of taxation, money, and markets, in combination with French political rule, produced a merging of the strata of Fulbe society. It should not be thought, however, that this process has taken place at the same rate or in the same direction for the different strata. During the colonial era the distinctions between the various Fulbe diminished, but the distinction between Fulbe and serf remained important until the present period of independence. Independence has ended much of the political significance of whether one is Fulbe or descended from serfs, and with independence all the remaining labor obligations of serfs were ended. However, there are strong social and ideological continuities with the past. The merging of former serf and Fulbe is not yet complete.

4

GUINEA

The Guinean government considers its citizens as Guineans first, members of their committee second, and only last as members of different language groups. All persons are theoretically considered equal, and earlier social distinctions are no longer recognized. This attitude on the part of the Guinean political leaders is in advance of the population as a whole. The Guinean revolution is young and time is needed to create a new society. Older social categories remain important for the population in the countryside. To refuse to recognize this would be to ignore a key feature in the life of former serfs.

The government and party of the Republic of Guinea believes itself to be socialist. In the writings of President Ahmed Sékou Touré one finds perhaps the most systematic examination of socialist policies and thought in a sub-Saharan African nation. President Touré has already published seventeen volumes—virtually all of them printed at the Imprimerie Patrice Lumumba in Conakry—setting out in great detail both the theoretical and programmatic aspects of his thought. Even though President Touré has been Africa's foremost radical leader there has been no biography of him and only a few articles concerning his political development and theories in English.[2] The Guinean leaders are committed to socialism. In their opinion socialism is both a goal and a process—the way in which Guinean development has and should take place. According to President Touré, socialism involves the transformation of the relationships of humans to each other, of society to nature, and will be the outcome of the present development of all societies (volume 16: 45). Moreover, socialism is not a state which once attained will last forever but is part of an ongoing evolution involving human society as a whole.

There seems to be little controversy among American scholars

2. R. W. Johnson of Magdalen College, England, appears to have begun this work.

that Guinea is in fact socialist, if not communist. In this connection William Attwood's account of his personal fight against the specter of advancing communism is particularly interesting. And among those who have constantly kept in touch with Guinean events, Victor Du Bois stands out for his vitriolic attacks on Guinea and her leaders. Significantly, the real questioning of the socialist character of the Republic of Guinea has taken place among French leftist scholars among whom the debate was touched off by B. Ameillon (apparently a pseudonym) in *La Guinée, Bilan d'une Indépendance*. Ameillon argues that Guinea will become neocolonialist and elite controlled as have other newly independent African nations. The debate has been picked up and continued by other scholars such as Yves Bénot and Jean Suret-Canale. While it is beyond the scope of this book to engage in extended discussion of the political character of Guinea, it is my hope to provide additional and substantial information about the evolving character of the Guinean countryside. Perhaps this study will be of greater import because it concerns the area of Guinea thought to be most recalcitrant to independence and the government of the Democratic Party of Guinea.

Two

Geography and History

THE PHYSICAL SETTING

The Fouta-Djallon, now the province of Middle Guinea (Moyenne Guinée), has been subject to long and intensive human occupation. Throughout the central Fouta-Djallon, villages are rarely separated by more than a few kilometers, and the isolated hamlet has become quite rare. There are few forests, as the land has been cultivated time and time again.

The Fouta-Djallon can be subdivided into three geographical areas: the central and northern plateaus (in the regions of Dalaba, Pita, and Labe); the eastern plateaus (in the regions of Timbo, Dalaba and Tougué); and the western transition areas of the regions of Gaoual, Telimele, and Kindia. The central and northern plateaus often are denuded of trees, intensively cultivated, and relatively densely populated. Here sedentarization has been fairly complete since the early nineteenth century. The altitude of this area varies from 1000 to 1515 meters, the highest in Guinea, and the terrain is marked by river valleys that extend into the province of Upper Guinea. In this area is the historic capital of the Fouta, Timbo, and Fougoumba, the place where the *al-mamys,* rulers of the Fouta-Djallon confederation, received the turban of office. The population density of the eastern plateau was, and is, less than the central.

7

In the past, there were three different kinds of villages: the *misside,* where the mosque, and usually the residence of a chief were built; the *fulasso,* a Fulbe village; and the *runde,* a serf village. All three kinds of villages were constructed in the same manner, but the Fulbe village was usually on high ground, and the serf village on lower ground. The *missides* were invariably on strategically important high ground overlooking large areas. Villages were and are permanent, and the history of each compound in a village is known precisely.

The climate of the Fouta is tropical, but because of the altitude there is neither overwhelming heat during the dry season, nor continuous rain during the rainy season. The rainy season is from May through November, but most of the rain falls during the July, August, and September. According to Guinean government figures the average yearly rainfall at Labe from 1959 to 1962 was 207.9 centimeters.

The population density of the Fouta-Djallon varies greatly from area to area. The highest density is found on the central plateaus, where the village of Hollaande is located. As of the last census in 1962, the population of the region of Labe was 271,632 people in an area of 7,616 square kilometers. This is a density of 35.6 inhabitants per square kilometer. Although the density of the region of Labe is high, it is not the highest in the Fouta-Djallon. Just south of Labe on the same plateau, but in the region of Pita, is an area known as Bantingnel, which has a density greater than 68 inhabitants per square kilometer (Richard-Molard 1951: 101).

There is another demographic statistic for the Fouta-Djallon of great interest. Jacques Richard-Molard observed that the greater the density of population in an area of the Fouta, the greater the percentage of serfs in the population. In his enquiry he found that serfs comprised 35.6 percent of the population of Labe whereas in the canton of Djimma (Koubia) in the eastern Fouta they comprised 29 percent. I agree with Richard-Molard's conclusion that the percentage of serfs grew with the density of population and that the highest percentages of serfs were to be found in

8

proximity to political and military centers such as Labe where the leaders took the lion's share of the booty of war (1951: 104).

In order to place Hollaande in its proper social and political context the traditional, the colonial, and the modern administrative organization must be considered. Traditionally, Hollaande was a satellite village of Popodara, the village where the mosque was located and where the chief of the area resided. Hollaande in Fulfulde means "plain." In particular it refers to those plains that absorb water and become muddy during the rainy season. Popodara was part of the *diwal* (traditional province) of Labe, which was much larger than the present region of Labe. After their conquest of the Fouta-Djallon the French adopted a different governing scheme. Ultimately they formed the *Cercle de Labé,* which was divided into fifteen *cantons*. One of these *cantons* was called Ore Koumba, but was also known as Popodara. The village of Popodara was the residence for the French-appointed *chef de canton,* or "chief." This system was brought to an end with the achievement of independence.

Today the Fouta-Djallon is one of the four provinces of Guinea —Middle Guinea. (The other three provinces are Maritime (or Lower) Guinea, Forested Guinea, and Upper Guinea). Middle Guinea is divided into a number of smaller administrative units known as *régions*. Hollaande is located in the region of Labe.

The villages are now grouped into committees, which are the functioning political groups in the countryside. There is now a Committee of Popodara, but it is tiny in size compared to the area and numbers of people formerly under the *chef de canton*. The size of committees approximates the size of the traditional groupings of villages around a mosque. However, the division of villages into committees has not necessarily followed the older lines of where people go to pray. Whereas the village of Hollaande was formerly directly under Popodara, Popodara is now in one committee, and Hollaande in another.

Popodara has served as the commercial center for the surrounding area, and the school and infirmary are there. To the south

9

and east of Popodara is the Regional Farm of Labe. Founded by the French in 1935, it is presently a government farm which serves as a source of employment for the local people. At the farm there is also a primary school and a new Collège d'Enseignement Rural.

A village that was a political and religious center during both traditional and colonial times, Popodara dominates its environs physically, being located on a hill that overlooks the plains and valleys in all directions. Both the mosque and the chief's former residence are located on the highest point in the surrounding area. Popodara no longer retains the political dominance it had during traditional and colonial times; the former chief still lives there, but he no longer has any real authority.

As one looks at the countryside from Popodara, one sees villages that seem, from a distance, to be wooded areas. The forests, however, have been destroyed over a long period of time by the peoples who have inhabited the Fouta, the extent of deforestation having increased even within the lifetime of the oldest men. My older informants were all very specific as to areas that are now treeless but which formerly were wooded. They attributed the deforestation to the great increase in the number of people.

The village of Hollaande lies one kilometer to the south of Popodara on a road built in the 1930s for a *chef de canton,* Alfa Yaya. The physical and social relation of Hollaande to Popodara can be exemplified by the fact that during the rainy season all the water from Popodara flows downhill to Hollande, turning much of the land into mud, while Popodara remains dry. The inhabitants of Popodara maintained that they would never go to Hollaande during the rainy season because of the mud. (The social implications of this statement will be discussed later.)

Hollaande lies against a small hill, where the market is located, and spreads out onto a plain that ends rather abruptly about one kilometer from the village where the terrain descends sharply into a large valley known as *ainde* Sombili, or "Sombili river valley."

Two roads pass through the village of Hollaande. The first,

still used for vehicle traffic, was constructed with forced labor by a *chef de canton* so he could drive his automobile to his private gardens, which he also had built with forced labor. The second road was built by the French in an attempt to bypass a bridge on the Senegal road which was continually being washed out. However, after they had constructed several kilometers of the alternative route and thus split the village of Hollaande in two, they decided against the alternative. As a result of the French mistake Hollaande was divided in two, and several inhabitants were forced to move their compounds. The former-serf villagers still speak bitterly of both road projects, and state that the Fulbe did not have to provide most of the forced labor for the chief's road or provide the shelter and food for the workers who built it.

Hollaande, with the exception of the two dividing roads, is now made up mainly of contiguous compounds. It has a population of 319 people who live in 129 houses. This represents a large and rapid increase in population during the recent past. Formerly the village limits were smaller and the compounds were not contiguous. At first, houses were built only on the tops of the termite hills that dot the plain so as to avoid their standing in water during the rainy season, which would have made them wet and uncomfortable and led to their rapid deterioration. However, building on termite hills had its obvious disadvantages, for the termites in the Fouta eat both the wood of the houses and the mud brick of which they are built. Then during the 1920s and 30s the pattern changed in a way unknown to me: houses were no longer built on the termite hills and villagers began building rock foundations two to three feet high for their houses. The houses are now dry and are no longer eaten by termites. Moreover, they now stand a minimum of twelve years without repairs. Further, the technological innovation in the building of houses gave a new appearance to the village. The houses are no longer dispersed, located on the tops of separated termite hills. The construction of rock foundations permitted the occupation of areas between termite hills, and the village coalesced as it grew, rather than expanding and dispersing, as would have been the case if the older pattern of housebuilding had continued.

THE HISTORICAL SETTING

To provide a background for the discussion of a present-day village of former serfs, I shall attempt a brief reconstruction of Fulbe society in 1880 based on accounts of French administrators and interviews with older informants. Crucial institutions of the precolonial period are now often unknown to young people. The description that follows is more an "ideal" view of the nineteenth century than of the "actual" organization.

PRECOLONIAL SOCIAL AND POLITICAL ORGANIZATION

The Fulbe entered the Fouta-Djallon as cattle pastoralists, filtering in from what is now the Republic of Mali during the fifteenth and sixteenth centuries. Until that time the Fouta-Djallon had been inhabited by an agricultural people known as the Diallonke or Yalunka.[1] A symbiotic relation, typical between cattleherders and cultivators, developed between the Fulbe pastoralists and the Diallonke cultivators. The Fulbe exchanged milk and manure for grains and rights to pasturage. According to Fulbe legends, they were not Islamic during this period, and they regarded themselves as guests in the lands of the Diallonke. The relatively peaceful relations between the two peoples ended in war. In what was probably the first Fulbe-led *jihad* in West Africa, beginning around 1727, Muslim Fulbe defeated and expelled the Diallonke.[2] Despite Fulbe claims in the *Tarikas* (written history

1. There has been no study of Diallonke history. Leland Donald has recently completed an excellent account of their social organization in Sierre Leone. However, he believes it too speculative to extrapolate from Yalunka social organization in Sierra Leone to what it might have been in the different ecology of the Fouta-Djallon in 1750.

2. Jean Suret-Canale views Laing and the *tarikas* as the only reliable sources for chronology during the eighteenth century.

in this context) extolling the swiftness and decisiveness of their victory one reads in the same *Tarika* that the Diallonke were "decisively defeated" in the same place four times over a period of many years. In fact, the warring between the Fulbe and the "pagan" Diallonke for control of the Fouta-Djallon appears to have lasted for fifty years, although little is known of the chronology of the *jihad*. The Islamization of the Fouta and the sedentarization of much of the Fulbe population seems to have taken place at around the same time. Thus in a relatively short period pagan Fulbe pastoralist groups became sedentary Islamic communities.[3]

The resistance to the Muslims was led by the Diallonke and some pagan Fulbe (the Poulli) with allies from the Susu, Baga, and Foulakunda, as well as from the Malinke and Wassoulanke.[4] The conquered Diallonke, Susu, and Poullis were reduced to serfdom (except for their earliest allies, who managed to keep their lands, and the last-minute converts, who lost their land but kept their freedom). Those who escaped went to the border territories—the Susu toward the coast and the Diallonke toward the east.[5]

Sometime during the course of the *jihad,* when the victory of the Muslim Fulbe was no longer in doubt, an assembly of the nine chiefs of the Muslim groups (accompanied undoubtedly by close important kinsmen) gathered to prepare the constitution for a confederation of the Fouta-Djallon. The name Fouta-Djallon probably indicates a union of the Fulbe and Diallonke elements (Suret-Canale n.d.: 73). The nine Muslim groups became the nine traditional provinces of the Fouta-Djallon confederation: Timbo and Fode-Hadji in the low area (*lei pelle*); Fougoumba,

3. The dating of sedentarization is speculative. Further research needs to be done.

4. According to one traditional written history (*tarika*), there were 22 leaders —12 Fulbe and 10 Malinke. If it is true Malinke were involved in the *jihad,* it is very interesting and important. However, to verify this account, one would need to do research in the Malinke areas bordering the Fouta.

5. Based on an unpublished manuscript, courtesy of Jean-Canale.

Kebali, and Bouria in the area between the rivers (*hakkunde madye*); and Labe, Timbi, Kollade, and Koin in the highlands (*dou pelle*). Chosen from among the nine chiefs of the Muslim groups, now chiefs of the nine provinces, was one chief to head the entire Fouta-Djallon. He was referred to as the *almamy* Fouta. *Almamy* was used in two senses: to designate either the head of the Fouta-Djallon, or the religious head of a mosque. The individual chosen to be the first *almamy* was Ibrahima Sambegu of Timbo, known historically as Karamoko Alfa. Thereafter the office of head of Timbo and *almamy* Fouta remained together. Whosoever became *almamy* Fouta also became chief of the province of Timbo. Only those who were direct descendants of a province chief could become a province chief, and only those who were sons of an *almamy* Fouta were eligible to become *almany* Fouta.

The power of the *almamy* Fouta outside of his own province of Timbo was limited. He served as the organizer for the defense of the Fouta from outside enemies. His authorization was needed when province chiefs wanted to war or to trade outside the Fouta. The office of *almamy* also provided the means for the resolving of inter-province conflicts and the most important prerogative of the *almamy* was the nomination of the other province chiefs. But, in all his acts the *almamy* was controlled by a council of elders (*tekung*) who had the ultimate right to depose the *almamy* (Demougeot 1944: 16).

Each province chief was equal in stature to the chiefs of the other provinces, all being the direct patrilineal descendants of the nine leaders of the *jihad*. The chief of each province had his own army and source of wealth. However, differences in power existed among the chiefs due to the variation in the size and wealth of the provinces. The largest province in terms of both area and population, and possibly in terms of power, was not the *almamy's* province of Timbo, but Labe.

Each province was divided into clusters of villages, each cluster having a mosque as its religious and political center. Each cluster of villages around its mosque was known as a *misside*. The word *misside* is used by the Fulbe in two senses: a cluster of villages around a mosque, or a village that has a mosque. Each *misside* was headed by a chief, *lando misside,* who was a member of the patrilineage of the chief of that province. The chief of the *misside* was appointed by the province chief from among the eligible candidates. With each *misside* were three kinds of villages: the *misside* proper, the village with the mosque; the *fulasso* or *marga,* a village inhabited by Fulbe but without a mosque; and the *runde,* a village of serfs.

This set of units—*diwal, misside, fulasso, runde*—furnishes the basic territorial grid of the Fouta-Djallon after Islamization. Those who have written about the Fouta-Djallon have described its sociopolitical organization as feudal (Vieillard 1939, 1940; Arçin 1911; Marty 1921; and Suret-Canale 1961) or theocratic (Sow 1966). Suret-Canale (1964: 21–42) has reconsidered his view and now argues that there are many African groups who can be included under the rubric of the Asiatic Mode of Production. The Fulbe of the Fouta-Djallon do not lend themselves to an easy classification, but in terms of the evolution of the Fouta-Djallon one can view the political territorial organization as having been superimposed upon an earlier kin organization. These two principles were always in contradiction; their synthesis was never attained. Cantrelle and Dupire reached a similar conclusion:

This patriarchal structure [refers to patrilineages, see below] is itself contained in a hierarchical political organization. There isn't any rupture between the primitive organization of these herders who became Muslim conquerors, and their new religious and political forms that were implanted and then came to dominate the Fouta. Hereditary social power, political power, and religious supremacy were united in the hands of several noble families (1964: 75). (All translations, unless otherwise noted, are mine.)

In sum, the state never became fully distinct from the earlier kin organization.

The kin organization of the Fouta-Djallon was based on patrilineages. These were the *lenyol,* the maximal patrilineage; the *gorol,* the major patrilineage; and the *suudu,* the minimal patrilineage. A *lenyol* is a geographically dispersed, patrilineal, agamous group with descent demonstrable from a common male ancestor. There were at least forty maximal patrilineages within the region of Labe. The distribution of a maximal lineage, was not restricted to one province. The maximal patrilineages were grouped into three ranked categories, each having a defined sociopolitical and economic status: the chiefly maximal patrilineage; the free maximal patrilineages (Fulbe *lassilibe*); and Fulbe of the bush (Fulbe *burure*). To these three can be added the fourth rank of serf (*mattyudo*).

There was a ruling, or chiefly, maximal lineage for each province. The maximal lineage of the *almamy* Fouta, the Seidiyanke, was not the maximal lineage of the other province chiefs; rather, there were five different maximal lineages that provided the chiefs for the nine provinces. The Khalduyanke provided the chiefs for Labe, Kankalabe, and Kollade. Although the chieftainship in a province was limited to one maximal lineage, the residence of members of the chiefly lineage of one province was not limited to that province. Thus one finds members of the Khalduyanke living in Timbi where another maximal patrilineage provided the chief. The Khalduyanke in Labe provided both the province chief and the chief of each *misside*. Accession to chieftainship was governed by a rule based upon genealogical closeness to a former chief. While the specifics of succession must remain beyond the scope of this study, it should be pointed out that succession to office was complicated by a division within all the chiefly maximal lineages between Soroya and Alfaya. This factionalism apparently had its roots in the succession to the *almamy*-ship after the death of the second *almamy*. The first *almamy,* Karamoko Alfa, went mad and was succeeded by his father's brother's son Sory. Upon the death of Sory there was a struggle between the sons of Sory and Karamoko Alfa for the succession. This resulted in the formation of two factions: the

Alfayas, those loyal to the descendants of Karamoko Alfa, and the Soroyas, those loyal to the descendants of Sory.

The *lassilibe,* the free maximal lineages (or literally "the free men"), were reckoned from those leaders who elected to follow and aid the *jihad.* In the province of Labe there were seven such maximal lineages. Because of the assistance they rendered during the *jihad,* they were free of obligations to the chiefly maximal lineage of the province.

The Fulbe *burure* or "Fulbe of the bush," comprised the largest number of maximal lineages in Labe. They are said not to have helped the chiefly *lenyol* during the *jihad,* and in some instances hindered it. They were subordinate to the chiefly maximal lineage, and when a Fulbe of the bush died, a significant, but varying amount of his wealth had to be given to the chief of his *misside.* This obligation, the *kummabite,* was typically paid in cattle, although it might be paid in land or gold. In addition, a Fulbe of the bush could be obligated to give part of his harvest to the *misside* chief in return for the privilege of living in the *misside.*

The *mattyube,* or serfs, did not have maximal lineages, but "took" the maximal lineages of their masters. However, this did not confer social position. The serf of a master who belonged to a chiefly maximal lineage did not have higher status than the serf of a lower-ranking master. Any Fulbe could own serfs, although a chief was likely to have more.

In sum, the population of the Fouta-Djallon can be divided into four horizontal strata.[6] The proportions of the strata, especially the proportion of serfs, varied from one province to another.

Another traditional social grouping was the four *yettore.* The term derives from *yettude,* "to greet," "to salute," or "to praise." *Yettore* refers to the four "family" names that still include all the Fulbe of the present-day Fouta-Djallon, and which cut across

6. We have excluded from this grouping the *griots,* known as *farba,* who derived from the Fouta-Toro. Another interesting group were the wood craftsmen, the *laobe.* They made wood stools and milk bowls. However unlike other craftsmen, they were considered Fulbe, not serfs. They are said to have been endogamous.

ranks. These family names are Ba, Bari, Diallo, and Sow. Most serfs took the *yettore* of their masters. Cantrelle and Dupire (1964: 74) have taken the *yettore* to be patriclans. In their genealogy (1964: 76), they list the four names as the common ancestors for all Fulbe. They observed that the social function of the *yettore* was the use of *yettore* names in salutation and in joking between a pair of *yettore*. Cantrelle and Dupire suggest that cross-cousin joking and cross-*yettore* joking are tied to the preferential marriage system (1964: 74). During my stay I was unable to discern any continuing significance of the *yettore,* except that family names are derived from the *yettore*.

The problem of the *yettore* raises the question of Fulbe accounts of their ancestry. On the one hand, members of the chiefly maximal lineages have claimed Arab origin (and therefore noble and Islamic) to justify and validate their chieftainship. On the other hand, members of the free lineages claim they are free because their ancestors assisted the Khalduyanke in the *jihad*. The former serfs of Labe attempt to show their ancestors' connection with the leaders who directed the *jihad* in Labe, thus proving their religiosity and longstanding residence in the province.

One account of Fulbe origins, transcribed from the narration of an elder of the former chiefly lineage, accords with the notion that a common genealogy relates all Fulbe. According to this myth, Fulbe history begins with the generation of Saidina Umaru Bun Cattabi of Missira. He sent some men to explore the world. He put them in a boat and named Umaru Bun Asi as their chief. Saidina told Umaru Bun Asi to spend two months in the interior of the country near Macina (Mali). If he found the inhabitants were Muslim, he should aid them in following the law of Islam. If he found they were heathens, he should make them pay tribute and convert them to Islam. Umaru Bun Asi left as he was told. Upon arriving at Macina, he found the inhabitants to be heathens. He called for their chief. He asked him to become a Muslim. The chief obeyed. The chief paid tribute and Bun Asi stayed with the chief for two months. At the end of the two months he asked the chief if he could return to Missira. The chief responded by appealing to Bun Asi not to abandon them, but to leave them a religious teacher. Bun Asi left Ugu Battu Bun Yasir; the others departed for home. Ugu Battu Bun Yasir married a woman from Macina. From this union there were four children: Ra'abu, the oldest, ancestor of the Ba's; Wunaiyu, ancestor of the Sow's; Bodewol, ancestor of the Diallo's; and Da'atu, the youngest ancestor of the Bari's, the chiefs of the Fouta-Djallon. The ancestors of Ugu Battu became numerous at Macina and they went into other countries, countries of the blacks. Among the countries where they went was the Fouta-Djallon. There they found the Diallonke.

According to this myth, all Fulbe are descended from the same ancestor. It is possible that because of the strength of Islam, this myth will become accepted by all Fulbe in the future. Presently, however, the origin tales of the maximal patrilineages do not concord with this myth of common ancestry. Two examples are the origin accounts of the Seriyanke and Seidiyanke maximal lineages, according to whom the nobles of the Fouta-Djallon originate from Fas, their maximal lineages connected to an Arab family. Two of their ancestors, Seidi and Seeri, went to the country of the Diakanke, where they visited the home of a saint of God, *el Hadj* Salimou Souare, ancestor of the Mande. They told him, "We have come to you to ask your benediction. Troubles have broken out in our country." He told them, "Continue until you come to a country called the Fouta-Djallon. There you will establish yourselves." He prayed for them. They continued on their way until they came to the Fouta. Upon their arrival in the Fouta they found their kinsmen living in a heathen state. Seidi and Seeri however, are the ancestors of only two maximal lineages: the Seriyanke of Fougoumba, and the Seidiyanke of Timbo.

An example of a genealogy (see Fig. 1) explaining the origin of two maximal lineages is that of the "royal" families of the Fouta-Djallon, the Seriyanke of Fougoumba, who had the right to wrap the turban around the head of the *almamy* Fouta, and the Seidiyanke, who furnished the *almamys* of the Fouta. This genealogy is from a written history obtained from a Fulbe elder in Labe. Seku Abbana is regarded as their common ancestor. His son gave birth to two sons, Fode Seri and Fode Seidi, the recognized ancestors of the two maximal lineages. Within the Seidiyanke are a great number of major patrilineages that originated after Nuhu and Maliki. Nuhu and Maliki were, respectively, the fathers of the first and second *almamy*, Karamoko Alfa and Sory.

The maximal lineages were geographically dispersed, quite often over noncontiguous areas, and sometimes over more than one province. Unfortunately, there are no population estimates for them during the nineteenth century. Each of the various maximal lineages had the same internal structure; it was composed of a number of different major patrilineages (*gorol, gori,* pl.). Mem-

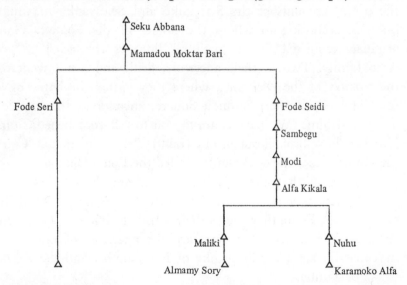

FIGURE I. Genealogy of the chiefly maximal lineage of the Fouta-Djallon.

bers of the same major patrilineage usually lived in the same *misside,* but not necessarily in the same village. Each major lineage was composed of a number of minimal lineages (*suudu, tyuudi,* pl.). Each minimal lineage was composed of households (*beinguure*).

The maximal patrilineage represented the widest unit within which close ties of kinship were expressed. The maximal lineage was agamous, although the four ranks tended to be endogamous. Thus marriage within the same social status was more frequent than between the different ranks. The maximal lineage, however, was not the key kin group; the major lineage was. It was through the major lineage that one entered society and obtained rights to land. Its members lived in proximity to one another, although not necessarily in the same village. In larger villages more than one major lineage would usually be found.

While I was living in Hollaande, the opportunity arose to visit three villages of the same small maximal lineage which were separated from each other by seventy-five kilometers. None of these villages was in the same *misside.* One village, the ancestors of whose inhabitants had helped the Labe leader of the *jihad,* Karamoko Alfa (the same name but a different individual than the *almamy* Fouta) against the heathens and thus became free men, was viewed by all as the oldest village. Not too long after the *jihad* some members of the maximal lineage founded a village near Labe, forty kilometers from the original village. As this village grew in size and available cultivable land became difficult to obtain, several members moved again fifty kilometers to the northwest and founded a third village. When people of all three villages were asked for specific obligations between maximal lineage members, there were no direct responses. There remained relatively close ties, however, between inhabitants of all three villages. These ties which were viewed as a function of their common maximal lineage, consisted of economic assistance, intermarriage and frequent visits.

In precolonial times the operational groups within the *misside*

21

were not the villages but the major lineages. The eldest active male member served as its head (*mowdo gorol*). One obtained this position regardless of whether or not one's father served in that capacity. The major lineage head acted in concert with the other elders of their patrilineage to look after its internal affairs. They concerned themselves with questions of marriage, divorce, inheritance, distribution of land, and furnishing of recruits for *jihads*. Expressions of solidarity and aid were expressed in terms of the maximal or major lineages, not in terms of *misside* (the basic territorial unit). In cases of conflict between two *missides,* if one had major patrilineage members in the other *misside,* one would not fight and one might even aid one's kinsmen. Such behavior suggests that a territorial form of organization was imposed historically upon a preexisting kin organization.

The relation between *misside* and kin groups leads us to consider briefly the political organization of the precolonial *misside*. Each *misside* had its own chief (*lando* or *lamdo,s.; or lambe,* pl.), selected by the province chief from the available candidates. Candidates for the chieftainship could be either sons of the deceased chief or his surviving brothers. The descendants of two brothers who had been chiefs often competed for the chieftainship. Moreover, the province chief retained the right to name as chief someone drawn from outside the *misside*. This was one of the means used by the province chief to thwart legitimate competitors seeking his office. At Popodara, the *misside* chief always belonged to the maximal chiefly lineage Khalduyanke and was not drawn from outside the *misside*.

The position of members of the chiefly lineage ultimately resided in their political dominance resulting from the *jihad*. Their tie to the rest of the Fulbe was the relation of superordinate to subordinate, not of kinsmen to kinsmen. Their political position found its expression in the territorial relation of *diwal* to *misside*. However, this expression was not complete, because the internal organization of the chiefly lineage did not differ substantially from other maximal lineages, and they therefore could not force their subjects to show a political loyalty that fundamentally transcended their own kin organization and the kin groups of their subordinates. An additional weakness of the chiefly maximal lineage was its division into the Soroya and Alfaya factions. The chiefly maximal lineage of every *misside* was either one or the other. The province chief could expect consistent support only from his own faction.

The *misside* chief's functions were those of both a decision maker and of an enforcer of decisions. His political superior was the province chief, and at the level of the *misside* he worked with the elders and judges of the mosque. The *misside* chief was not exempt from economic tasks; he was not a full-time political specialist. The primary source of his "fund of power" was the *kummabite,* his right to part of the inheritance from Fulbe of the bush. He also received gifts throughout the year and in turn redistributed much of what he received.

The last aspect of the *misside* to be considered is the role of the *almamy* and the mosque. In precolonial times the mosque played a significant political role in addition to its religious ones. The *almamy,* three judges (*nyawoore*), and the *misside* chief interpreted the Koran and Islamic law and served as the regulators of disputes. They ruled on the payment of compensation (*dia*) when the blood of a fellow believer was shed, land disputes, and knotty problems of inheritance and divorce. The mosque handled problems that arose between major patrilineages or which the major patrilineages were unable to resolve themselves. Although political office was restricted to the chiefly lineage, positions within the mosque were not. The selection of the *almamy* was made by the elders of the mosque. This group comprised all Fulbe learned in Islamic law and the *misside* chief. The maximal lineage of the *almamy* was not necessarily the chiefly lineage of his *misside.*

In areas where the chiefly lineages were newcomers, they permitted the position of the *almamy* to remain in the hands of the maximal lineages that had been there before them. At Popodara the two indigenous maximal lineages were the Ragnaabe (see

23

figure 2) and the Seleyaabe. Only after the *jihad* had been fought in the area did the Khalduyanke settle at Popodara and assume the chieftainship. At both Popodara and at Labe itself, the *almamy* has never been a Khalduyanke. However, in other areas of the province of Labe there were large and older groups of Khalduyanke who served not only as chiefs but as *almamys*.

The judges of the mosque were chosen from among those who obtained the status of *tierno*, a religious status open to any Fulbe regardless of his maximal lineage—but not to serfs—upon completion of the translation of the entire Koran from Arabic into Fulfulde. This accomplishment, known as *firugol* or *timingol tafsir*, carried high prestige and led one to be automatically included among the most important members of a mosque. For a chief to rule effectively he had to have the support of these elders of the mosque.

In conclusion, the dual role of Islam in the precolonial sociopolitical organization should be discussed. Islam provided the model and the means by which greater political integration was achieved. The territorial units *misside* and *diwal* stem from Arabic words and are connected with the importance of the

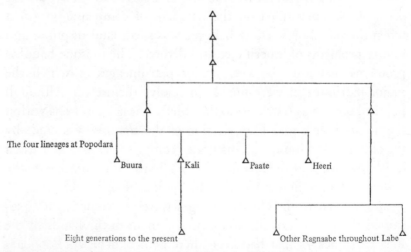

FIGURE 2. Genealogy of the maximal lineage Ragnaabe and its division into major patrilineages. The Ragnaabe had been masters of many of the former serfs of Hollaande.

mosque. However, Islam also prevented the concentration of power in the hands of one group. Status and positions of power within the mosque were open to all except serfs. It is significant, therefore, that the serfs became Muslims, even though Islam provided the ideological justification for their status. Before discussing the precolonial serf village (*runde*), it is necessary to note briefly some features of the precolonial Fulbe economy.

Although the Fulbe as an ethnic group are best known for their cattle raising, agriculture was and is the dominant economic activity of the Fulbe in the Fouta-Djallon (with the exception of such small groups as the Fulakunda in the western part of the Fouta). The agricultural sector of the economy is based primarily on fonio and rice crops, grown in fields (*ngesa*) on mountains and plains, and on corn, taro, and manioc crops, grown in women's gardens (*sunture*). The fields are cultivated by means of a slash and burn technique with fallow periods of 12–20 years and cultivating periods of 1–3 years. The women's gardens, located next to the houses and enclosed by fences to protect them from animals, are cultivated intensively and annually. Gardening is the responsibility of women, who are aided by their children. The men are responsible only for the upkeep of the surrounding fence.

Although Fulbe and serfs followed the same agricultural practices, cattle raising was the exclusive preserve of the Fulbe.[7] Serfs did all sorts of work for their masters, but they never served as cattle herders. With the sedentarization of the Fulbe, cattle declined in economic importance. By the end of the nineteenth century, nomadism had virtually ended (except at the edges of the Fouta) and cattle were kept primarily for social and ceremonial

7. The type of cow in the Fouta-Djallon is the *ndama*. They are small, sturdy, humpless, thickset cattle with long lyre-shaped horns. They are apparently resistant to trypanosomiasis, but their milk yield is low. See G. Doutressoulle (1947) and FAO Agricultural series (1957). The study draws its material for the Fouta-Djallon from Doutressoulle. The work of Doutressoulle is dated, and his statements must be carefully evaluated. No justification or evidence is presented for his view that the *ndama* bovines originated in the Kade region of the Fouta-Djallon (1947: 81).

reasons. Besides cattle the Fulbe kept goats, sheep and chickens. There were seasonal movements of the cattle from the lowlands to the highlands during the rainy season to avoid the tsetse, and from high areas to river areas during the dry season to find adequate pasturage.

Within the past two centuries, at least, cattle have been owned by individuals. Serfs, like cattle, were also "owned" by individuals. The individual ownership of serfs and cattle made the transition to a market economy easier. Land was not individually owned, but was held collectively by major lineages. It was not worked collectively, however, but was divided among the various minimal lineages, which in turn divided the fields among the households composing each minimal lineage. According to informants and observations each household head divided his share of the fields held by his minimal lineage among himself, his wives, and perhaps his older unmarried children. Each individual received the harvest of his own area, although the field was worked collectively by the household.

Markets were indigenous to many parts of West Africa, but they were not found in the Fouta-Djallon. Trade was carried on by barter. A series of measures were used, and an extensive system of equivalents was established. The Fulbe also engaged in long-distance trading. Salt, gold, and kola were the most important items of trade, later to be supplemented with slaves. The Fulbe of Labe had extensive contact with the Portuguese and later the French at the ports of the Rio Nuñez, where they obtained cloth and guns, in exchange primarily for slaves. They also traded with the English in Freetown.

An indication of the concentration of wealth and political power in the hands of the province chiefs is provided by a list of the possessions of one province chief, Alfa Yaya. The French did not expect Alfa Yaya to cooperate or to accept passively the dismembering of the province of Labe, and so sent him into exile to prevent his opposition to their program, thus making him a victim of their destruction of the traditional territorial organization of the Fouta-Djallon. They made a survey of his possessions which is preserved in the National Archives of Guinea (1907). Alfa Yaya's wealth came from three different geographic areas. In Kade, where he was born, he owned 973 cattle, 70 horses, and there was no list of his serfs. At Yambering, he had 384 serfs and 53 cattle. In the town of Labe he had 306 serfs and 5,000 kilograms of grain. Whether such concentration was possible prior to colonization is not clear. However, there was a great difference in the wealth of the province chief and that of the *misside* chief.

PRECOLONIAL SERFDOM

The serfs of the Fouta-Djallon during the precolonial period do not fit easily into the categories of either serf or slave.[8] There were aspects of their position which fit the common definition of

8. Use of the terms *serf* and *slave* is subject to difficulty. Trimingham (1959, 1962) refers to the lowest stratum of the Fouta-Djallon as slaves in some places and serfs in others. Thus he notes there are 300,000 descendants of slaves in the Fouta-Djallon (1962: 29). But later in the same work, in discussing the hierarchical social organization of the Fouta, he states:

Finally came the serf and slave groups. These became very numerous, increasing not merely in consequence of wars of aggression, but also because conquerors like al-Hajj 'Umar bartered their prisoners in exchange for cattle. They were divided into categories, domestic serfs who enjoyed some measure of independence and trade-slaves living a hard life in special villages (*runde*) under the control of an intendant appointed by the fief-holder (1962: 170).

Here he is making a distinction between "domestic slaves," which for Trimmingham are equivalent to "serfs," and "slaves proper," whom he calls "captives" (1959: 133). The distinction is their legal status, which arises by virtue of whether they were offspring of slaves or were captured or purchased from non-Muslims. Thus Trimingham distinguishes "household slaves" (*rimaybe*, pl. and *dimajo*) from captives or "trade-slaves" (*sodabe*, pl. and *sodado*). For the Fulbe, however, such a distinction, although made, did not reflect Fulbe practice in terms of the work serfs did or where they lived. This distinction is not at all clear, for Trimingham notes that under Islamic law slaves born in the house were still chattels (1959: 133). The problem is further complicated when, rather than assessing the economic and political position and importance of the "serfs" and "slaves," he views the system as one in which the lot of slaves was ameliorated with each generation as slavery advanced through the various grades of serfdom and ultimately to clientship (1959: 134).

a slave. According to Nieboer, a man is a slave if he is "the property or possession of another beyond the limits of the family" (1900: 6). Tuden and Plotnicov view slavery as the "legal institutionalization of persons as property" (1970: 9–10). What is critical about both these definitions is the nature of content of "property" in any given society, and why and how slavery and serfdom are distinguished from each other. Much of the discussion up to the present has been a series of preferences. Thus Stenning and Hopen refer to Fulbe slaves, whereas Vieillard, Froelich and Lestringant refer to Fulbe serfs and servitude. At this point what is most important is a discussion of the characteristics of a subservient population, and how subservience continues or does not continue among the Fulbe in particular and in Africa in general. Tuden and Plotnicov contend that slavery (and I understand them to include "serfdom") was an "ephemeral and transitory status"; that slavery "has had no major influence on the systems of stratification that have since emerged, and which exist today, with the possible exception of South Africa" (1970: 15). Their conclusion appears inaccurate for the Fulbe populations of West Africa.[9] I

9. Serfdom and slavery, or both, were found among many different Fulbe groups. Froelich (1949), in his article on the organization of a Fulbe-chieftainship in Adamawa, suggests a complicated system of slaves, serfs, captives, and vassals. And according to Froelich, these are all subsumed under the Fulbe category of *mattyube* (Froelich spells it *matchoube*). Froelich further distinguishes between the *mattyube* of the chiefs and the *mattyube* of free Fulbe as follows: Serfs of free Fulbe were the property of their masters. They worked exclusively for him in exchange for food and the payment of their taxes.

The serfs of the *lamido* were divided into three subcategories. The first, vassals, paid a *zakkat,* presented several gifts, and upon the nomination of a chief paid 1,000 francs. Froelich's category of vassals refers to non-Fulbe, nonserfs, who paid tribute to the chief. This situation (although I would not refer to it as vassalage) did exist on the borders of the Fouta-Djallon where villages paid tribute to the Fulbe chief of the area in return for peaceful relations. The second subcategory, serf dignitaries or notables, had the same obligations as free Fulbe serfs, but had a superior position vis-à-vis other serfs. The third, house servants, were in the same position as the serfs of the free Fulbe. He also includes the Mboror'en, who were equivalent to the Fulbe *burure* of the Fouta-Djallon. In Adamawa, however, they paid *soffal,* one cow per herd for the right of entry to the pastures of the chief. If they stayed for a period of time in these fields they

would contend that rural stratification systems continue to reflect earlier social divisions. These earlier social divisions themselves are reflected in patterns of land ownership and land tenure, and in the rural power structure. The inability of the P.A.I.G.C. in Guinea-Bissau to integrate the Fulbe into their guerrilla army has much to do with the continuation of the Fulbe stratificational system.

Among the Fulbe the "owner" of the woman serf was the "owner" of her children. Because a master regarded his serfs as his property, one needs to know the specific social meaning and definition of "property." In the Fouta, there were ill-defined limits to ownership. The story is told of a famous judge from a village not far from Hollaande who was faced with a difficult case. A Fulbe in his village gave the child of one of his serfs to the *misside* chief as a gift. The chief accepted, although the judge maintained that the transfer was not proper according to Islamic law. The judge did not have convincing arguments, how-ever, and shortly thereafter left the Fouta to study in North Africa. Upon his return several years later, he reopened the case, arguing that according to Islamic law, no one, regardless of status, had the right to separate a child from its mother. In short, the limits of the rights of masters over their serfs were not clearly defined.

Although the status of the serfs of the Fouta contained strong elements of what has been considered slavery, there was also a significant way in which they were not slaves: they were eco-nomically self-sufficient. They lived in their own villages, they cultivated their own fields and women's gardens (although they did not own the land), owned property, and had their own

---

paid a *zakkat*. The percentage of serfs (or, as Froelich refers to them, "servi-teurs") in Adamawa equaled that of certain areas in the Fouta-Djallon, 50 per-cent. In the village of Ngaoundere there were 6,400 Fulbe and 6,700 serfs; in the *lamidat,* or chieftainship as a whole, there were 16,450 Fulbe and 20,000 serfs. There were also 14,300 Dourou, who were independent.

While comparison with the Fouta-Djallon is tempting, Froelich's work is difficult to use because he draws no dividing line between the precolonial and colonial period.

kin groups. On the basis of their economic self-sufficiency we have referred to them as "serfs." However, use of the term does not imply that their social position was the same as that of serfs in Europe.

Serfdom was part of the Fouta-Djallon since at least 1750. Nineteenth-century European observers of the Fouta all commented on serfdom and Fulbe dependence on their serfs. Noirot stated that "l'esclavage est la plus grande source de richesses" (1882: 43). The most detailed comments were made by G. Mollien.

The *rumbdes* which I have several times had occasion to mention, are establishments truly honourable to humanity. Each village, or several inhabitants of village, assemble their slaves, and make them build themselves huts close to each other, this place is called a *rumbdé*. They choose a chief from among themselves; if his children are worthy of the distinction, they succeed to the post after his death. These slaves, who are so but in name, cultivate the plantations of their masters, and accompany them to carry their burdens when they travel. They are never sold when they are born in the country, any departure from this practice would cause the desertion of the whole *rumbdé;* but the slave who conducts himself improperly is delivered up by his comrades to their master that he may sell him (1820: 299–300).

Today both French and Guinean scholars believe that the majority of serfs are descendants of the earlier, non-Fulbe population of the Fouta who were bound into serfdom by the Fulbe during the *jihad*. There are indications that this is in part correct, but in the course of my own study I observed that much of the serf population was built up by trade and by war. Evidence to support the contention that at least a large proportion of the former serfs were descended from war captives brought into the Fouta comes from the genealogy of the village of Hollaande. There are eight minimal lineages in the village, seven of them descendants of war captives brought to the village during the nineteenth century. Within the area around Hollaande, at least one village was founded solely for the war captives and serfs brought to the area by members of the chiefly lineage.

The Fulbe have common origin myths written in Arabic

script. The former serfs have no common or written accounts of their origin. They have linked their myths to the coming of the Fulbe to the Fouta-Djallon. A Fulbe is proud of his past and his ancestry. He will without reluctance or hesitance relate his genealogy. Former serfs are hesitant, ill at ease, and will not tell their true origins without confidence in the interviewer. Below is a widespread account of the origins of serfdom (*mattyagaaku*), according to the Fulbe, and obviously based on Genesis. This account was related by four different Fulbe.

Adamwa and Haawa had two sons, Haabiila and Gaabiila. During this time, as there weren't enough people on earth, brothers and sisters could intermarry. Adamwa said that Haabilla ought to marry his twin sister. Gaabilla would then marry his sister closest in age to him. But the girl Gaabilla had to marry was nasty and mean. He protested against marrying this girl and in desperation killed his brother. He took the corpse on his head to bury it. No one would aid him in interring the corpse; even the earth refused to receive the body since Gaabiila had killed his own brother. For three days he carried the cadaver on his head; it began to smell bad. The hideous smell detached itself from the body and stuck to Gaabiila. Since that day the serfs have always smelled bad. Afterward God told Gaabiila that his descendants would work forever more for the children of Haabiila. Then God asked what had become of the blood spilled during the murder. The earth wasn't able to recover it, because the blood had run inside it. After that day, God forbade the earth to absorb blood as the earth absorbed water. Since that day, the earth no longer would absorb blood.

The history of one of the families of Hollaande illustrates the serfs' attempts to connect their ancestors with the Fulbe. This family claims descent from the original inhabitants of the Fouta. At the time of the *jihad* their ancestor took fright and fled into the mountains. Subsequently, there was a large battle at Toule, just southwest of Popodara, where they were living. The Fulbe, under Karamoko Alfa, were victorious. After the battle the ancestor debated and debated with himself about what to do. He ultimately went before Karamoko Alfa and explained how he had fled. Karamoko Alfa asked him if he would accept the religion, and he replied yes. With the acceptance of Islam, he was given a compound at Hollaande Tosokere (a village near Hollaande). Both former serfs and Fulbe say his descendants are the only indigenous serfs of the area.

There are two social categories within the former serf population: *ndima,* or "indigenous," and *ardoobe,* those who have been brought. These distinctions are not absolute, however, for families who were brought five generations ago are called *ndima,* whereas those who were brought three generations ago are referred to as *ardoobe.* Moreover, among the *ndima* no one could maintain with any certainty that they were descended from the Diallonke. These categories, it would seem, are important only for one or two generations; a serf was a serf regardless of his earlier origins.

The way new individuals were bound into serfdom during the nineteenth century is interesting. The Fulbe did not attempt to make adults serfs. They sought children preferably under ten years of age. These children, either bought or captured, were brought back from the frontier zones of the Fouta-Djallon and placed with the other serfs of the children's owner. It then became the responsibility of one serf to raise the children. According to informants, the children learned Fulfulde quickly and did not speak their native language once in their new home. They were cared for by the serfs as their own children with the consequent obligations and privileges. Upon marriage of such a serf girl the "adopted" parents would receive their share of the bridewealth; if the child was a boy they would have to give their share of the bridewealth.

The relative proportion of the autochthonous Diallonke population to that of serfs brought by war and trade within the total population of serfs cannot be assessed at this point. Moreover, there is probably regional variability in this matter. However, for the area around the capital of Labe there appear to be very few, if any, descendants of the original Diallonke. Most serfs came as a result of war or sale. Suret-Canale (1967), using the results of the 1954–1955 demographic study of Guinea, cites the ethnic origins of the population of Tyoukou, a *runde* in Labe. Of 121 persons, including only married adults or widows, 45 came as a result of the wars of Samory: 18 Kouranko, 9 Kissi, 8 Wassoulanke, 7 Toma, 3 Konianke. There were 33 from the former Soudan, who were probably made captives as a result of the activities of the Toucouleurs of Segou. Among them were 30 Bambara and 3 Sarakolle. Two-thirds of the captives had been acquired by purchase, and none were from ethnic groups that bordered the Fouta-Djallon. A third group of 26 captives lived in areas raided or acquired by the *almamy* of Labe during the nineteenth century. These ethnic groups include 13 Malinke of Gabu (Portuguese Guinea), 6 Tyapi, 3 Tenda, 2 Fulakunda, 1 Diakanke, and 1 Dioula. Finally, there were 15 former serfs of Diallonke origin (21 percent of the whole) from Sangalan, a region subject to perpetual raids by the Fulbe of Labe.[10]

Suret-Canale concludes that the figures from Labe are probably different from those of other parts of the Fouta-Djallon. And he is also quite right that it would be very difficult to redo such an enquiry in light of the political position of the Democratic Party of Guinea that such differences no longer exist and that reference to anterior economic and political subservience is destructive to current efforts toward national integration. In another generation

10. Rodney, in an important reanalysis of the history of the Fouta-Djallon, observes that as a consequence of the Fulbe *jihad* "the most important social institution which emerged was the *rounde*—a village of conquered Djalonkes . . ." (1968: 277). He also suggests that the *runde* inhabitants were a majority of the population held down by a Fulbe minority (1968: 278). Unless new evidence can be found such conclusions concerning the serf population will have to be rejected. I suspect that the *rundes* were not as important as Rodney suggests since they are present, albeit in a slightly different form, among both the Wassoulanke and Malinke. Other ideas presented by Rodney are stimulating, for example, his suggestion that the serf population was quite important for providing the food necessary for slaves awaiting shipment in Sierre Leone.

it will probably be impossible to have an accurate census, because the descendants of serfs already know little of their familial origins.

The serf population of the Fouta-Djallon was potentially self-increasing without new wars or trade. This was demonstrated by the fact that after French conquest ended the wars and thus denied new sources of serfs to the Fulbe, the serf population increased, and the former serf population continues to do so.

The serfs spoke Fulfulde, and the organization of their villages was fundamentally like that of their masters. Serfs were owned by individual Fulbe, both men and women, although the latter was rare. They lived in their own villages (*runde*), and the serfs of many different masters (who might be from different villages) would often be found within one serf village. This was possible in part because of the relatively high population density of the Fouta and the close proximity of villages.

There were villages near Hollaande where there were both Fulbe and serfs. These situations were of recent origin and came about for two reasons. A few Fulbe desired to have their serfs live in the same village with them, as in one such instance at Popodara which involved a few Khalduyanke. Some Fulbe had little land in their natal village (members of a land-poor minimal lineage probably) but owned land in a nearby *runde,* where they would then reside. There was one such example at *misside* Popodara which took place during the colonial period.

Serfs did not own land, but cultivated and lived on land borrowed from the Fulbe. Both the master of the serf and the owner of the land (the two were not necessarily the same) retained the right to throw a serf off the land, although they were subject to certain customary restraints.

The origin of Hollaande, founded around 1870, demonstrates the Fulbe's power to expropriate the land of serfs. The first inhabitant of the village, founder of the part of Hollaande called Binde Pellung, originally came from another village several kilometers away. When the Fulbe owners of the land he was living on wanted it for their own cultivation, he and his wife moved to another village. There they settled on land owned by the chiefly maximal lineage, the Khalduyanke. Soon after, a wife of the *misside* chief asked to have this land and they were forced to move again, this time to the present location of Hollaande. The family grew and remained together for about forty years until their masters' village split, and half the Fulbe moved one-hundred kilometers away in search of new land, taking their serfs with them. In the process brothers were separated and, in one instance, husband from wife.

The second section of the village, known as Hoore Tane, was founded slightly later. This case involved a serf woman from a village four kilometers from Hollaande. One day the cattle of her master entered her compound and ate the corn. She asked for compensation and was refused. She retaliated by entering the compound of her master one night and destroying his corn. He in turn demanded that she leave his land. Her husband found land for a new compound at Hollaande, where they both settled.

Ten percent of a serf's harvest from both field and garden was given to the proprietor of the land. The ten percent (*farilla*) was paid for all crops from the fields, but only for corn from the gardens. It was not obligatory for taro, manioc, other root crops, and the fruits of trees, although these were often given as gifts to the land owner. This payment was not the main economic exploitation of the serfs, for all Fulbe, by their interpretation of Islam, were obligated to give away ten percent of their harvest. A land owner, however, could give his *farilla* to whomever he wanted, whereas serfs had to give it to the proprietor of the land. Further, a serf who refused to pay the *farilla* would be denied land, whereas a Fulbe who did not pay only rendered the harvest impure.

Lands for the fields had to be obtained each year from the owner of the land, usually from the serf's master. The owner of the fields and the serf's Fulbe were most often, but not always, the same individual, because the most desirable arrangement was to have the fields of a serf next to those of his master. This provided for more efficient exploitation of labor, because less time would be lost in travelling. The land for the compound was not renewed annually but was granted in perpetuity. Due to the Fulbe mode of inheritance, the owner of the land and the owner of the serfs were less likely to be the same individual than in the case of fields. Despite examples of serfs who were removed from their natal compounds, the compound was generally considered as belonging to the serf. It was expected that a serf's compound would be "inherited" by his children; that is, under normal circumstances, they would continue to live there with their families. The serfs developed rights to their compounds through usage. These rights were limited by the payment of the *farilla,* and if a serf wanted to expand his compound (which was continually being done to provide land for his sons), he had to obtain the permission of the proprietor of the land.

The serfs' most important obligations to their masters were in the form of labor. This labor was of decisive importance for the economic wealth of the Fulbe. Men, women, and children worked five days a week for their masters from early morning until early afternoon at the various key economic tasks. The men cleared and cultivated fields, brought wood for drying corn, built and maintained the houses and the compound fences of their masters. The women cultivated the women's gardens of their master's wives, brought water, cleaned clothes, helped prepare food, and cared for the children. Children did domestic work. This pattern of labor appears to be relatively old. René Caillié, in visiting the Mande village of Kampaya (which borders on the Fouta-Djallon), observed a serf village where the serfs were cultivating rice. "I was informed that, in the Fouta-Djallon, the negroes [serfs] are allowed two days in the week to work in their own fields, that is to say the ground which furnished their subsistence" (1830: 212).

The great amount of labor that serfs had to do for their masters hindered their own production. Prior to more recent developments, they are said to have been mainly dressed in rags—discards from their masters—and to have eaten little fonio and rice, but primarily the root crops from their own gardens. Their houses were smaller and poorly constructed, and they did not own cattle, except in exceptional circumstances. In sum, as a group they were significantly poorer than the Fulbe.

The masters had certain obligations toward their serfs. They provided food during the time the serfs worked for them in the fields or in the household, provided clothes if their serfs had none, provided animals for slaughter at life-cycle ceremonies if their serfs and kinsmen had none, attended the life-cycle ceremonies of their serfs, and provided ritual services when required.

There were many Fulbe who did not own serfs or lived in areas where the number of serfs in the population was lower, thereby reducing the overall economic significance of serfdom. As we have seen, the number of serfs in proportion to Fulbe was directly proportional to the density of the population of the region as a whole, and to the proximity to a large political, military, or religious center, for the greatest number of prisoners became the serfs of the chiefs. Moreover the province chiefs had groups of male serfs who served as their armed body guards and also fought for them. This group was known as the *suufa*.[11] The area of Popodara, relatively close to the capital of Labe, and in one of the most densely settled areas of the Fouta-Djallon has a very high proportion of former serfs to Fulbe, and this study is meant to apply only to the central plateau area. All three ranks of Fulbe could and did own serfs.

The serfs served the Fulbe in capacities other than as agricultural laborers. There were (and are) a great number of specialized crafts in the Fouta-Djallon. The most important craft among the serfs was that of blacksmith (*baillo,* s.; *wailube,* pl.). Blacksmiths performed a variety of tasks, including smelting and

11. In struggles for the position of *lando diwal* or *almamy* Fouta the *suufa* were of great importance because they were the only ones of the chief's followers who owed him complete and unambiguous loyalty. The *suufa* did not live in the serf village, but in the compound of the *lando diwal*. This group fits the notion of "personal slaves" so common throughout West Africa.

forging iron, making iron tools (hoes, axes, knives, adzes, and a tool resembling a machete, and the tools necessary for making these tools), jewelrymaking (goldwork primarily), and wood work (doors, fence, gates, and wood posts for the houses). Whereas blacksmiths constituted a separate caste in other parts of West Africa, they did not in the Fouta-Djallon. A blacksmith had an owner just as any other serf, and was obligated to work for him without compensation. Other Fulbe paid in kind for the items they needed. It was common practice for a *misside* chief or a Fulbe elder to apprentice one of his serfs to a blacksmith, who could refuse such a request only with difficulty. Blacksmiths cultivated their own fields and gardens, but were released from much agricultural labor in order to make tools.

The next important group of artisans among the serfs were the leather workers (*garankedyo,* s.; *garankebe,* pl.). They were few in number compared to blacksmiths and their tasks were more limited. They made sandals, sheaths for swords and knives, the leather coverings for written sayings inside amulets, saddles for horses, sacks, and leather covering for the Koran and other Islamic works. They worked primarily during the dry season, but were freed (although not completely) from working in their masters' fields. Their masters could ask them to make what they needed without reimbursement. The apprentices of the leatherworkers were usually their sons, although, as in the case of blacksmiths, apprenticeship was also open to other serfs' children and to serfs selected by their masters.[12]

The third and fourth groups of artisans were the cloth weavers (*sannyowo,* s.; *sannyoobe,* pl.) and the bamboo-basket makers. Their tasks were less specialized, required less training, and did not free them from work in the fields of their masters. Bamboo-basket makers were regarded as the least skilled and the least important artisans.

Many tasks, now regarded as specialties, were formerly per-

12. There were leather workers among the Diakanke who were known as *sylla,* just as were the serf leather workers. The former, however, were free.

formed as part of the labor obligation of serfs. These included the building of fences, the construction and maintenance of houses, and the roofing and re-roofing of houses. In any serf village, particularly a larger one, were found serfs with skills in the various crafts. They lived in and participated in the life of the village as would any serf. In the environs of Popodara, none of the artisan groups were endogamous. The products of the artisans were not important components of the long-distance trade carried on by the Fulbe. Each *misside* had its own set of artisans who worked on command and whose products were primarily bartered for grain. However, not all artisans were serfs. Certain crafts were reserved for the Fulbe; these included, for the men, the embroidery of robes and hats and copying the Koran, and, for the women, the making of raffia bowl covers. Other ethnic groups within the Fouta-Djallon also had specialties. Thus, the remaining Diallonke continued to make pots, which until very recently were found in every house to keep water, and vessels for cooking.

The internal organization of a serf village was an imperfect replica of a Fulbe village. Major patrilineages and minimal lineages existed, but not the maximal lineages. Although kin groups played an important part in the lives of the serfs, many strategic decisions about the key areas of life—handled by the elders of the major lineages in Fulbe villages—could only be made with the counsel of the appropriate Fulbe. The most important Fulbe for any serf was his owner. It was the serf's owner (or husband if the owner was a woman) who received part of the bridewealth, whose consent was required for marriage, who provided animals for the life-cycle ceremonies when necessary, and who would receive at least one-half of his property when he died.

The Fulbe followed the general Islamic pattern for the inheritance of serfs. The owner of a woman serf became the owner of her offspring. Women serfs were of greater importance than males because they would produce more serfs. The prices for serfs at the end of the nineteenth century reflected this, for the cost of girls

39

was higher than that of boys. The fact that the owner of a woman became master of her children also had consequences for the marriage of serfs. The owner of a woman quite clearly would not want his serf to marry far away, and from the owner's point of view the most desirable marriage was between his own serfs. The reasons for such a preference do not lie only in a wish to maintain geographical proximity, but in a drive to reinforce the social ties binding master to serfs.

Relations between master and serf varied. The expressed ideal for the master was that he treat his serf well and fairly and share with him during times of scarcity. We have already mentioned the numerous reciprocal obligations between master and serf. However, a serf had little recourse against a bad master except appeal to either the chief or to the judges of the mosque.

The precolonial serf village was not in any sense an independent or autonomous community. Many of the institutions of the serf village were no different from those of the Fulbe, but the serfs lacked political control over them. Political leadership within the serf village lay with the *manga*. The *manga* was either a serf of a chief, when the chief owned serfs in that particular serf village or the serf of another notable. The role of *manga* was to represent the chief in the serf village. He was therefore responsible for seeing that the serfs met their obligations and served as a communication link between the serf village and the chief.

Disputes within the serf village were generally handled by the elders of the village, with the *manga* having a strong voice in such matters. However, any dispute between a Fulbe and a serf, or even disputes between serfs of different masters when compensation was involved, were settled by the Fulbe. All men were not considered equal in Fulbe precolonial legal practices. The testimony of a serf was not equal to that of a Fulbe, and the penalty for a Fulbe who killed a serf was compensation paid to the owner of the serf, whereas the penalty for a serf who killed a Fulbe was execution.

The political ties of the serfs were vertical. A serf was tied more to his master than he was to the other members of his village. In a conflict situation, for example a feud between two Fulbe lineages, the serfs of the two lineages would fight at the sides of their masters, regardless of their own kin relationship. In certain contexts the Fulbe considered their own kinship ties in conflict situations more important than territorial ones. If there were a conflict between two *missides* and a man had kinsmen of the same maximal or major patrilineage on the other side, he would either fight with his patrilineage or not fight. The way serfs were inherited reinforced their vertical ties. Because residence was patrilocal but the inheritance of serfs passed through the mother, the serfs of many different masters came to live in one serf village. Moreover ties between serfs of the same master were strong enough to produce a fictive kin category known as "serfs of one master" (*dyom gooto*), which entailed much face-to-face contact and mutual assistance.

Marriage between Fulbe women and serf men was prohibited. Two forms of union between serf women and Fulbe men existed: concubinage, the children from which would be returned to the serf village and remain serf; and marriage, the children from which became Fulbe. Such marriages were frequent, particularly between the members of a chiefly lineage and their serfs, and it provided a way for members of a chiefly lineage to avoid marriage with other maximal lineages, thereby avoiding affinal relationships and obligations. Fulbe-serf marriages were also advantageous because bridewealth payments were lower. However, this only applied when the Fulbe spouse was the master of the girl he married. When a Fulbe man wanted to marry a serf girl of another master, he had to secure the consent of the master and give him a substantial part of the bridewealth, in addition to the normal bridewealth due to the parents of the girl.

Ties of marriage between Fulbe and serf did not increase the status of the serf. Affinal obligations between Fulbe and serf, although nominally carried out, tended to lapse over time. The marriage of a serf daughter to a Fulbe was viewed by the serfs as the loss of a daughter and her children, not the gain of Fulbe affines and potential advantages.

In Islam, and therefore in Fouta-Djallon, provision was made for the freeing of serfs. Fulbe freed serfs, although rarely, to atone for major contraventions of Islamic practice. We have only one account of a serf revolt (Gordon Laing 1825) said to have taken place in 1756. However, during this time the Fulbe had not yet consolidated their control over much of the Fouta-Djallon; thus it is not clear whether those who fled were serfs of the Fulbe or were indigenous Diallonke, who paid tribute to the Fulbe but had not yet become serfs.

Fulbe dominance over the serfs was not simply political and economic. The serfs were dependent on the Fulbe for religious direction of all their major ceremonies. A significant part of most ceremonies (including birth, death, circumcision) required the sacrificial slaughtering of an animal. The serfs had to call upon their master to slit the throat of the animal. The status of serfs was reinforced by other Islamic practices, although these do not necessarily derive from the Koran, but rather reflect the fusion of Islam and Fulbe practices.

Serfs could not attain positions as religious teachers or leaders. Achievement of these religious statuses in Fulbe society took many years of study. The ability to read and write Arabic was crucial. Serfs were Islamic, but they were given only the most minimal education and thus denied the means to attain such statuses. The serfs performed their prayers and other religious obligations, but there were certain aspects of their life which the Fulbe regarded as non-Islamic—the playing of drums, the dancing of men at male circumcision ceremonies, and the extensive practice of sorcery. Although the Fulbe were dependent upon serfs for the circumcision of Fulbe boys and the clitoridectomy of Fulbe girls, the serfs were dependent on their masters for the religious direction necessary to live an Islamic life and attain Paradise.

THE IMPACT OF FRENCH COLONIAL RULE

Traditional Fulbe society in the Fouta-Djallon was altered radically by French colonial rule. In this section I will: 1) present a summary of political changes, including the failure of indirect rule and the changing role of chieftainship; 2) consider the economic impact of colonialism by examining the French position on the serfs, taxation, the introduction of money and markets, and new labor demands. The reasons for the decline of serfdom and the creation of a peasantry will then be discussed.

THE POLITICAL IMPACT

The Fouta-Djallon excited the interest of both the French and British during the early and middle nineteenth century (Newbury 1965, Crowder 1968, Suret-Canale 1959, 1970). Both countries considered the Fouta a wealthy and desirable area and competed for the trade of the Fulbe. The British attempted penetration primarily through Sierra Leone and secondarily through Rio Nuñez, the French primarily by way of Cayor and Boundou in Senegal. British and French expeditions to the Fouta alternated throughout the nineteenth century, while the Fouta remained independent, viable, and united. Toward the end of the century both the French and British sought to make the Fouta a protectorate. The Englishman Gouldsberry obtained the signature of one *almamy*, while the Frenchmen Noirot and Bayol obtained the signatures of representatives of both the Soroyas and Alfayas. By obtaining the signatures of both *Almamy* Ahmadu, the ruling Alfaya, and the Soroya nominee, *Almamy* Ibrahima Sory, and thereby paying attention to the political realities of the Fouta, the French were able to exert greater influence than the British. Moreover, the French agreed to pay each one an annual rent of three thousand francs.

From 1888 until 1896 the leaders of the Fouta experienced in-

creasing French presence and influence. They attempted to coun-
teract it by increasing contact with the English. However, the
almamys apparently were unaware of the Anglo-French accords
of 1889, by which the French had the right to place a resident at
Timbo, and the English could no longer intervene (Crowder
1968: 94). As late as 1891 the major French purpose was to extend
commerce. Thus the instructions for Mr. de Beeckman, a French
colonial official sent from Senegal to the Fouta-Djallon, were to
attempt to obtain a greater amount of trade through French controlled areas (removed from Sierra Leone) and to sign another
protectorate agreement maintaining the integrity of the Fouta-
Djallon, but establishing greater commercial rights for the
French.[13]

In 1896 the French decided to take political control and sent a
military expedition against *Almamy* Bokar Biro. The result was
the defeat of the Fulbe army at Poredaka and the death of Bokar
Biro and his son. The French success in dividing the leaders of the
Fulbe was critical in the conquest of the Fouta-Djallon. To this
end a separate treaty was signed the same year with Alfa Yaya,
chief of the province of Labe, the largest and most powerful
province. This treaty insured that Alfa Yaya would not come to
the aid of *Almamy* Bokar Biro.

During the years 1896 to 1905 the French retained the Fulbe

13. Conakry, 16 October 1891.

Instructions for Mr. de Beeckman, charged with a mission to the Fouta concerning commerce: We would like to insist strongly that if possible, to obtain a written argument with the *almamys* that the *almamys* spend money
along the Southern rivers, that they send the Foulbe caravans directly to the
coast, and to definitely renounce their relations with the English. You will
be able to easily demonstrate to them that they will be able to find the same
articles at the same price in Conakry as in Sierre Leone.

The instructions go on to say that Beeckman should make the *almamy* understand that the French respect the Fulbe mores and customs, that the French
intention was only to develop commerce, not to occupy militarily the Fouta nor
in any way oppose the laws and ways of the Fulbe (from the National Archives
of Guinea, 1891).

political organization but removed chiefs opposing their rule.[14] However, by 1904 the large indigenous political units were found to be interfering with effective control over the population (Suret-Canale 1966). Therefore the French initiated a political reorganization that took control out of the hands of the traditional province leaders. Alfa Yaya was arrested and exiled in 1905, and shortly thereafter the *diwal* of Labe was divided into three *cercles* (which were quite different from the *diwal*) each with a *chef de cercle* appointed by the French. The function of these new chiefs was only administrative: "The new province chiefs are only to be the agents of transmission, to be, as it were, the liaison between administrative authority and the population" (Demougeot 1944: 81).

The *missides* were judged the key political units in this new organization. The *misside* chiefs were appointed by and responsible to the French. However, because there were so many *missides* and only a small number of French administrators, any real political control was precluded.[15] In 1913, the *missides* were grouped into districts, each with a French-appointed chief. In 1919 these districts were grouped into *cantons,* each headed by a chief chosen by the French: "Between the *misside* too small and the *cercle* too large, the *canton* has been destined to become the basic administrative area" (Demougeot 1944: 81).

From then until the end of the colonial period the *canton* remained the most important political unit, and the *chef de canton* the most important Fulbe political figure. Thus the French pattern of rule proceeded from indirect rule, through the destruction of the larger traditional political units and direct French administration, to a compromise, the *canton,* which met their

14. The provisions of the treaty of February 6, 1897 stipulated that the French would respect the actual constitution of the Fouta, and that the *almamys* would continue to rule the entire Fouta subject to the supervision of a French administrator who would take the title of *Résident du Fouta-Djallon.*

15. In 1912 the *cercle* of Labe, which was much smaller than the original *diwal,* included 84 principal *missides* and 156 secondary ones.

needs for greater control while making fewer demands upon them for direct administration.

Chieftainship had been hereditary within the agnatic line, but the French attempted to find a compromise between legitimacy, subserviency, and ability. Thus the chiefs tended to come from the collateral lines of former chiefs, at least in the early years of French rule. These were men who under ordinary conditions would not have acceded to chieftainship, but who nevertheless had some legitimate claim to the office. In the face of the well-defined political organization of the Fulbe, the French attempted to maintain the legitimacy of the chiefs, while at the same time dismembering the larger territorial units of the Fouta-Djallon. Their view of the position of the *chef de canton* is summarized by the French administrator Demougeot: "Chosen from among the elite of the elders, the *chef de canton* joins representation of French command to that of his personal prestige, and to his knowledge of the whites he adds his knowledge of the native" (1944: 81). The *chefs de canton* of Ore Koumba were always selected from among the Khalduyanke of Popodara, and almost all were descendants of chiefs of the *misside*.[16] The last *chef de canton* of Popodara was the youngest son of a *cercle* chief of Labe.

The province of Labe had become the *canton* of Labe by 1920. Its traditional borders were redefined, two parts being ceded to the Portuguese, and four other relatively large areas becoming separate *cercles*. The capital town of Labe, which had been the seat of the chief of the *diwal,* became a *canton*. The *chef de canton* for Labe was neither politically nor administratively higher than the other *chefs de canton*. The *misside* of Popodara was first made part of the French-conceived *misside* Hinde, and then became the seat of the *canton* of Ore Koumba. Within the *canton* of Ore Koumba there were approximately 30 *missides*.

Political reorganization was coupled with an end to the tradi-

16. However, in several instances in Labe, the French appointed as chiefs members of maximal patrilineages other than the Khalduyanke.

46

tional economic source of power of the chiefs, the *kummabite*, and with efforts to make revenue from French taxation the major source of wealth for the chiefs. The French conquest also led to an end of warfare and the slave trade, which further diminished the sources of wealth of the chiefs. In sum, the confederation of *diwals* that made up the Fouta-Djallon was ended. The position of *almamy* Fouta was eliminated as was that of province chief. Moreover, for those who now sought power it was obtained by virtue of their relation to the French, and much less through genealogical relationship to other chiefs or through building up an independent political base of support.

The chief in French West Africa progressively lost his traditional authority while his new functions of taxation, recruiting of forced labour and troops and checking on anti-French movements within his area of supervision, together with the authoritarian way in which he was treated by the Commandant, transformed him from the embodiment of the collective will of the community into an agent of some of the most hated aspects of French colonial rule. (Crowder 1968: 193)

However, we must distinguish between levels of chieftainship. The *chefs de canton* who replaced the province chief fit the description of Crowder (1968) and Suret-Canale (1966). Even though the French attempted to give them some aspect of legitimacy by selecting them from the collateral lines or even occasionally a direct line from former chiefs, they were viewed by the population as agents of the French. The situation was much less clear with respect to the chief of the *misside*. The establishment of the *chef de canton* did not bring an end to the *misside* chief. Rather, the chief was appointed by the *chef de canton* with the approval of the French *commandant*. During the colonial era, it was the *misside* chief who was both colonizer and colonized.

Village chiefs were placed under the dependence of the *chefs de canton*, their administrative role was much less marked than the latter, except as a relay in the fiscal system. Village chiefs conserved their customary characteristics and their representative nature, since, as in the tradi-

47

tional system, the nature of their powers was democratic and their authority depended much more upon the agreement of the group than upon the nomination by a superior official. Lombard 1967: 110)

The *chef de canton* was surrounded by kinsmen of his major patrilineage (referred to as *dyagafara*) and by his courtiers (known as *mbatula*), who came from different lineages, including serfs. These two groups became as hated as the *chef de canton* because they were executors of his orders. They were tied to the chief, and the more resources they drew from the population, the better their relationship to him. The *misside* chief did not have a "court" of his own. His accession to office depended on nomination by the *chef de canton*. His retention of the position depended on his ability to balance the exactions of the *chef de canton* with the needs of the residents of his *misside*. There were, of course, *misside* chiefs who allied themselves with the *chef de canton* but there were many who attempted to carry out their mandate as representatives of their *misside* to the higher political authorities. Whereas the former *chefs de canton* are now discredited, former *misside* chiefs have attained political office in the committee system.

The position of *manga* continued in the serf village during the colonial period. At Hollaande and surrounding villages, the *manga* was appointed by the *chef de canton*. His main role was to organize and supply labor for the *chefs de canton* and the French, but he also played an important role within the village by virtue of his position and relation to the powers that be.

The system of social stratification based on maximal lineages diminished in importance during the colonial period. Whether one was a member of a "chiefly," "free," or "bush" maximal lineage mattered less, since the basis of accession to chieftainship as well as its economic base had changed. Since the Fulbe of the "bush" no longer had to pay the *kummabite,* the earlier status distinctions between them and the "free" Fulbe lost their significance. However, it took much longer for the serf-Fulbe distinction to decrease in importance, and the process has not yet come to an end.

THE ECONOMIC IMPACT

French colonial policy ended warfare and the slave trade on the one hand, but maintained the social status quo on the other. The French administrators of the Fouta were clearly cognizant of the situation of the serfs, but let administrative convenience provide an excuse for maintaining the institution of serfdom. Only in specific political circumstances did the French act to free serfs. For example, one of the tactics used to reduce the power of the *almamy* Fouta was to free all his serfs and resettle them in a new *canton* near Timbo, with a former serf appointed as *chef de canton*. Another example was the retaliation against a religious leader, Tierno Ouali from Goumba, who was accused of leading a revolt against the French. As part of his punishment all of his serfs and those of his close followers were freed. In 1918 Paul Marty, who was engaged to survey Islamic movements in Guinea to obtain information about their anti-French and anticolonialist potentialities, recommended that serfs be left under their masters. He argued that to free more serfs would increase even further the opposition and resentment of the "notables" of the Fouta. To buttress this position he stated that because the serfs were ". . . brutalized as a result of centuries of ignorance and servitude, the greatest part of serfs today are of a heart-breaking intellectual inferiority and it is necessary that they have several generations to reach the level of the other blacks" (1921: 448).

Although the French did not deliberately attempt to destroy serfdom, the series of changes wrought by them led nevertheless to its gradual undermining.[17] These processes were both political

17. A decree was issued by the French in 1905 prohibiting "an agreement having as its object the alienation of the liberty of a third party." The decree also suppressed domestic slavery, although, according to both Crowder (1968) and Suret-Canale (1964a), no measures were taken to enforce this. Crowder gives four reasons to account for the French reluctance to end slavery or serfdom:

First of all, the French used a system of forced labour in their occupation of West Africa which was tantamount to Africa domestic slavery. Secondly, they had used 'captifs' as a reward for their African troops, and could hardly with-

and economic, the latter being more important. One of the major factors in changing the nature of Fulbe-serf relations was taxation. It is instructive to read the French administrators' monthly reports, whose dominant queries seem to have been how do we count everybody and make sure that the Fulbe pay their taxes? [18] The amount of money collected in taxes seemed the index of the success or failure of both the French administrators and their Fulbe subordinates. Taxes were imposed as soon as the French gained control of the Fouta. Thus the first collection of taxes in Labe occurred in 1897. Although it was theoretically a head tax, the censuses had not been completed at the time. Thus it was in fact a house tax, based on the assumption that there were five inhabitants per house; 252,700 francs were collected. By 1902 this had risen to 771,660 francs (Gauthier MS.).

A large share of the tax money allocated to the Fulbe was given to the chiefs. In 1897, before political reorganization, the allocation of taxes was 10 percent to the *almamy* Fouta, 10 percent to the *diwal* chief, 20 percent to the *misside* chief, and 60 percent to the French (Gauthier MS.). The province chief of Labe, Alfa Yaya, received 20 percent; taxation was one of the mechanisms used to detach Labe from the confederation by providing greater tax revenues

---

draw them overnight. Thirdly, so many of the slaves in French West Africa were 'captifs' as distinct from domestic slaves that it was feared social dislocation of enormous proportions would ensue. Finally, the question of the domestic slave, born to the role as distinct from subjected to it, was a problem the administrators found difficult to tackle in the early years of colonial rule (1968: 183).

18. There were a variety of reports used by French administrators. I found one particularly useful. This was the Rapport Politique to the Governor-General of Afrique Occidentale Française which included the following: "Analyze. Questions en Cours: leur suite—FAITS NOUVEAUX: appréciation, conclusions—IMPÔT: faits d'ordre politique et administratif relatif à la rentré de l'impôt—ESPRIT DES POPULATIONS: attitude des chefs et des personnages influents—QUESTIONS MUSULMANES: mouvement islamique, marabouts, leur influence—ECOLES: laïques, catholique, protestantes, musulmanes—MISSIONS: catholiques et protestantes—JUSTICE INDIGÈNE: causes importantes, attitudes des magistrates indigènes—DEMANDS." These reports are found in the National Archives of Guinea.

to the chief of Labe than to the other province chiefs of the Fouta-Djallon. By 1908, following the first political reorganization, the percentage of the tax money allocated to the Fulbe fell from 40 to 8 percent, with 5 percent going to a *misside* chief, and 3 percent to a district chief. With the division of the Fouta into *cantons,* the *chefs de canton* and the *chefs de villages* (the *misside* chiefs) received the same percentage as their earlier counterparts. In sum, the French at first gave the chiefs a large share of the taxes collected to obtain their loyalty. Having gained their loyalty, they reduced the percentages. Their dependence on tax revenues rendered them economically dependent on the colonial power.

At the turn of the century, very little money circulated in the Fouta-Djallon. Taxes were at first paid in kind, principally in rubber. During the early years of colonization rubber was the most important export of Guinea, and many wild rubber trees in the Fouta-Djallon were soon tapped by serfs so their masters could pay their taxes. Rubber was used to pay taxes from 1899 to 1914.[19] When its price fell dramatically after the opening of rubber plantations in the Far East, the French refused to accept taxes in kind any longer. The Fulbe were then forced to find various other ways of making money.

When taxation was first introduced, it was more or less assumed that the master would pay the taxes for his serfs, but the change from the payment of taxes in kind to payment in money broke down the traditional reciprocity of Fulbe-serf relations. A rising tax rate, combined with a scarcity of money, created a situation in which the Fulbe could no longer pay or even contribute to the taxes of their serfs. All serf and Fulbe informants indicated that from this point the serfs began to spend less time working for their masters. With real political power in the hands of the

19. The height of the rubber boom in Guinea was 1909 to 1910, when the price of a kilo of rubber was 15 to 20 francs at Conakry. In the interior it was 12 francs. By 1915 the price had fallen to 2.50 francs for a kilo at Conakry (Suret-Canale 1964a: 66).

French, the Fulbe could no longer employ force legitimately to enforce their demands for serf labor. In addition, the serfs were subjected to contradictory demands for labor by their masters, the French, and the *chefs de canton*. The combination of the breakdown in reciprocal Fulbe-serf obligations and the competition between the masters and the colonial authorities for the labor of the serfs led to the gradual decline of serfdom.

The impact of taxation was felt in other ways as well. The French administrator Gilbert Vieillard describes some of these effects.

The young people who left to earn [the tax] often did not return; taxpayers who have emigrated are in hiding, in flight or dead, but they are inscribed on the tax roles, and this makes the charges for those remaining even heavier. Too bad, the money had to be found: the people were reduced to selling goods of those who had paid, but who did not dare to complain too much. First animals were sold—cows, sheep and hens; then grain, cooking-pots, Korans, all that could be sold. Prices were very low. The chief's men and the Syrians fished in troubled waters: the taxpayers rarely received any change between the sale prices and the figure of the tax due. When there was nothing left [to sell] the coming harvest and the children would be pawned. (1940: 171)

The Fulbe's search for tax money had two desirable consequences for the French: it created a supply of cheap labor and made it necessary for the Fulbe to sell their goods for money and to buy French manufactured goods. The need for money began the gradual end of the system of exchange in kind for goods and services, and it changed several traditional patterns of exchange. The cloth weavers traditionally worked on command for payment in grain or small animals, either when they needed goods themselves or when asked to do so by their masters. With the introduction of money taxes, they often became itinerant traders, moving with their looms from one area to another, attempting to earn the amount necessary for themselves and their families. The blacksmith's established rates of exchange (a hoe was exchanged for 4 measures of fonio or corn, an axe for 8 to 10 measures of fonio or corn, and a door for 40 measures) were changed into money.

Interestingly, there is no Fulfulde word in the Fouta-Djallon for *butcher*. There are only words for the slaughtering, skinning, and cutting-up of an animal. The French word *boucher* refers to someone who sells meat for profit, something that was not done in precolonial times. The need for money led to an increase in the slaughtering of cattle. Fulbe cattle owners who had no other way to earn money could either trade an animal by bringing it to Nuñez, Conakry, or Freetown, or sell its meat. During the period from 1915 until the establishment of markets, money was usually so scarce that a man would sell about one half of a cow for money and exchange the rest for grain. The sale of meat was irregular in both time and place until the founding of the local markets. The new job of butcher opened up opportunities for serfs never before possible. The first butcher at Popodara was a former serf, who had been placed in charge of the cutting-up of the slaughtered animals by the *chef de canton*. As his own funds increased, he began buying cattle from those who needed money and selling the meat for a profit. He is presently the richest butcher at the market.

Precolonial Fulbe trade patterns were complex. They involved long-distance trade under the supervision of the province chiefs. Only those merchants who had the explicit approval of a province chief could traverse the Fouta. Most trade took place at the residence of a province chief.[20]

The French created a marketplace in what is now the city of Labe in 1900. Merchants from other parts of Guinea came to trade and initially there were fights between the Fulbe and the alien merchants (Susu and Malinke). An anonymous French administrator described these hostilities.

---

20. Caillié stated he met several merchants going to the market of Labe to sell some calabashes and earth pots but gives no further details. He could have been referring to the residence of the *province* chief (1830: 300). My informants maintained the French introduced the marketplace to Labe.

There is between them [the African merchants, the Dioulas] and the Fulbe both a caste and racial hatred, a preexisting hostility toward any business dealings. The Fulbe, whose chiefs only recently had been pillaging and looting the caravans descending from the Soudan, sensed well that the freedom of commerce and encouragement given the Dioulas were the result of the French administration. The Dioulas wanting this protection, and on the look-out for any offenses they could commit, continued in their vexatious behavior. It should be understood that the wandering merchants practiced theft in the guise of commerce, selling and buying only stolen animals. (1903: MS.)

The same administrator proposed a solution to the conflict between Fulbe and merchants.

The most efficacious solution to adopt hasn't been suggested yet. The necessary change is simply a transformation of the Fulbe mind, a struggle against their Islamic spirit; pushing the Fulbe to engage in trade themselves, having them bring their own animals from the market at Labe to Conakry. (1903: MS.)

Whether or not the Fulbe became merchants as a result of deliberate French efforts is not clear; but it was not long before the Fulbe themselves realized that in order to survive and prosper under colonial rule they would have to become merchants.

Despite the increasing use of money for exchange, marketplaces developed only in the regional capitals during the first three decades of French rule. Some trade was carried out by itinerant merchants, but otherwise the Fulbe had to go to a regional center to sell merchandise or to obtain needed manufactured goods or money. It was not until the road from Labe to Senegal was completed in the 1930s that markets were established in rural areas.

The market of Popodara was established in 1937 and was the first in the *cercle* of Labe.[21] The story of how it was created illustrates the role of the *chef de canton* as an administrator of

21. Although I searched for the archives relating to the opening of the markets at Popodara and in the surrounding areas I did not find them. Thus I did not learn the reasons the French had for creating markets.

French policy. All household heads were told they had to bring some item to sell. The day of the first market hardly anyone showed up. The *chef de canton* sent his courtiers to order the people to the market under threat of punishment and confiscation of their property. The scene was repeated, and further markets were held until the population became aware that their goods were not being stolen from them and that they were allowed to keep the money they received for the food they sold. Then attendance and participation at the market grew. It is interesting to note that the first official of the market, who collected the market tax and supervised the trading, was a serf.

With the success of the market at Popodara, other markets were started in the region of Labe. From the beginning almost all transactions at the market involved money; an earlier barter system had been transformed into an exchange system based on money.

Markets were also important in creating the new situation of competition between serf and Fulbe. New occupations, such as merchant and transporter, became available to both Fulbe and serf. Positions of relatively high status thus became open to serfs.

Money created a new kind of equality, and older, unchangeable statuses became transformable. Among the new saleable items was the status of Fulbe itself. We have briefly discussed the ceremony of *rimdingol,* the freeing of a serf by his master, usually to atone for breaking an Islamic law. During the colonial period, this ceremony became available for a price. It was possible for serfs who accumulated a great deal of wealth to approach their master and a religious leader and ask what they would have to pay in order to become "free," that is, to become a Fulbe, and to change their name. Although it became possible to change status in this way not many serfs took advantage of the ceremony, for it involved moving from a serf to a Fulbe village, thus severing one's kin ties. Most serfs who had the ceremony performed lived in towns or cities and did not intend to return to their natal *misside.*

Taxation and the introduction of money and markets acted to break down the labor obligations of serfdom, but new labor demands were imposed on the serfs by the *chef de canton*. As an administrative agent for the French, he had to obtain men to work on the roads and other "public works," obtain conscripts for the French army, and make milk, vegetables, and fruits available to the French. The *chef de canton* attempted to fill his quotas for laborers and army conscripts from the population of serfs. Moreover, the *chef de canton* needed labor to maintain his own fields and household; again he called on the serfs. The procedure for furnishing military conscripts to the French followed similar lines. The number of men needed was announced to the governor of the *cercle,* who in turn divided the quotas among the dfferent *cantons*. It then became the responsibility of the *chef de canton* to bring the men to Labe. The two Fulbe I knew who had served in the French army had both been volunteers. The recruitment of serfs on the other hand was forced, although some individuals did enlist.

Although the serfs did not like serving in the French army—many informants said young men fled to Senegal and Portuguese Guinea to avoid military service—it did provide a source of income. Many men sent home money from France to buy cattle (which serfs did not formerly own), and upon their return from service they used money and credit obtained from the French to buy cattle and plows or, perhaps, to establish themselves as merchants. Those who served fifteen years or more in the French army received an annual pension which could be applied to the same purposes. Thus, on the one hand, the suffering and exploitation of the serfs increased under colonial rule because the burden of forced labor fell mainly on them; on the other hand, the colonial period presented new opportunities for escape from their status and poverty.

Three

Fulbe Society

THE FULBE AS PEASANTS

An analysis of contemporary society in the Fouta-Djallon leads to the real and important problems of how to characterize the former serf population, which should be examined before discussing their social organization. In the nineteenth and early twentieth centuries there were clear social, economic, and political differences between serfs and Fulbe. However, since the end of serfdom, these differences are no longer so pronounced. Moreover, the study of the present involves a study of change.

One solution is to characterize former serfs by saying that they are, or are becoming, "Fulbe." However, to do so implies that the other strata among the Fulbe have remained unchanged. In attempting to understand the new sociopolitical and economic conditions in which the population lives, and the likely direction for the future, the concept of peasantry seems most applicable. This is not to say, of course, that the earlier society did not condition and determine responses to the processes of transformation in the Fouta. However, to simply consider the present population of the Fouta as Fulbe is to accede to the notion that in some sense the Fulbe remain a "tribe."[1]

1. It is also interesting to note that although use of the term *tribalism* has been called into question (Wallerstein, for example, uses *ethnicity*) the term *tribe* has not. Also see William Bascom (1962) and Paul Mercier (1965). Cohen and Middleton hedge on the question and appear to use *tribe* and *ethnic unit*

57

The Fulbe of the Fouta-Djallon are a group who have strong continuities with the past, but should, as Skinner urges, be viewed as a new entity.

Some of the names which are now used as symbols for group identity do refer to distinct socio-cultural entities in the past. However, many of the so-called tribal groups were creations of the colonial period. But even those groups for which continuity with the past could be claimed have lost so many of their traditional characteristics that in fact they must be viewed as new entities (1966: 182–3).

One reason the term *peasant* has been rejected in the discussion of African societies has been the traditional concern with "tribal" peoples. It is interesting that British social anthropologists do not use the term *peasant* for African populations despite the very broad definition of peasantry given by Raymond Firth. Firth states that "peasant refers to a socio-economic category. It describes a socio-economic system of small-scale producers with a relatively simple, non-industrial technology" (1964: 17). He goes on to say that "definition of a system as 'peasant' implies that it has its own particular local character, partly because of intricate community interrelationships and partly because, in economic and social affairs, it both contributes to and draws upon a town in trade, cultural exchange and general ideology" (1964: 17). This definition by Firth is more complex than his earlier definition: "By a peasant economy one means a system of small scale producers, with a simple technology and equipment often relying primarily for their subsistence on what they themselves produce. The primary means of livelihood of the peasants is cultivation of the soil" (1951: 87). This makes it even more surprising that the terms *peasants* and *peasantry* have not been used in the analysis of African material.[2]

interchangeably (1970: 4), a procedure I find further muddles the question. My own view is that if *tribe* is to be used, it should either be used to mean the form of sociopolitical organization that arose during the Neolithic and was superseded in many areas of the world by different forms of states (see Sahlins 1969; Service 1965; Ribeiro 1968), or it should not be used at all (Fried 1968).

2. In a recent article Firth seems to expand even further the notion of peasantry. He observes that the notion of a peasant economy usually links a par-

The social anthropologists, more than others (except journalists), have used the term *tribe* to describe African societies—past or present. Gluckman (1965) has attempted to give *tribal society* a very general meaning: "the kind of community which was once described by the term 'primitive society' " (1965: xv). Gluckman emphasizes that "tribes" were something Europe once had but no longer has, which inadvertently gives justification to those who see *tribe* used in the African context as something atavistic and primitive. Furthermore, because Gluckman defines the interest of the social anthropologist as "the role of persistent custom in maintaining a social system in equilibrium" (1965: 299), we can see the link between the notion of tribe and the theoretical studies of societies in equilibrium which emphasize the study of the institutions that maintain the tribe. The focus is not on the transformation of the tribe, but rather on how the tribe maintains itself against impinging forces. An example of this approach is the dissertation of Butcher on the Fulbe of Sierra Leone.[3]

The purpose of raising this problem is limited in this study to the question of how to analyze most meaningfully the field material gathered on the Fulfulde-speaking people of the Fouta-Djallon. I have attempted to look at the social forces operating on one group, forces which are leading the group into new lines of development. These processes would be obscured if viewed through the notion of "tribe." The creation of a peasantry in the Fouta-Djallon was the result of French colonial rule, urban

---

ticular kind of economic system and a particular kind of social structure. "The simplest formulation" according to Firth "is probably the one which defines peasant farming as that which relies primarily or completely on family labor" (1969: 25). While I look forward to the application of the notion of peasantry to the study of Africa I must continue to point out the paradox of British social anthropologists formulating overly general definitions of *peasantry* but not applying them to their analyses of Africa.

3. Butcher's thesis on the Fulbe in the town of Lunsar, Sierra Leone, is of particular interest because almost all of the Fulbe in Sierra Leone originate from the Fouta-Djallon. He provides important data on the economic system and occupational stratification of the Fulbe in an urban environment. Unfortunately many of the conclusions which he reaches are based on incorrect or partial information about the Fouta-Djallon.

areas having been unknown in the Fouta-Djallon prior to colonization. Although the residence of the province chiefs tended to be
larger than most villages, it was not until the colonial era that
urban centers developed.

The case of Latin America where the creation of most of the
peasantry resulted from colonization offers a useful perspective
for viewing African rural populations. If we draw on the Latin
American example, we can perhaps recognize our own past
biases in emphasizing the "tribal" nature of African societies. We
have, by dwelling on tribes, not given enough attention to the basic social processes that have produced, and are producing, a
peasantry in Africa.

As late as 1961 an anthropologist (Fallers 1961) argued that
African cultivators are not to be called peasants. His reasoning
was that although Africans are "peasant-like" economically and
politically, African societies lack the distinction between a "high-
culture" and the "folk" culture that characterizes true peasants.
However, in the conclusion of his article, Fallers does suggest
that Christian and Islamic societies, with their accompanying
"high cultures," were and are structurally ready to receive peasant
cultures. There has long been a literate tradition in certain Islamic
areas of West Africa. The people of the Fouta-Toro in Senegal,
the Fouta-Djallon in Guinea, and the Macina region in Mali are
well known for the emphasis they put on a written Islamic education. Timbuktu was a great center of Islamic learning in the
fifteenth and sixteenth centuries. Yet despite the existence in
these areas of a written tradition, which would fit Faller's description of a "high culture," we are still faced with the question
as to whether we would want to describe these areas as peasant
before colonial contact. My answer for the Fouta-Djallon is no.
The Fulbe were transformed into peasants during the colonial
period, whereas many became Muslim by 1727. In my view the
notion of peasantry is not applicable to precolonial Fulbe society
due to the lack of development of a state in the Fouta. "It is
only when a cultivator is integrated into a society with a state—

that is when the cultivator becomes subject to the demands and sanctions of power-holders outside his social stratum—that we can appropriately speak of peasantry" (Wolf 1966: 11). There are three other reasons that lead to the conclusion that the concept of peasantry is inappropriate for the Fulbe prior to 1900. First, the majority of the population, through their major patrilineages, were landowners. Second, chiefly maximal lineages were not exempt from key economic tasks (with the exception of the chiefs of the different provinces, and the *almamys* of the largest *missides*). And third, the power of the chiefly maximal lineage of a *diwal* to extract a surplus from the other Fulbe was severely limited, the system of exaction being that of tribute and not taxation. While one stratum of precolonial Fulbe society, the serfs, approximated a peasantry, the precolonial organization differed greatly from a "feudal model" in that serfs did not constitute a majority of the population, and there were areas of the Fouta where there were few, if any, serfs.

Two recent discussions of peasantry are useful in placing the Fouta-Djallon in a peasant framework. The first discussion is that of Wolf (1966), who considers peasantry in general, and the other is by Dalton (1962, 1964, 1969), who is specifically concerned with Africa. Their approaches are complementary for they emphasize a slightly different aspect of the category of peasant.

In Wolf's view, peasants are "rural cultivators whose surpluses are transferred to a dominant group of rulers that use the surpluses both to underwrite its own standard of living and to distribute the remainder to groups in society that do not farm but must be fed for their specific goods and services in turn" (1966: 3-4). Wolf contrasts the peasant economy with that of primitives: "In primitive society, producers control the means of production, including their own labor, and exchange their own labor and its products for the culturally defined equivalent goods and services of others" (1966: 3). He then goes on to consider the critical difference between primitive and peasant cultivators. This critical difference is the production of a "fund of rent." "Where someone exercises an effective superior power, or domain, over a cultivator, the cultivator must produce a fund of rent" (1966: 9–10). Before we turn to the question of the "fund of rent" in the Fouta let us first set out Dalton's criteria for peasantry and see whether the population of the Fouta-Djallon meet such criteria.

Dalton distinguishes between the economies of primitive and peasant cultures in two ways. First, in a peasant economy most people depend for the bulk of their livelihood on production for market sale. Often resource markets are present. By *resource markets* Dalton means that labor, land, tools, and equipment are available for purchase, rent, or hire at a money price. He concludes that "it is the relative importance of markets for resources and products and cash transactions that is the principal difference between peasant and primitive economies" (1969: 13). Second, in a peasant economy, capitalist features (he does not say socialist) are present, but they are incomplete and underdeveloped compared to market organization in a modern national economy: "By incomplete is meant that within a given peasant community, some markets may be absent or petty—land may be frequently purchased or rented but labor is not, . . . or vice-versa; and that subsistence production may still be quantitatively important in some households" (1969: 13). It is clear that Dalton's distinction between subsistence (or primitive) and peasant economies will have to be further refined and analyzed.

In contrast to Wolf and Dalton, and in a very recent continuation of the discussion of the existence of African peasantries, Brokensha and Erasmus (1969) argue that no matter what conception of peasantry is applied to Africa, the fit is very poor. Thus for Ghana and Uganda they note that the rural populations have not been the "subordinate masses of a bifurcated, dual or 'feudal' society suffering from the inhibitions of a limited power image" (1969: 95). Rather they are subsistence-oriented cultivators in the process of becoming farmers. Structurally, culturally, and eco-

62

nomically they are not peasants. Brokensha's and Erasmus's analysis, it would seem, rests on at least three incorrect assumptions: that there is complete absence of a ruling class in "traditional African societies" (a phrase used as though its meaning is apparent, which it is not); that whether or not land is owned by Africans (presumably as opposed to Europeans or non-Africans) is critical for a definition of peasantry; and that African cultivators do not belong to a subordinate social stratum.[4] One of the critical areas of my disagreement with Brokensha and Erasmus is the interpretation of the impact of colonial rule and the nature of contemporary African states. In my view the state—both colonial and postcolonial—remains highly exploitative of the rural peasants, or cultivators. African peasants are coming to form an increasingly subordinate segment of the population, a trend that began during the colonial era. At the same time I would hold to the classical view (Ribeiro 1968), which interprets the rise of peasantry as connected with the rise of urban centers. There have been, and will be, some areas in Africa where peasantries will not form (as among the cocoa farmers of Ghana), but for the most part the concept of peasant is now applicable or will be. In contrast to Brokensha and Erasmus, Reining concludes that the Tanzanian Haya are peasants on the basis of a typology

4. Again, the definition of *peasantry* according to Norbeck, and cited with approval by Joel Halpern and John Brode, is:

A peasant society is a sub-society of a large stratified society which is either pre-industrial or only partly industrialized. It is further characterized by most or all of the following traits: rural residence; familial agriculture on self-owned small land holdings or other simple rural occupations providing a modest or subsistence livelihood; the family as the centrally important social unit; low social status; economic inter-dependence in varying degree with urban centers; simple culture; and attachment to the soil, the local community and tradition (in Halpern and Brode: 49).

Quite clearly this is a definition that attempts to embrace all aspects of what has been defined as constituting peasantry without specific economic, political, or cultural focus. Yet, one of the aspects is low social status. In my view this is critical, for it specifies the relation of the peasants to centralized political power. And, this is why I view the role of the colonial state as critical to the development of peasantries in the Fouta-Djallon, as well as in Africa generally.

that combines the works of Barnes, Redfield, and Wolf. Reining's argument is particularly important because East Africa has been discussed in tribal terms even more than has West Africa.

Within the Fouta-Djallon there are key economic features that lead me to regard the population as peasants. Purchase and sale transactions with cash are frequent and quantitatively important. Labor, tools, and equipment are available for purchase and hire at a money price. However, one commodity stands out above all others in its relative absence from the market, namely land. The inalienability of land remains one of the key features of peasantry not only in the Fouta-Djallon but in West Africa as a whole. During the colonial period it was possible to buy and sell in the Fouta despite the wishes of the land-owning units (patrilineages), but this process has been reversed by the present government of Guinea.

A major problem exists in analyzing the Fouta in terms of Dalton's criterion that peasants depend mainly on production for market sale for their livelihood. Many Fulbe of the Fouta-Djallon are dependent for their livelihoods on leaving the area to work for wages. The simple fact that the Fouta produces large numbers of migrant wage workers, of course, does not make it a peasant region.[5] However, where money has become the dominant form of exchange, and where there are inadequate internal means of earning money, we might reason that what the people of the region have to sell on the market is their labor.[6]

5. See Watson (1958). He argues for retaining the perspective of "tribal" structure and values in discussing an economy in which it is expected that men will leave for wage work while the organization of the "tribe" remains stable and strong.

6. The discussion of African peasantries has been continued in three recent articles: Goldschmidt and Kunkel (1971), Saul and Woods (1971), and Dalton (1972). Goldschmidt and Kunkel have continued the analysis of Fallers and Brokensha and Erasmus. My arguments against that line of approach have already been given but for a further analysis see Derman (1972). Saul and Woods have reached the same conclusions that I have, namely that African peasantries are "primarily the result of the interaction between an international capitalist economic system and traditional social-economic systems within the context of

Another major problem for considering the Fulbe as peasants within Wolf's criterion is the question of what constitutes "rent." Wolf argues that rent takes many different forms and should be very broadly defined. In the Fouta-Djallon rent took the form of taxation and labor corvée imposed by the French. Not paying taxes or refusing to work could lead either to prison or confiscation of one's property, including land. The result was the extraction of a surplus in money and labor from the inhabitants of the Fouta-Djallon. Taxation, of course, was imposed in all French colonies, but its results were not the same because of the different kinds of organization that existed prior to colonization.

THE SOCIAL ORGANIZATION OF
A FORMER-SERF VILLAGE

The social organization of Hollaande, a village of former serfs, is being restructured in the context of a new economy fundamentally unlike that of the precolonial period. The individualization of both the subsistence and commercial sectors of the economy has emphasized the small kin groups at the expense of the larger ones, while the end of serfdom has reinforced the social, and particularly the ceremonial, functions of the larger kin groups within the village. The social organization of the former serfs, as a result of their participation in the new economy and nation state, has become fundamentally the same as that of their former masters.

---

territorially defined colonial political systems" (1971: 106). Dalton (1972) takes great pains to separate his position from that of Eric Wolf. Nevertheless I still think that Dalton's earlier position is entirely compatible with Wolf's. I find myself in much less agreement with Dalton's position in his latest article. He argues that there are basically two types of peasantries, traditional and modernizing. He implies that contemporary peasantries are recapitulating the stages of European peasantries from serfdom through modern farming. Dalton's notion appears to lump under traditional and modernizing so many factors and so many time periods that the scheme loses its usefulness and I prefer the approach and analysis of Wolf (1966, 1969).

Unfortunately, all of these articles appeared too late for me to incorporate them fully into the discussion of peasants.

The kin groups and their roles are essentially the same in both populations. In the past, the serfs lacked maximal patrilineages and their major patrilineages were without genealogical depth. Present tendencies point to an ever increasing convergence between the social organization of the Fulbe and the former serfs.

In describing the social organization of Hollaande it is necessary to first discuss kinship terminology and the social relations that obtain between individuals in the various kin relationships. Although this is not directly relevant to the major points at hand, a discussion of the important kin relationships is necessary to an understanding of the composition of the larger kin groups. We will then turn to a consideration of the composition and operation of the various kin groups: the household (*beinguure*); the compound (*galle*) and minimal lineage (*suudu*); the major patrilineage (*gorol*); and matrilateral kindred (*deewol*). We have already dealt with these groups in the abstract in describing the precolonial organization of the Fouta-Djallon, but here we shall delineate them concretely in terms of one village.

KINSHIP TERMINOLOGY

The kinship terminology of the Fulbe of the Fouta-Djallon is like that of other Fulfulde-speakers in Senegal, Nigeria, and Niger. Eight generations are included in this system. The male line is distinguished from the female line. Cross and parallel cousins are distinguished. Parallel cousins and siblings are referred to by the same terms. These terms are *mownyiraawo* for an older brother (*koto* is used as well), *minyiraawo* for a younger brother, *dyaya* for an older sister, and *minyiraawo* for a younger sister. *Bandiraabe* refers to all siblings of the opposite sex. Men can refer to female maternal parallel cousins as *reemiraabe* also. *Dendang,* or cross cousins, are not distinguished by seniority.

Father and father's brothers are not usually terminologically merged (*beng* or *baaba* for father, *bappa* for father's brother), whereas mother and mother's sisters and father's other wives are

66

terminologically merged as *neene*. However, when asking about one's biological mother, it is polite to use *yumma* as opposed to *neene*. Further, one uses *neene* for his own mother and *neene ang* ("my mother") with first name for other individuals.

Seniority can be distinguished in one's father's generation. I found this practice in Fulbe villages but not in Hollaande. If father has an older brother, he is referrred to as *baaba mowdo*, "eldest father." Kinsmen (*musibbe*), which includes both the male and female lines, are terminologically distinct from affines (*esiraabe*).

For any individual there are two sets of kinsmen—his major patrilineage and his matrilateral kindred. Dupire (1962) notes (and this is the same for the Fulbe of the Fouta) that paternal kinsmen are said to be of the same blood. All members of a major patrilineage are one blood (*dyiidyang gootang*), whereas the maternal kinsmen are said to be from the same breast or to have been raised on the same milk. Milk and sucking are used as synonyms for affection.

An individual's rights to a kin group derive from the lineage of his father. A bastard is literally a man without a lineage. His counsels will not be followed; he will receive no inheritance. The maternal line of an individual provides warmth, support, and love. There is a saying to the effect that "love comes from the matrilateral kindred" (*Giggol ko ka deewol iurata*). There is another saying which incorporates a borrowing from the French: "The world changes, fathers change, but two things don't change, mother and the *deewol*" (*Aduna sansi, baaba sansi, kono pidyi didi sansalli; Neene sansalli e deewol sansalli.*) [7]

The last kin group of importance to an individual (after his marriage) are his affines. One's affines are the major patrilineage

---

7. There is no Fulfulde word for *to change*. They have adopted the French *changer,* but as there is no 'ch' sound in Fulfulde, it becomes an 's' along with the verb ending: *sansugol*. The closest word to *change* is *hailagol*, which is much closer to *transform*. Just the phrase itself provides striking evidence of the Fulbe consciousness of change.

of his wife, with the exception that those whom his wife calls "younger sibling" he calls *kenang*. His affines and the *kenang* become the matrilateral kindred of his children.

The most important "non-kin" of an individual are his age-mates (*goree*). Because members of a village are considered kinsmen, *non-kin* may not be appropriate, but insofar as relations between age-mates are not determined by a precise genealogical relationship, the term *non-kin* accurately portrays the quality of relationship. Age-mates are an individual's friends for life and the group with whom he will spend most of his time before adulthood.

The last point to be noted before a detailed presentation of the relations between kin categories is the pattern of residence. Residence is highly virilocal. Only four of the living adult males at Hollaande were not born of a member of one of the two major patrilineages. Two had been brought as children by the *chef de canton* to Hollaande, and had become adopted members of the major patrilineage of Hoore Tane. The other two individuals returned to Hollaande after the deaths of their fathers to live with their maternal grandparents. They both have received land at Hollaande, the land of their maternal grandmothers. Within the past thirty years no individual has voluntarily left Hollaande to live in another village in the Fouta.[8]

SOCIAL RELATIONS AMONG KINSMEN

Traditional Fulbe society was not egalitarian. There were marked status differences depending on sex, age, descent, and rank. Rank was the position an individual occupied in the precolonial hierarchy—member of a chiefly lineage, free Fulbe, Fulbe of the bush or serf. Polite address was used between Fulbe of different statuses,

8. We have mentioned individuals who were forced to leave, when we noted how a family was divided because a Fulbe village left the area and took their serfs with them. We have also mentioned those who are now leaving "voluntarily" to work permanently in the cities.

as between a master and his serfs, a chief and his "subjects," the *almamy* of a mosque and the members of the mosque, a man and his wives, or a man and his children. The polite form of address between unequals was not used reciprocally; it was used by those of lower position when addressing those of higher position. In addition, there was a special vocabulary of respect used to address those in a higher position, only part of which is now known.[9] The vocabulary of respect which can be conceptually distinguished from the older system of titles (chief, *almamy,* etc.), concerned the body of the honored person, the clothing he wore, and the objects he used. For example, the respectful form of *to speak* is *maakagol* instead of *woulugol*. The respectful word for *head* is *sala* instead of *hoore*. The decline in the use of the vocabulary of respect mirrors the decline in the social institutions that supported such usage.

Behavior toward one's kinsmen paralleled behavior toward those of higher or lower social, political, and religious status. The seniority and authority etiquette therefore was not simply a domestic etiquette. It was, rather, an etiquette that originated in the descent system and in social differences, and which in turn supported them. Older forms of respect have not disappeared in certain non-kin contexts. The leader of the religious center at Koula, who is referred to as *Shaiku,* is today treated much in the same way chiefs and religious leaders must have been treated fifty years ago. The *Shaiku* is not spoken to unless he speaks first; he is greeted with extreme deference and respect; and if he is seated, a visitor will seat himself before speaking to him. The *Shaiku's* sons use the polite vocabulary in speaking about him. His former serfs are even more deferential to him than are his fellow Fulbe villagers. Respect shown the *Shaiku* represents the continuation of traditional forms. A committee meeting is a situation in which earlier forms are not followed. In committee

9. Vieillard (MS.) has compiled a list of fifty-three such words of respect which can be found in the Fonds Vieillard at Dakar. I made a list of thirty-five words.

meetings old and young speak directly to each other without great attention to polite usage. Fulbe and former serfs, former chiefs and youths, will argue without regard to earlier status differences.

There are behavioral and terminological manifestations of respect that remain today in the behavior of kinsmen. For instance, when a visitor approaches a compound and asks if the head of the household is present, the response of his children or his wife is "They are here" or "They aren't here." A man's children and wives do not refer to their husband or father by name, nor by the familiar or impolite usage "He is not here." [10] There are other indications of household status. Children will do errands for their father. The eldest of the children can employ his younger siblings. If the father's younger brother comes for a meal, he will be deferential toward his older brother. Younger brothers and sons will typically be subdued in front of their elders and will be reticent unless they have come for a specific reason.

Before discussing the appropriate behavior expected between relatives of the same household, let us note Hopen's description of the household of pastoral Fulbe of Gwandu.

The structure of the household is . . . visualized as a series of households each of which is, at a given moment, at a specific level in its development. The interests, ambitions, roles and status of the members vary according to the level of development of that household; so also, therefore, must the nature of the relationships among the members change in time (1958: 135).

Father-Child. The two most important characteristics of the behavior of a son toward his father are obedience and respect. As a child (ages six to fourteen), the son will carry out his father's commands, will do his chores, and will be disciplined and punished by his father.

A man's position in the village, as well as his own sense of self-esteem, rests on the number of sons he has. Thus a man is very proud of his sons and of their exploits, even though he is cul-

10. The singular pronoun denotes familiarity; the plural pronoun respect. This is true for both second person (you s.—*a;* pl.—*ong;*) and for third person (he, she—*o;* they—*be*).

turally inhibited from showing such emotion. In public—particularly at ceremonial gatherings—he shows extreme constraint, and usually one would not know from their behavior who is father and who is son. As in many societies, an old or infirm father is supposed to be supported by his sons. A father often justifies the expense and difficulty of rearing children by pointing out the support he expects from them in his old age. The behavior expected by a father is likewise expected by a father's full and half-brothers.

As Hopen (1958) points out, at the age of ten a boy looks to his father as a man whose authority cannot be questioned. As the son gets older, however, there are many sources of conflict. The potential for conflict is greater today than it was in the past for several reasons—the problem of obtaining land for compounds, labor migration out of the Fouta-Djallon, the failure of sons to furnish their families with assistance, and general resentment between the generations over the lack of proper respect shown by the young for their elders. Although the young people's lack of respect is the most frequently heard complaint of the old, the existence of outside labor markets has been the most important factor in undermining the authority of the parental generation.

During the early years of a girl's childhood her father will play with her, but this period does not last long. The relationship between father and daughter is minimal after the girl's clitoridectomy at about the age of ten. Following the operation, the girl is her mother's charge. The father retains responsibility for her, but the relationship is not close.

Mother-Child. Within the kinship ideology of Fulbe society, it is the mother and her kinsmen who give warmth and love to the children. After a girl's clitoridectomy she assumes more and more of the household work—preparing food, obtaining water, cleaning clothes, and gardening. Girls typically have much less free time and work much harder than do boys of the same age. Mothers discipline and oversee the girls.

A mother gives her sons love, support, and discipline until they are seven or eight. From about age ten a boy no longer sleeps in the house with his mother and sisters, but with his age-mates or those slightly older in a house for already circumcised boys.

The Fulbe express, at least consciously, greater ambivalence toward their fathers than toward their mothers. Even the most educated Fulbe retain a love and feeling for their mothers. Because of the self-sacrifice and support mothers give their sons, a son can only with the greatest difficulty reject a request by his mother.

The relationship between mother and daughter is characterized by greater ambivalence than the relationship between mother and son because of the direct and constant control a mother exercises over her daughter. Nevertheless, ties between a daughter and mother remain close all during their lives, and a daughter continually assists and helps her mother during peak work times.

Brother-Brother. The relative age of brothers is of decisive importance in determining their relationship. An elder brother is to be shown respect and obedience, the same as is shown to the father. If the father dies, it is the eldest son who will assume his role if he has reached adulthood. (If a father leaves no mature sons, his brother will assume responsibility for the children.)

The closest of all childhood relationships is between brothers of the same age but of different mothers. They are typically inseparable. But as the brothers grow older the most important determinant of their relationship comes to be the relationship of their father to their respective mothers. In contrast, brothers of the same mother retain a closeness and love not found in any other relationship.

The relationship between brothers of different ages is characterized by reserve and restraint. The fact that an elder brother is the "affine" of his brother's wife heightens their reserve, for on the death of a man, his brother will almost always inherit his wife, or wives.

Brothers will conflict with each other over inheritance and the division of their father's land. But they will also cooperate, for it is upon brothers that responsibility for the economic support of ceremonies falls.

Grandparents-Grandchildren. The relationship between grand-children and grandparents is characterized by unconditional love and warmth. Following a dispute between a child and his parents, it is typical for the child to seek refuge with his grandparents. The grandparents' role is to give support to a child without criticising or disciplining him.

When there are gatherings of young and old, the only inter-action between members of different generations is between grandparents and their grandchildren. In particular, a grand-parent will tease his grandson by pulling out his knife in a mock attempt to circumcise him. Only in the interplay between grand-parent and child is a child permitted to strike an adult.

The only adults to whom children are free to express them-selves are their grandparents. They often spend evenings with their grandparents listening to the numerous folkstories and legends or accounts of earlier times.

Father's Sister-Ego. The relationship between an individual and his father's sister is one of respect and restraint. His father's sister is a disciplinary and authority figure for the child. Her role is quite important in all the ceremonies of the life cycle. How-ever, her interaction with the child is limited.

Mother's Brother-Ego. In general, the relationship between an individual and the kinsmen on his mother's side is characterized by warmth and familiarity. Of all the maternal kinsmen of his matrilateral kindred, his mother's brothers are the most impor-tant. In times of crises or difficulty, he can always go to his mother's brothers for assistance.

Sister-Sister. This relationship parallels that between brothers, although it is less influenced by age difference. The respect shown by brothers for one another was not observed among sisters.

Brother-Sister. The relationship between brother and sister is marked by restraint, unless they are of the same age. An older sister, particularly if she is much older, serves almost as a second mother to her younger siblings. An older brother has a restrained relationship with his younger sisters. If his father dies, he will become father to his sisters. Between siblings of the same age there is great familiarity, joking, and they share the same friends. As we will have occasion to discuss later, religious ceremonies require the accumulation and consumption of much wealth—wealth that exceeds the resources of any one individual. Economic support for these ceremonies is shared among siblings.

As we noted for brother-brother relations, a brother and sister of the same mother will be much closer than will those of the same father but different mothers.

Husband-Wife. An individual's first marriage, at least until recent times, was always an economic and social arrangement between two families. The preferences of the woman, in particular, were little followed. Quite often the marriage arrangements were already formally completed prior to the girl's first menstruation. Later marriages may reflect the personal desires of the man, as well as continuing social, economic, or political needs. After her first marriage a woman has a strong say in accepting a new husband.

Relationships between husbands and wives are quite variable, as in our own society. The stereotype of the husband-wife relationship, however, is one of discipline and respect. A wife is supposed to obey her husband, cook, wash, garden, and raise children. A husband provides the house, land for the garden and fields, and clothing for his wife. The relationship between a husband and wife will vary depending on the stage of the household: prior to children, while the wife can bear children, and when the wife is past child-bearing. At first, the husband will be very solicitous as the new wife learns the skills of managing her section of the economy. However, this is also a time of probation, as most divorces take place before the wife has children. The birth of a child marks the entrance of both husband and wife into adult status. A wife's relative importance frequently, although not necessarily, depends on the number of sons she bears her husband. A wife has great economic responsibility, because her success in managing the garden is significant to her husband. As a wife approaches the end of her child-bearing stage, her relationship with her husband changes. If they have maintained a companionship prior to this time, it will continue, but if the relation has been distant, this will become accentuated, and if the woman is not in her natal village she may well have to face a period of loneliness unless she has her children. Women often prefer to marry within their natal village so they will have kinsmen and age-mates close at hand.

The relationship between husband and wife during the child-bearing years tends to be very restrained in public—husband and wife do not speak to each other, nor is there ever any expression of affection. If a husband needs to call a wife, or vice-versa, when others are present, an intermediary is almost always used. If a couple remain childless, but want to remain married, they can adopt children. However, as they become older and the wife can no longer bear children their relationship either becomes minimal or they interact more freely with each other.

Women today enjoy greater mobility and independence due to their participation in markets, just as the husband has greater independence from his father due to the growing importance of the household at the expense of larger kin groups.

Co-wives. In polygynous households every wife has the right to occupy a separate house provided by her husband. She also has personal food supplies and domestic equipment. She rears her own children and in both productive and recreational activities is free from the interference of any of the other wives. Each wife has to prepare food daily for the husband. Relationships between co-wives are informal in character and depend on individual temperaments and the particular husband. There are no clear-cut rules of behavior between co-wives, nor of domestic cooperation. The first married, or senior, wife does not have formal prerogatives over the other wives. The only formal rule for involving co-wives is for the husband. The inhabitants of

Hollaande state that, according to Islam, all wives should be treated equally. Each wife should receive the same amount of grain, money, clothing, and attention. However, there are differences of attitude on the part of both husbands and wives, as well as different abilities. The difference in the treatment of wives is a source of tension, manifesting itself not only in ill-feelings between the co-wives, but between the brothers of the different mothers.

Relationships between Affines. The relationships between affines are characterized by restraint, respect, and sometimes by avoidance. Complete avoidance is not prescribed, aside from being impractical because marriages take place in the village. Rather, various situations are defined in terms of whether avoidance is to be followed or not. Thus affines should not eat together out of the same bowl but can and should work together.

When affines meet formally, both individuals squat on the ground, look away from the other, and use the polite forms of greeting. However many no longer practice this form of salutation. If affines are from the same village, they will not use the polite forms of greeting except perhaps at ceremonies. Younger people are much less likely to use such a greeting than are older people. A simplified form of greeting is often substituted, in which the one who has to show respect kneels partially, holds his left hand to his right arm, and shakes the hand of the other while using the polite forms of salutation.

Affines are called on for work assistance, and they provide specific items for ceremonies. A husband sends many gifts to the major patrilineage of his wife, primarily to her father. The obligations of an affine are to his "daughter" and to her children. An individual's affines will be the matrilateral kindred of his children.

Age-mates. Age-mates are those born in a village within the same one-year period, although before the recent large population increase the period was three years. This relationship is life-long, includes both sexes, and can be viewed as a kin relationship based on age.

Behavior between age-mates approximates our "true friendship."[11] Whereas the relationship between siblings is determined by their relative ages, with consequent restraints and responsibilities, age-mates are equal. From the earliest age, mothers teach children that age-mates share equally, no matter how little they may have. Children spend most of their free time with their age-mates, and this is the one relationship in which they are permitted to dispute, fight, and experiment sexually. Age-mates undergo circumcision or clitoridectomy at the same time.

As they become older, age-mates see less of each other, particularly the women who marry out of the village. However, lovers are still taken from within the age-mate group. In general, age-mates remain very close, and it is one of the rare joys of old age to have a true age-mate living. There was one such relationship in Hollaande, and the two men were inseparable. As one gets older there is also more flexibility with the age span, so that men of fifty, fifty-five, and sixty are often considered age-mates.

There are no real social and economic obligations between age-mates. The free sharing of childhood declines gradually after circumcision and ends with marriage, but age-mates remain confidants who share the details of all their experiences, including the problems of married life and extra-marital affairs.

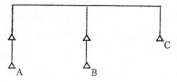

FIGURE 3. A kin relationship among age-mates.

11. Another word used for *friend* is *dyatigi*. However, *dyatigi* connotes inequality in the relationship. A chief who gives a stranger land becomes the *dyatigi* of the stranger. Among French-speaking Fulbe age-mate is translated as *copain*.

Age-mate relationships occasionally supersede requirements of other kin relationships. In one case, one age-mate was the brother of the father of the other two. Although the boys did call him "uncle" (*bappa*) and showed slight restraint with him, the boys played inseparably, something which patrilineal uncles and nephews do not do. They were also circumcised together. In another case two adult men became age-mates when all of their true age-mates had died as a result of the common experience of fifteen years in the French army. Their age-mate relationship superseded their relationship as affines. (One man was the older brother of a wife of the other, acting as father since the real father had died.) The two men do not carry out the formalities of in-law behavior, although they do carry out the economic obligations of affines.

THE KIN GROUPS

The importance of the village as an economic and political unit has increased during the periods of French colonial rule and independence. The village was traditionally of minor importance, the major political and economic units being the patrilineages. Living in the same village was of less significance than membership in the same major patrilineage. This is no longer the case. The village has supplanted other institutions as the focus of activity.

A village is composed of a series of compounds.[12] Within compounds the houses are not attached, and the entire compound, including the gardens, is enclosed within a wood fence. The adults of a compound typically have their own houses. However, poorer individuals will have only one house where they sleep with their wives and children, and a young married man sometimes prefers to live in the same house with his wife. Richer families who can afford to build cement houses have a living

12. Hollaande had 40 compounds; larger villages have up to 100 compounds; the smallest villages, only have 2 or 3.

area, an adjacent bedroom for the husband, and then a series of bedrooms with separate entrances for the wives and children. Houses within a compound are generally grouped together toward the center, where there is a small courtyard that serves as a meeting and prayer area for the compound. The courtyard is marked by an orange tree around which are placed many stones.

The physical area of the compound, enclosed by a fence, is called the *galle*. *Galle* also refers to the social unit living within one compound. Earlier, extended families were the typical living unit within one compound and still are in more remote areas. The extended family consisted of the father (or eldest male), his married sons, unmarried sons and daughters, and possibly his younger brothers and their wives. The compound was therefore roughly equivalent socially to the minimal lineage when younger brothers and wives also lived in it.

Today, the most important kin group for an individual is the household, consisting of a man, his wife or wives, and his children. More and more the compound has become socially synonomous with the household, although taxes are currently determined by compound. The head of the compound is referred to as *dyom galle* (*dyom* derives from *dyeyugol,* "to own"). A man is always considered the head of a compound, even one in which a woman lives by herself with her children. The compound as a physical unit belongs to the compound head, even in a former serf village.

In earlier times, however, the serf compound was owned by a Fulbe, who had the right to drive them from their land. Nowadays little can prevent former serfs from becoming land proprietors, and thus the proper owners of their compounds. There is no way a former land holder—a Fulbe—can expel them. (We have already mentioned two examples of land expropriations, one of which led to the founding of Hollaande.) Most former serfs consider that they are the owners of their compound; even if they are not the owners *de jure,* no one can expropriate their compound. However, despite changes in the *de facto* ownership of compound land by former serfs, tradition can be difficult to break.

79

The Democratic Party of Guinea has waged a campaign in the countryside to convince the peasants that the land on which they live belongs to them, but there are still many former serfs who continue to pay *farilla* on their corn harvest to the nominal Fulbe "proprietors" of their compounds, and who go to them for permission to expand their compound. Further, despite the current illegality of selling land, many young former serfs still think they have to buy land from the Fulbe in order to start their own compounds. This is of critical importance for young men, because the compound head has to give each wife a house and a garden within the compound.

The eldest son, regardless of the order of marriage of the mothers, inherits the house of his father. If the eldest son inherits any land at all, it is the courtyard (*tande*) by his father's house. The youngest son of each wife inherits her house and her garden. All sons except the youngest have to make their own compound. Except for the eldest son (*afo*) and the youngest (*tola*), sons have to make their own way. There is a saying which expresses their difficulty: "Between them [the first and youngest sons] they are like bastards in the division [of their father's land]" (*Hakkunde be beng faida no wai wa fattu ka sendugol*). This refers to the fact that intermediary sons are treated like bastards in the inheritance of the land of their father; a bastard, of course, receives nothing. A father may expand his compound for the potential use of his sons, but he has no obligation to do so. Land is divided among the sons of serfs and the sons of Fulbe in the same way.

Inheritance directly from the father is not the only way to receive land. If a father's brother were to die leaving no sons, his land would be inherited by his brothers, who could give it to their sons.

In Hollaande the result of the system of inheritance is that brothers of the same mother live in the same compound or in contiguous ones, whereas brothers of the same father by different mothers typically live in noncontiguous compounds. There are two reasons for this. First, when Hollaande was originally settled, the compounds were dispersed and noncontiguous. A husband, therefore, usually created new compounds away from his own for his second, third, and fourth wives. The expansion of the original compound by the father for his sons or by the sons themselves separated the compounds of the sons of different mothers. Second, as the compounds became contiguous and there was no room for further expansion along the immediate boundaries, sons would be forced to build their compounds away from those of their father. Brothers of the same mother tended to do this together.

The Household. The household is the most important economic and social unit in Hollaande. It consists of a man, his wife or wives, his children, and sometimes his mother if his father has died. In the former serf villages, the acquisition of land is the responsibility of the male head of the household. He has to provide land for all the fields and his wives' gardens. The fields are cultivated jointly by the whole household, although each adult member of the household has his own section of the fields. Ideally, the husband is supposed to give each of his wives an equal part of his fields. In practice, this is not necessarily done due to variations in the numbers of children, or in the husband's attachment to his wives. This is a frequent cause of tension within the household. The *farilla* is drawn by the man from the household as a whole, because it is his responsibility as head of the household to pay the *farilla*. Moreover, taxes are paid by the man for his household as a whole. All individuals over fourteen are taxed, and most men pay for their wives.[13] The man also pays the taxes for his mother, but his wives are expected to aid her in cultivation and preparation of food.

The household has a strong and continuing interest in its chil-

---

13. There are some women who pay their own taxes for their market activities, usually at the insistence of their husbands. However, this is not typical. In one instance of divorce, part of the wealth to be returned was the taxes paid for four years by the husband.

dren. Although co-wives zealously attempt to have extra consideration given to their own children, each wife knows that should she die, the others will become mother to her children. The children, while they of course know who is their biological mother, view all their father's wives as "mothers." Depending on personal factors, and emotional closeness, their relationship may or may not approximate that existing between the real mother and child. There were several examples in Hollaande of individuals raised by a co-wife of their mother after their real mother's death or divorce.

All the co-wives have the right to discipline the children and to intervene whenever necessary. In all the ceremonies involving children the wives share both the work and the joys of the occasion. When one wife gives birth to a child, the others take care of her other children, cook food for her, and prepare the food for the ceremony. The same is true when there is a clitoridectomy or circumcision.

We have emphasized the extent of cooperation possible among co-wives. Equally striking are the limits of cooperation within a polygynous household. Each wife prepares every meal for herself, children, and her husband. The preparation of food is often a social occasion, but it is spent with close friends or kinsmen, not with co-wives. Eating is not a special time for the household. A wife eats with her daughters and younger sons. A father eats with all his older sons, unless a rebellious teenager does not choose to eat with him. A man also eats oftentimes with his full brother, the younger brother going to the house of his elder brother with the food his wives have prepared.

Each individual stores his own portion of the household food supply. Although work in the fields is done cooperatively, the fields are initially divided among the husband's wives—and sometimes among his older unmarried children—and the harvest of each individual is threshed separately so that it can be stored separately. The husband takes the largest field and gives his grain to his wife or wives over the year. In addition, each wife has complete responsibility for her own garden and stores crops in her own house.

The care of animals, is again individual.[14] Animals, whether they be goats, sheep, cattle, chickens, dogs, or cats, are individually owned by both men and women. The women receive animals either through inheritance or as the part of the bridewealth that becomes their personal property (*tenge*.) If it is the woman who owns the animals, the responsibility for their care is clear. If it is the husband who owns the animals, he delegates responsibility for certain animals to his wife or wives. If there is a lactating cow, the husband has to decide who will receive the milk. In general, preference will be given to a mother of a very young child.

The economic independence of the members of a household is great. As individual ownership now predominates over other possible kinds of collective ownership, each individual has the right to dispose of his property as he wants. Thus a woman can sell the surplus crops from her garden at the market and keep the profit. However, she has to plan first for the food needs of her children and husband and for ceremonial obligations.

The household is interdependent insofar as it hinges on the father. It is he who has to find land, maintain the compound, provide money for clothes for his children and wives, and furnish the necessary grain and gifts for the various ceremonies in which the household participates. It is the husband who organizes crop production, selects the grains to be planted, and decides whether to expand the gardens for his sons and daughters. However we should note the growing economic importance of the woman's garden for the sustenance of the household. Because of the decline in both the availability of fields and their yield, and the labor migration of men, the burden of providing food has

14. There is a difference in the division of labor for the caring of animals between Fulbe and former serfs. Among the former serfs, women play a much greater role in the care of all animals. Perhaps the Fulbe heritage of cattle herding manifests itself in this continuing difference.

fallen on the woman. This emphasizes the limits of economic cooperation within the household, rather than expanding them.

The Minimal Lineage. The word for minimal lineage, like that for compound, has two meanings: a house, or the patrilineal descendants, male or female, of a paternal grandfather. We are concerned only with its second meaning. The affairs of the minimal lineage are directed by the compound heads. The line of cleavage within a minimal lineage runs through the paternal grandmother, as there is continual formation of new minimal lineages made up of the sons of the same grandmother. Figure 4 shows a minimal lineage and the point of fission in it.

The head of the minimal lineage is either the eldest living male descendant or someone who by virtue of his descent has seniority over the other members of the minimal lineage. For example, if a grandfather has a younger brother who is younger than the son of the grandfather's deceased elder brother, it is quite clearly the younger brother who will be the head of the minimal lineage.

In the past the kin group that lived in one compound, or at least in contiguous ones, was the minimal lineage. In Fulbe villages, fields were worked collectively by the members of a minimal lineage and its head served as the organizer of the household economy. In outlying Fulbe areas the minimal lineage retains more of its functions than in those areas closer to cities and

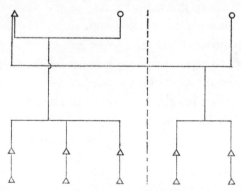

FIGURE 4. Model of a minimal lineage.

84

administrative centers. In more distant areas the head of the minimal lineage still assigns fields to the male members, and the clearing of fields is still done together. All the rest of the labor in the fields and the distribution of the harvest, however, is done by the household.

The economic role of the serf minimal lineage was minimized by the fact that both field and compound land was owned by individual Fulbe. Thus, a serf minimal lineage had no authority in terms of land distribution. Further, because the location of a serf's fields was dependent on where his master lived, labor co-operation among serf members of a minimal lineage was normally not possible.

At Hollaande today fields are acquired, distributed, and worked by the household. The minimal lineage plays no role in the process. Brothers might have fields next to each other, but they work them individually, although they may assist each other, particularly if one brother has no children old enough to help him. Sometimes an individual can call on his minimal lineage, age-mates, and his affines to work with him in his fields.

The kin group most often called on for labor assistance in the fields, gardens, and compounds are the children of siblings of the same mother. The fission of a minimal lineage between descendants of the same grandmother is clearly seen here. Thus, elder full brothers with older children frequently permit or ask their children to help younger brothers or sisters whose children are too young to help in the key economic activities.

During the month of Ramadan, the Islamic month of fasting when adult Muslims cannot eat between sunrise and sunset, the men of each minimal lineage unite for the evening meal.[15] The women of their households eat together with their children, although some women will eat with their mothers or eat alone with their children. This is the only time of year when there is

15. *Suumayee* is the Fulfulde word for Ramadan. The word Ramadan is not used by most Fulbe.

communal eating (*huntagol*). In Hollaande there are eight places for communal eating. Seven of them are located where the elder of the minimal lineage lives, and one is the house of a recently deceased woman who gave rise to a minimal lineage.

The key importance of the minimal lineage is its ceremonial role. It is the minimal lineage that is responsible for the major economic support for ceremonies. To understand this role we must examine the major patrilineage.

The Major Patrilineage. The major patrilineage has a clear, fixed, and defined membership and is, in short, a corporate group. The oldest male member usually serves as the head of the major patrilineage, which is a position of high prestige, demanding great respect, but which is not a position of power. For both the Fulbe and former serf the major patrilineage is the key to entrance into society. It is within the major lineage that every individual proceeds through the various stages of his society. Membership in it is what gives an individual specific rights to the economic, social, and physical support of his kinsmen, their assistance in all life-cycle ceremonies, and, for the Fulbe, rights to land.

Depending on the size of a village, all inhabitants may or may not belong to the same major patrilineage. There are two in Hollaande, each composed of four minimal lineages. They are based as much on proximity as on descent, whereas Fulbe patrilineages are based primarily on descent. The reason for this difference lies in the diverse origin of the inhabitants of a serf village. If we examine the genealogy of Hollaande, we find that each of the major lineages has a geographical name, in contrast to those of the Fulbe, which are named after demonstrable ancestors.[16]

At Hollaande the two major lineages correspond approximately but not exactly to the geographical division of the village. This

16. For the first few months, the people of Hollaande told me "preferred fictions" about the genealogical relations of the different kin groups. Descent from a captive was at the root of deception.

division results from the original settlement of the village, one compound being established at the head of a stream (*Hoore Tane*) and the other by the side of a small hill (*Binde Pellung*). There is one minimal lineage within the area inhabited by the Binde Pellung which is genealogically a part of Hoore Tane; there are also two compounds belonging genealogically to Binde Pellung located in Hoore Tane because a road constructed by the French divided the village. Aside from these three cases, the geographical division of the village reflects the kin division of the village into two major lineages. Figure 5 is a chart of the genealogy of the two major lineages and their component minimal lineages.

If we examine the genealogy of Hollaande we find there are now eight minimal lineages. In 1900 there were only two, the families of the founders of the village of Hollaande. The heads of the two major lineages were Tyoro, the founder of Hoore Tane, and Beng Mata, the son of the founder of Binde Pellung.

In precolonial times there was a way an individual became a member of a major lineage aside from agnatic descent. Captives and their descendants became members of the family assigned

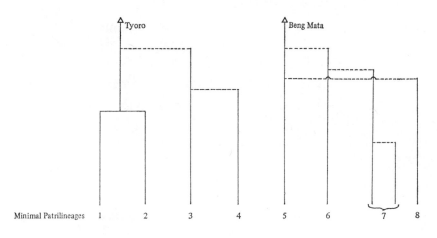

FIGURE 5. Outline of the genealogy of Hollaande.

the task of raising them. We have noted that captives were usually young children and were given to the owners' serfs to be raised. Today an individual, either Fulbe or former serf, can become a member of a major lineage through his mother's father's family. For a variety of reasons an individual may have to leave his father's village and rejoin the family of his mother. He is then raised by his mother's family and becomes a member of their major lineage. His mother's brother is the individual most likely to give him land.[17]

To be a bastard is to be without lineage. "A bastard," the saying goes, "will inherit like a dead man." The sole exception is if the father of the bastard has no other sons, in which case the bastard might inherit. To be a female bastard does not present the same difficulties. Because descent is agnatic, the fact that a woman is a bastard is not of great importance for her children, and therefore she will be able to find a husband.

If a husband is present and hasn't slept with his wife for several months, but she becomes pregnant, he may say the child is not his. The accused man and the husband's wife will be questioned by the elders of the husband's lineage as to who is the real father. In earlier days the woman would be beaten until she announced his name, but this practice has been discontinued. When the identity of the father has been established, he is called before the elders and asked to admit his guilt. If he does so, or if the elders judge that he is the proper father, then his lineage becomes responsible for performing the child's naming ceremony. The same procedure is followed when the husband of the pregnant woman is not present. An older brother of his (an affine of the woman) will act on his behalf. In fact, this situation is currently more

17. An example from Hollaande: A woman born in Hollaande married a man in a neighboring village and bore a son. When the father died, she gave her son to her mother to be raised. She remarried elsewhere, and the son grew up with his maternal grandmother. Had the father not died, he would have remained with his father. He was given a wife in Hollaande and borrowed some land for his compound. He became the founder of one of the minimal lineages of Hollaande.

common due to labor migration. The naming ceremony will be performed by the real father's lineage, but the child most often remains with its mother and will not be a member of either lineage. If the identity of the husband is not discovered, the naming ceremony is performed by the major lineage of the woman, but the child does not become a member of that lineage.

The provision of goods for life-cycle and religious ceremonies is the responsibility of the elders of the major lineage. When it is time for a life-cycle ceremony for a member of a major lineage, the elders with the father concerned, make a series of decisions about what goods will be needed and how much. The elders then divide the amount needed among the minimal lineages of the major lineage. In general, approximately an equal amount is contributed by each minimal lineage except the minimal lineage of the individual involved in the ceremony which is much larger.

The head of each minimal lineage decides how much each household will contribute. A rotation system is often set up so that every household does not have to contribute to each ceremony. There were differences in contributions depending on the wealth of the households. Within Hollaande, however, there was less economic differentiation than in other villages. The contributions of the various households in Hollaande, therefore, tended to be of equal value.

It seems that the share of the cost of ceremonies met by kinsmen outside the household and minimal lineage has diminished, and that a larger burden now falls on the smaller units. Certain gifts are now standardized. Each adult male is expected to give 50 francs ($.20) to the father of a new-born child, and each young man 25 francs ($.10). If the person was a member of the same minimal lineage as the father, his contribution would be around 500 francs ($2.00).

The importance of the major lineage is not simply ceremonial. Key decisions affecting the lives of the members cannot be made without the consultation and approval of its elders. Such decisions include marriage, divorce, and inheritance. Moreover, the former serfs presently exercise a greater degree of autonomy over these questions than they did in the past. This point can be exemplified by considering the question of inheritance. In the case of the Fulbe, decisions about inheritance were and are made by the elders of the major lineage of the deceased. When difficulties or conflicts arise, they can be brought to the mosque, where there still exists a group of elders known as "judges" (*nyawoore*). When a serf died, the decision about the disposition of his possessions was made not only by the elders of the serf's major lineages but by his Fulbe master.

In a legal sense, serfs were "owned" by their masters, and therefore did not inherit as free men. Masters had the right and power to take the possessions of their dead serfs, and according to former serf informants, this is precisely what they did. If a serf had accumulated any wealth at all (goats, sheep, clothing, or money), the master would take the lion's share. Fulbe informants maintained that the serfs were so poor that they really took quite little.

Today the Fulbe no longer have any say in the distribution of a former serf's possessions and usually receive none. In one case at Hollaande an elderly man died and left three wives and ten sons. At the time of his death he had six cattle. Of those, one was slaughtered for the sacrifice required at his funeral, and the rest were given to one son. This case is interesting for two reasons: The Fulbe did not receive any of the former serf's most important possessions, and in no way was Islamic law followed when he gave the cattle to the son he loved best.

The circumcision of boys is a matter for the major lineage. The decision when to circumcise is made by the father and the elders of the major lineage. It is expected that age-mates will be circumcised during the same year. One year six boys in the same age-mate group were to be circumcised on the same day; only four actually underwent the ceremony. The case of one boy, who was not circumcised, although his brothers and his father's brothers were, serves to illustrate the limitations of the authority of the major lineage. The boy was the only son of his mother, who had been the youngest wife of her deceased husband. She had not remarried but lived by herself in a compound separated slightly from the rest of the village. The boy, although an uncircumcised child, had to work as a man. He maintained the compound fence, repaired the house, and cultivated the small fields his mother was able to obtain. He had many older half-brothers, the eldest of whom was considered to be the primary father. The decision was made by the "fathers" to have the boy circumcised along with five other boys. But, the mother of the boy said she didn't want her son circumcised. She never made her real reasons explicit, but claimed she did not have the resources and had not received notice early enough to prepare properly for her son's circumcision. The men stated that she was preventing the circumcision of her son to keep him close to her and to prevent him from leaving the village. In either case, he was not circumcised with his age-mates—a matter of great shame to him. And, significantly, the boy was not circumcised despite the wishes of the major patrilineage. In retrospect, it appears that the half-brothers—especially the eldest, who was particularly miserly—were not willing to aid the mother in assuming the economic burden of the circumcision ceremony. The limitation of the authority of the major patrilineage is obvious from this example.

The village of Hollaande can be treated, in certain political or ceremonial contexts, as a single major patrilineage, and its inhabitants often expressed this view themselves. In a ceremonial context the village is referred to as a *bolonda*. There is no clear demarcation between *bolonda* and the major patrilineage, but the former term carries a strong connotation of proximity as well as kinship. The tendency for Hollaande to act as one major lineage is particularly evident at ceremonies in which the matrilateral kindred of the individual concerned are from another village. At the naming ceremony of an infant whose mother originates from another village the entire village of Hollaande acts as the major patrilineage of the child. Similarly, when a delegation is formed to carry the name of the child to the village of the mother, a member will be selected from every minimal lineage in Hollaande. Another example is a sacrifice made twice a year for the health and well-being of the community. This sacrifice is performed by the village as a whole, led by the elders of the village. The feast held at this time is eaten in groups arranged by age, not by membership in one or another major patrilineage.

Hollaande is treated as one major patrilineage in a political context when census-taking and taxation are imposed on the village as a whole. Taxes were collected at the compound of the second eldest man in the village. He was chosen over the eldest because he knew French and could write. However, both the elders of the village as a whole and the members of the committee worked together to see that taxes were collected from all those listed in the census. It is true that such phenomena are a result of colonial rule and independence, but on such occasions the village does act together in a single unit, expressed in a kinship idiom. And this would seem to be the trend for the future.

Matrilateral Kindred. We have described the household, the minimal lineage, and the major lineage. The last "group" to be discussed is the matrilateral kindred, which is not actually a corporate group. If one asks anyone in a village how many major lineage and minimal lineages there are and who the members are, the answer is clear and unambiguous, and it will be the same from anyone in the village. If one asks someone about the matrilateral kindreds of the village, the answer will vary with each person. The matrilateral kindred can be distinguished from one's affines. The affines of a male are both the major lineage and matrilateral kindred of his wife. (See Appendix I for exactly whom ego calls affines.) One's matrilateral kindred are the patrilaterally related kinsmen of one's mother.

The distinction between affines and matrilateral kindred is clear in practice, but it is also true that a married man's affines receive their shares from the various ceremonies (money, food, parts of slaughtered animals) as members of the matrilateral kindred of the married man's children. A man's wife's kinsmen are his affines; these same kinsmen are the matrilateral kindred of his children. The distinction can be seen in the following example. A man had taken a woman from another village as his second wife. Under the agreement he had made with his wife's parents he would finish paying the bridewealth only upon the birth of the first child. The wife became pregnant shortly after the marriage, and the husband began preparing to finish paying the bridewealth and to obtain the food and gifts necessary for the child's naming ceremony. The bridewealth was given the parents of the wife as affines, at the same time that gifts and food announcing the child's name were given to the same individuals in their capacity as matrilateral kindred of the child.

The most important member of one's matrilateral kindred are his mother's brothers. It is they who in traditional times sometimes gave one of their daughters in marriage to a man at the time of his circumcision. Although this happened infrequently in fact, it nevertheless indicates the importance of the relationship. Moreover, the boy to be circumcized spends a few days before his circumcision with his mother's brother, who will give him important gifts of money and food.

The matrilateral kindred, unlike the major patrilineage, does not hold common property or rights, but the matrilateral kindred of an individual contributes economically and socially (by attendance) at his life-cycle ceremonies. Moreover, at such ceremonies, a separate share is set out for the members of one's matrilateral kindred.

Almost all the major ceremonies—at birth, circumcision, completion of the reading of the Koran, attainment of religious title (*tierno*), *tabaski* (slaughtering of sheep), and death—are marked by the slaughter of a sacrificial animal and the distribution of its meat. The distribution of meat reflects and reinforces kin ties and kin groups. Giving, distribution, and consumption of the meat of slaughtered animals is an important means of validating kin ties. The acquisition of the animal is usually the responsibility of the individual for whom the ceremony is held. In the case of birth, circumcision, and translation of the Koran, responsibility falls on the father. Formerly, when serfs had many fewer animals than they do now, a master would often provide the animal for at least the naming ceremony of a serf's child. The meat of the animal slaughtered at a naming ceremony is divided among the child's major patrilineage, his matrilateral kindred, his mother, and his father's minimal lineage. Among the maximal patrilineage Ragnaabe of the village of Khaliyaabe the matrilateral kindred receive approximately half of the animal, including a front leg, the chest, and half of the back, as its share from the naming ceremony. The share for the major patrilineage—a front leg, a back leg, and half of the back—is divided among the three minimal lineages of the major lineage, the half of a back going to the minimal lineage of the father. The mother receives lungs, heart, pelvis and the stomach with its contents. The head and the feet were in traditional times given to the serfs of the father. The giving of these parts, which contained almost no meat, validated the subordinate status of the serfs.

The distribution of the meat of a sacrificial animal at death is quite different and involves the validation of the ties of one maximal lineage to the other maximal lineages of the surrounding area. To again take our example from one minimal lineage in the village of Khaliyaabe, we find the following distribution of the meat of a cow at a death ceremony: a back leg and half of the chest for the Seleyaabe (maximal lineage), a front leg and half of the back for the Ragnaabe (maximal lineage), and part of the chest and a front leg for the Khalduyaabe (chiefly maximal lineage). These are the three maximal patrilineages of the area. Within these lineages the meat will be redivided first among the major patrilineages and then among the minimal lineages: a back leg (formerly for the *misside* chief of Popodara) for the minimal lineage of the deceased, half of the chest for the matrilateral kindred (*deewol*) of the deceased, and head and feet for the serfs. To the serfs' share has been added the first thigh attachment and part of a side for the former serfs. As one can see, affines receive no share as affines. The matrilateral kindred are always recognized, but are obviously not a fixed group and will vary for each individual.

MARRIAGE

As in most African societies, a Fulbe's attainment of full economic and social participation in the life of his village does not come until he establishes a household. Marriage, in addition to meaning the creation of a household, is an economic and social arrangement between two families.

The first determinant of marriage in precolonial times was the desire of a Fulbe to have his own serfs intermarry rather than marry serfs of another master, thereby gaining economic advantage and maintaining greater control over his serfs. Moreover, as the Fulbe acquired captives and made them serfs, they married them to the serfs they already owned. A second determinant of marriage in Labe was that the chiefly lineage Khalduyanke preferred marriage (as did the other chiefly lineages) with their serfs to marriage with members of other maximal patrilineages. By marrying their serfs a chiefly lineage avoided affinal ties with other lineages. A third example of precolonial marriage considerations involves the Fulbe of the bush, who were engaged in cattle herding more than were the other strata of the Fulbe. When a Fulbe of the bush died, part of his wealth was given to the *misside* chief. This practice was known as the *kummabite* and was an important economic resource for the chiefs. The chiefs opposed marriage between a Fulbe woman of the bush and a member of a free lineage, for the members of the free lineages did not pay the *kummabite,* and when the woman died, her sons, who would be free would inherit her wealth and the chief would not receive his *kummabite*. Although there were no apparent economic reasons, it appears that marriage between free women and Fulbe of the bush was also discouraged. It is clear that marriage in pre-colonial days had a political and economic significance different from what it has today.

In an article celebrating the transformation of the Fouta, while regretting many of the changes, the Guinean anthropologist Ousmane Diallo wrote:

Parents no longer dare to marry their children. Future couples choose freely, and simply inform their close kinsmen and friends. Isn't this because the children themselves meet their own subsistence needs? They are the wealth of their families—they take on part of the daily responsibility for obtaining food, clothing and taxes. They assure the continuation of life of their elders and the elders' ability to continue the occupations suited for elders. And, the parents prefer to have this happen for they are content to affirm that "I raised you, and it is now left to you to fill my old years." (1961: 85)

Although Diallo points to some important changes that are occurring, he has overstated the case. During my stay I learned of a marriage of an adult from the same village as Diallo; this individual had left his natal village to work in a city. While residing in the city, he began an affair with a woman. Ultimately they decided to live together, and after a year of such an alliance he wrote to the elders of his major patrilineage, without fully describing the situation, asking them to begin preparation for his marriage to this woman. Unfortunately for the young man, someone had already communicated the common-law nature of the marriage to the elders. They refused the request of the man and insisted that he take a bride of their choice from a nearby village. After much haggling, the young man renounced his earlier intention and accepted the will of the elders of his major patrilineage. In sum, there has been less change than Diallo described.

In another frame of reference Diallo deplores the loss of other social customs.

Politeness, deference, respect—they have lost their hold as values. Respect for the human person is empty of content. Consideration is not given to others. The right of the elders is scoffed at, if not contested. At public meetings no one is concerned enough about the presence of others to give up one's place or to avoid pushing. This isn't the use of freedom but the abuse of license; it is the deprivation of customs. (1961: 84)

Diallo appears to be arguing for a transformation of the Fouta without the destruction of the fine qualities of indigenous social organization. His statements are significant because he is a scholar looking at his own society. He is both Guinean and a Fulbe, and the contradictions and the problems he points out are the problems of the Fouta.

Choosing a Spouse. The Fulbe observe the Koranic prescription:

You are forbidden to take in marriage your mothers, your daughters, your sisters, your paternal and maternal aunts, the daughters of your brothers and sisters, your foster-mothers, your foster sisters, the mothers of your wives, your step-daughters who are in your charge, born of the wives with whom you have lain (it is no offence for you to marry your step-daughters if you have not consummated your marriage with their mothers), and the wives of your own begotten sons. Henceforth you are also forbidden to take in marriage two sisters at one and the same time. (The *Koran,* Sura 4.)

They likewise follow an Islamic pattern of marriage that Murdock (1967) has called quadrilateral marriage; that is, marriage is allowed with any first cousin. We have already noted that a terminological distribution is made between cross-cousins and parallel cousins, the latter being referred to as siblings.

Whereas there are no differences in the kin terminology used by Fulbe and former serfs, there are differences in the choice of spouse (see Table 1, p. 101). Cantrelle and Dupire (1964:80) have noted that the Fulbe express a strong preference for marriage with FaBrDa, and after her for either MoBrDa or FaSiDa.[18] They go on to state that the actual choice of spouse is based on social and economic considerations. When a man marries the daughter of his paternal uncle the major patrilineage will thereby

18. Cantrelle and Dupire obtained their data from the 1954 French Demographic Mission.

more easily control her conduct and her wealth. Social considerations enter if one segment of the patrilineage wishes to consolidate its interests in the face of other segments (Cantrelle and Dupire 1964: 81). There is not enough new data from Fulbe villages either to support or reject these conclusions. Differences in both practice and preference due to differences in social status and political position would not be surprising. Thus, considerations of political alliance, or marriage for control of inheritance of land and cattle, would have been important for the Fulbe—though not for the serfs—even in 1954, when there were still *chefs de canton* and their entourages. One would guess that with the end of chieftainships, the marriage patterns of members of the lineage of the chief might also have undergone some change. Thus, during my stay the first marriage took place between a member of the former chiefly lineage Khaludyanke and a Fulbe of the bush of the lineage Khaliyaabe.

Cantrelle and Dupire (1964) have emphasized the reasons for marrying FaBrDa and other "cousins," but they have not mentioned certain Fulbe notions that such marriages should not be made. The Fulbe have a term for marriage between close kinsmen and a particular saying that expresses their reluctance to enter into such an arrangement: "Marriage with one's close kinsmen makes us ugly" (*Loundu no kanini meng*). *Loundu* refers to marriage within the major patrilineage. There is an opposite saying that expresses the desirability of ties with one's affines: "To have desirable ties with affines, they should come as strangers" (*Futu koka dyananiri*). What the Fulbe express in these sayings are the potential conflicts and difficulties that will arise between close kinsmen if their children marry. This difficulty has been summarized in another pithy saying: "If you search for marriage with a close kinsmen you have hate" (*A dabai mbeldiga heba ngaingu*).

The ideal for which both Fulbe and former serfs strive in relations with their affines is respect (*teddungal*). And as we have noted affines should practice a mild sort of avoidance. This avoidance includes not eating with affines. This avoidance becomes impractical in the case of marriage within the patrilineage. In short, in terms of actual day-to-day behavior, it is not possible for the proper respect to be shown if the affines are of the same patrilineage and thereby located in the same village.

These considerations do not mean that the Fulbe do not practice marriage with their cousins; they show that the Fulbe are explicit in pointing to potential stress and difficulty in such marriages. These views were elicited in asking several Fulbe informants about their marriage preferences for either themselves or their children. One of the most interesting results was simply that there was no uniformity of opinion. An elderly neighbor of the man who gave me the saying about the danger of close marriage (they were from the same major patrilineage, but not minimal lineage), expressed a different point of view, and just as strongly. He maintained that the most highly preferred marriage was with MoBrDa, much more so than with FaBrDa. He justified his view by saying that this kind of marriage was more in accord with the wishes of Allah. And he went on to point out that from one's matrilateral kindred love was unconditionally forthcoming. He tempered this general remark with practical considerations. Someone who is poor and cannot find enough wealth to arrange a marriage with a "good" family can ask his MoBr to help him, implying that the MoBr will give him his daughter. Moreover, if your MoBr has no sons, your wife will inherit his wealth; it will then be passed on to your children.

Former serfs also vary in their marriage preferences. Some maintained that they would look first within their major patrilineage for a wife; others insisted they wanted a stranger (*dya-nano*) from another village as a wife. Whereas there was disagreement about marriage preferences, all agreed that if one's marriage with a close kinsmen were good, it would be very good; however, if it were bad it would be horrendous, and there would be difficult problems with one's close kinsmen. In general, the villagers of Hollaande thought that marriage within the village tended to diminish respect for affines because respectful relations between affines are hard to maintain within the daily life of the village.

In sum, for the former serfs of Hollaande there are no longer any fixed rules for marriage, if indeed there ever were, given the Fulbe voice in such affairs. Marriage choices are flexible and result more from individal circumstances than from any societally defined rules. To find within one village one half of the men saying that marriage out of the village is preferable, while the other half maintain the opposite, reflects the actual contemporary situation.

Table 1 presents data on marriages in the village of Hollaande. Of 109 marriages only 28 were between individuals defined by the villagers as "related," related in the narrow biological sense, both Fulbe and former serfs being quite conscious of the difference between classificatory kinsmen and biological kinsmen. The rest of the marriages were with individuals who were said to be unrelated. The villagers were quite clear about true genealogical relationships. There is also a classificatory aspect to the kinship terminology as well, all former serfs in nearby villages being termed "kinsmen" (*musibbe*). In short, to say that marriages were exogamous (outside the village) with unrelated individuals holds true in one sense, but may not be so in a very broad sense.[19] Many of these exogamous marriages were between a man or woman of the village and a captive placed in the village. Quite clearly the introduction of captives, who are viewed as unrelated to the villagers, increases the probability of marriages between individuals who are unrelated. It is interesting that the Hoore Tane, who in comparison with the Binde Pellung on the other side of the village have a greater genealogical unity, also have a higher percentage of marriages with genealogically related individuals. This percentage becomes even greater if one subtracts

19. An example of a marriage listed in table 1 as "no relation" is between a woman and her FaBrWiBrDa. Although there is clearly some relation between the two individuals, her answer to whether they were related to one another was no.

Table 1. Marriage Patterns in Hollaande

Maximal Lineages	Total Number of Marriages	Within Village	Outside Village	FaBrDa	MoBrDa	FaSiDa	Other	No Relation
Hoore Tane	55	26		5	1	5	MoMoSiDa–1	14
			29	1	1	1	MoSiDa–1	25
Binde Pelung	54	28		1	–	1	MoSiDa–2 MoMoSiDaDa–2 FaMoMoSiDa–1	21
			26	1	–	1	MoSiDa–2	22

Endogamous Marriages:

	Binde Pellung	Hoore Tane	
Hoore Tane	11	11	22 marriages
Binde Pellung	10	11	21 marriages

(11 marriages with captives brought into village.)

captives. When an individual was brought to the village as a captive and integrated into the village, his origins were not forgotten. As we pointed out there is a slight difference in status between those among the former serfs whose families are said to be indigenous and those who were brought as captives.

Marriage is viewed as a necessary step in the life-cycle. There were only two unmarried individuals in the village who by virtue of their ages should have been married. (For men it is more difficult to know what is an appropriate age, because there are some instances when they don't marry until the age of thirty). One was a middle-aged man, a midget with limited intellectual capacity who had been abused by a chief and was cared for by a household in Hollaande because of a remote kin tie. He was surprisingly not cared for by his maternal niece who lives in the village. The other individual was a girl about sixteen. Exactly why she was not married I never found out; she gave the appearance, however, of not being quite right. Not to marry is unthinkable, and to have more than one wife is desirable, although the Islamic limit of four wives is now followed. In the village of Hollaande no individual had more than three wives. Of the 41 household heads 2 had no wives (having been divorced), 23 had only one wife, 14 had two wives, and 2 had three wives.

Marriage is a very serious affair, for it establishes relations between two groups of kinsmen which may last indefinitely. The kinsmen of the bride will become the matrilateral kindred of the couple's children. Moreover, marriage involves the exchange of much wealth. Because of the importance of the decision, older individuals maintain that such matters should not be left to the young and inexperienced, that is, to the prospective bride and groom. However, the economic leverage kinsmen of the groom can exert on him is decreasing as he provides a greater and greater share of the expenses required for marriage. The trend is clearly for an individual to have an increasing voice, even in his first marriage.

It is usually the parents of a boy who decide he is ready for marriage. Even now, when a son may be away working in a city, the parents will begin to make preliminary arrangements without his knowledge. Ultimately, however, the son's consent is necessary. Once a suitable girl has been found, the boy's paternal aunts are the first to discreetly approach the girl's mother or kinsmen. If the initial response is favorable, the formal series of steps toward marriage are begun.

The Fulbe make a distinction between obligatory acts (*farilla*) and recommended acts, or acts that please Allah (*sunna*). This distinction is made, for example, between the two fast months of Raadyibi, which is *sunna,* and Ramadan, which is *farilla.* The former is observed only by the most devout; the latter is obligatory for everyone. These distinctions are also applied to marriage. In the eyes of Allah there are three obligatory steps to marriage: the mother's permission, the father's permission, and a gift from the husband to the new bride which becomes her property (*tenge*). "Even if nothing else is done but the giving of *tenge* and the mother's and father's consent the marriage will please Allah" (*Ko tenge e si neene e baaba okki paikung ong. Hai si haifus adaaka harai dagike.*) [20] However, first marriages rarely take place without execution of the following steps: the asking (*toragol* or *tornde ndeng*); the engagement (*dyamal ngal*); the asking again (*landital*); the seeking of news (*kumpital ngal*); the marriage ceremony (*peera ong*); and the return of the bride (*artirgol dyomba*). Nevertheless, these acts are considered *sunna,* and therefore not obligatory.

The Asking. Following the girl's parents' acceptance of the initial inquiries, a formal delegation is sent with a gift from the boy's major patrilineage to that of the girl. The Fulbe present either kola nuts or a blanket for the girl's father and a shawl for her mother. Former serfs present mats. If the gifts are kept, the first step has been completed.

The Engagement. Following the asking, there are a series of

20. Of course, in precolonial times serfs also had to have the permission of their Fulbe masters.

informal meetings between representatives of the two major patrilineages concerning the amount of the bridewealth. There is no
fixed amount, but it is expected that those who are richer will
give more. The traditional bridewealth was comprised of father's
robe (*dolokke baaba*), mother's skirt (*wudere neene*), gifts for
the bride's father's brothers and sisters, and gifts for the bride's
older brothers and sisters. In addition, a sack of salt (*saladyang*)
and kola nuts (*goro bolonda*) were given to the father, who then
redistributed them to the members of his patrilineage. All gifts
were intended for the major patrilineage of the bride, none for her
matrilateral kindred. In earlier times all the gifts were given in
kind. Now all but the salt and kola nuts are given in money. Once
the bridewealth has been completed it is very rare for the engagement to be terminated, because that would mean the wealth would
have to be returned, no matter who asked for the termination.
The *tenge* obligatory under Islamic law, is separate from the rest
of the bridewealth because it becomes the bride's property. The
two preferred gifts for *tenge* are cattle and gold. However, the
ability to give either gold or cattle depends on an individual's
wealth. Goats, sheep, or money are also acceptable as *tenge*. The
items and amount to be given are decided on before the marriage
by the major patrilineages of the bride and groom. However, it is
not given until after the completion of the marriage ceremony
itself. The *tenge* is always given to the wife with witnesses present, because if a woman leaves or divorces her husband, she
would have to return it to him. In Hollaande the *tenge* was
almost always a goat or a sheep. The only time I observed a
cow being given as *tenge* was at a marriage between two Fulbe.
However, there were at least three instances within the past ten
years when a cow was given. There is a short saying which states,
"A goat or a sheep is unacceptable as *tenge* to a free (Fulbe)
girl" (*Dimon tengetaake mbewa maa balli*). In short, the giving
of goats and sheep is associated with former serfs.

Following the actual engagement, the prospective groom gives
gifts to both his prospective bride and affines.

The Asking Again. In recent years this has been performed on the day of the marriage. A delegation from the groom's major patrilineage visits a similar delegation from the bride's patrilineage. Among Fulbe the delegation brings a gift, formerly a goat or a sheep, now money. Serfs formerly brought mats and a roll of cotton. Former serfs now usually bring the price of either of these items. The groom's delegation is then given food. If it is found that the arrangement still holds, the next step is taken.

The Seeking of News. Those "who seek news" (*humpitoobe*) are from the bride's major patrilineage. They go to the groom's major patrilineage, who presents them with gifts. Formerly they were given raffia covers (*bedi*), little spoons (*nyeddukoi*), and much food. Now they are given food and some money. This step is said to serve as witness that the girl has been given as a bride: "It is the news seeking which is the witness that (she) has been given' '(*Ko kumpital woni seede okkaama*). With the completion of this step the marriage decision is irreversible.

Marriage Ceremony. According to tradition, a girl's impending marriage is to be kept a secret from her. She is supposed to be told on the night of her marriage, when a delegation arrives from the groom's village to escort her to the ceremony. In practice it is quite rare for the girl not to know. Most often she knows she will be married and to whom, but does not know the day of the marriage until the day itself. Secrecy is attempted only for a girl's first marriage, and its emphasizes the importance of the lineage and family, for, according to tradition, in second, third, and fourth marriages the consent of the woman is required. According to Guinean law, a girl's consent is always required for her marriage, and the law is gaining acceptance.

The night before the day of the marriage there may be dancing and singing in the village of the groom. The day of the marriage, if all the arrangements have been completed, a small delegation sets out from the groom's compound or village and arrives at the bride's compound or village at night. The delegation is made up of the persons who ask the father's formal permission for the girl, those who carry the girl on their backs from her compound to the compound of the groom's father, and a sister of the groom who brings the bride's clothes.[21] The delegation proceeds to the house of the bride's mother. The bride, upon learning of her fate, begins to weep, and her mother joins in the weeping. Their crying attracts all the women of the village. She is dressed by her paternal aunt, who covers her in white cloth so that no part of her body including her face is exposed. All the women of her village then accompany her to the site of the marriage in the groom's village.

There is a particular statement made by the father when he gives approval for taking his daughter which is a formal expression of the importance of the ties of marriage.

We give you a child, we don't know her, we don't know her personality or soul. If she and her husband stay together, let them stay. If she and her husband don't stay well together, let them separate. That's fine (it's the same). Nothing has been done to the relation between us. It is this we beseech you.

Meng okki ong paikung. Kono meng andamo. Meng anda dyikku makko. Si homo wondo yoo wonu. So o wondatakko yo be seedu, edyam. Hara dung waddallieng. Ko dung doo meng tori ong.)

The man sent to ask for the girl leaves ahead of the main party and notifies the groom's village of the impending arrival of the bride. Thereupon the kinsmen of the groom gather. The marriage ceremony is primarily an affair for women. Few men actually go to the ceremony, and those who do so look after the division of the food and gifts and see that all goes well. As the bride approaches the compound of her new husband's father, the women are divided into two groups—those accompanying the bride and those of the groom's village. Both groups sing and dance while slowly approaching one another, and the bride is carried in and placed on a mat in front of the house of the groom's father. Among Fulbe the bride is placed directly on the mat; former serfs carry the bride three times around the orange

21. In a Fulbe marriage the girl is carried on the backs of her father's former serfs. In the marriage of a former serf, age-mates of the groom carry the bride.

tree in the courtyard while everyone says, "The tree bears fruit, let her bear fruit [children]" (*hiki dyido, himo dyido*). She is then placed on the mat, where she stays while the women dance and sing around her. If it is the man's first marriage, he has to hide himself and not be seen by anyone until the rite that formally symbolizes the marriage union. If it is a second or later marriage, he has to avoid being seen only by the bride.

The major gift (aside from food and kola nuts) given the night of the marriage is called the *kilasakke*. In the case of the Fulbe the *kilasakke* is given to the former serfs of the father of the new bride, who refuse to admit the bridal party into the village unless they receive their proper gift. Formerly, the *kilasakke* was a goat or sheep. Now it is 1,000 or 2,000 francs—less than an animal's value. In the case of former serfs, younger brothers of the bride block the path of entry until they receive their gifts.

The other gifts presented are money to the older sisters of the bride, money to the women who accompany the bride (*fanda futu*), money and a plate of food for those who have carried the bride, kola nuts for the matrilateral kindred and major patrilineage of the bride (the latter receive more) and finally money for the dancers, drummers, and other musicians who are there.

Toward midnight the last part of the marriage takes place. The bride is taken inside the house of the groom's father, where the elder women of the groom's major patrilineage are gathered. Immediately afterward the groom is escorted inside. Inside there is a calabash of sour milk (*kosang*) from which the bride and then the groom each drink three times, after which the ceremony is over for the night. The rest of the night is given to the division of food and kola nuts among the guests, and there is dancing and singing into the early hours of the morning. The groom departs with his age-mates, while the bride stays in his father's house for awhile and then goes to sleep in the groom's mother's house. The new couple will not sleep together for at least three nights, and often longer. Frequently, depending on the wishes of the bride's mother and father and whether the bride is from a distant village, she will spend a few days following the marriage (but not the nights) with her parents. This makes the separation from her mother less abrupt. In the few marriages I observed, the bride spent the night in the compound of her new husband, but was escorted back to her natal village at dawn for a week following the night of the ceremony.

The Return of the Bride. This ceremony follows consummation of the marriage. The groom's paternal aunt presents the bridal sheet to the mother of the newly married girl. If there is blood on the sheet, the sheet is returned with red kola nuts. If there is no blood—if the girl wasn't a virgin—the sheet is returned with white kola nuts and there is no ceremony due to the shame of the bride's family, although the bride does return to her natal village on that day.[22] When the bride is proved a virgin, she is brought by the women of the groom's village to her mother's house, accompanied by the same singing and dancing that took place at her wedding. The bride sits on a mat in the center of a circle formed by the women dancing around her. She is then put on the shoulders of one of the women, who dances while the bride throws her head from side to side. The bride is dressed in a black skirt, no blouse, with a red scarf over her head. Following the dancing, gifts are given to the bride and food is distributed to all attending. As with the marriage ceremony, the return of the bride is primarily an affair for the women. The men do not participate in the singing and dancing.

The bride stays a week with her mother and then returns permanently to the household of her new husband. The return of the bride typically concludes the process of marriage.

The following tabulation is a list of the expenses of one marriage in Hollaande. This marriage was not viewed as particularly expensive, but was representative for Hollaande, where there are few wealthy individuals.

22. It is unusual for there not to be blood on the sheet. When brides are not virgins, various methods are used to stain the sheet.

The asking:	500*
The engagement (bridewealth to patrilineage of bride):	
Father	7000
Mother	5000
Father's sisters	1500
Father's brothers	1500
Bride's older sisters	1000
Bride's older brothers	1000
Mats	1500
Salt	variable—about 2000
The asking again:	5000 (one goat)
The seeking of news:	1500
Wedding:	
Bride's older sisters	2000
Bridal party	2000
Bride-carriers	150
Kilasakke	1000
Token gift to bride's former master	2500
Tenge:	6000 (one goat—goats vary in price depending on age, sex, condition)
Clothing for the bride:	20,000
Kola nuts:	2500

* (247 francs equal $1.00)

The total cost of one marriage, then, is approximately 62,500 francs ($250.00), and it has become the responsibility of the groom to obtain this amount.

This list does not include the cost of the wedding ceremony, which is divided among the members of the groom's patrilineage and sisters (*bandiraabe*). Nor does it include the gifts the groom sends to his affines and fiancée during the long period between engagement and the wedding ceremony. In addition, among the

Fulbe the meat of a slaughtered cow is sent to the bride's major patrilineage the day before the wedding.

There are two other important economic aspects of marriage—*dotitungal* and *sooge*. *Dotitungal* are the household objects given to the girl by her mother, such as pots, enamel bowls, calabashes, spoons, wooden bowls for milking cows, and taro and manioc plants to start a garden. The number of plants needed depends, of course, on whether the wife must start her own garden or will inherit her husband's mother's garden. *Sooge* refers to what a father gives his daughter to begin her household. If the father is wealthy, he will give her one or more cows. In the past a Fulbe father might have given her a serf.

There is a fixed order to the marriage steps, which is usually followed, but no fixed length of time specified for their being carried out. In the cities, where less time is spent on ceremonies, the engagement, the asking, the seeking of news, and the wedding ceremony itself can take place on the same day. There formerly existed a customary understanding that the seeking of news and wedding ceremony could not take place on the same day. This custom is no longer respected, even in the countryside.

In one marriage, noted previously, the bridewealth was not given to the bride's family until the birth of the first child. This was indeed unusual, but was a precaution taken by the man to be sure their marriage would last before he gave so much wealth. It is also important to note that the marriage steps are followed only when it is the girl's first marriage. If it is the woman's second or third marriage, the affair often involves only the man, his prospective wife, and her parents, and all that will be given is the *tenge*.

There is an institutionalized way for a man to reduce the expenses of a marriage. This form of marriage is known as "to steal the child" (*wuddyugol paikung*). All the marriage steps are followed, but the expenditure for each step is usually less, and the wedding is considerably smaller. Although this is an acceptable form of marriage, it is not desired. It is used by men seeking

as a second or third wife a girl who has not been married previously. Another option for a man without sufficient wealth to
finance marriage is to ask his mother's brother for help in seeking
a wife, which normally means requesting the hand of his
daughter without following the usual expensive marriage steps.
However, it is important to note that most marriages with one's
maternal uncle's daughter do not fall into this category.

very common [margin annotation]

DIVORCE

Divorce is infrequent in Hollaande and in the surrounding villages. However, distinction should be made between separation
before and after there are children. The former is far more frequent than the latter, there having been four instances within
the past twenty-five years at Hollaande.

The following two examples of divorce procedings in Hollaande, one involving no children and ending in divorce, the
other involving children and ending in a reconciliation will indicate the seriousness with which divorce is viewed after children
have been born. The first example is the divorce of two young
people from the same major patrilineage of the village. They
had been engaged for two years (that is, the bridewealth had
been determined and paid) and then married for two years. The
girl refused to sleep with her husband and returned to her
mother's house each night after having prepared her husband's
meals during the day. Finally, she refused to wash his sheets.
That was the final straw. Because the situation shamed him,
he had no choice but to ask for a divorce. The girl's family accepted the situation. Apparently they had mixed feelings about
the marriage, but in any case they were unable to control their
daughter. The girl's father was obligated to return the bridewealth, but he did not have enough money to repay it. He was
obligated to leave Hollaande in order to earn enough money.
He was gone for several months. Not once did anyone criticize
him or express any impatience about when he would return.

One day he returned, and that evening there was a meeting at the house of the husband's father's sister's son to discuss the return of the bridewealth. In affairs of this kind an intermediary is always used. In this case he was a fellow villager, a *tierno,* and not a member of the minimal patrilineage of either party. The girl's father and his two brothers attended the meeting. At first neither the husband nor his father were present, but it was necessary to call them when details arose. The discussion of the bridewealth took place without the husband, because it was felt that only the elders knew about that. However, for the question of taxes and clothes it was necessary to call the husband. The responsibility for the payment of taxes becomes the husband's after an engagement, but in this case the man had paid for his wife for three years, and everyone agreed that he should be repaid, as it represented a relatively large sum of money. On the day of a wedding a husband presents clothes to his wife. In this case several outfits had been given. He was asked whether he expected the money spent for that returned. He answered no, that he knew the difficulties involved and did not expect or want that money returned.

The question of the clothing was the last legal point raised that evening. Following that, everyone spoke of how well village relations had been kept, how everyone had fulfilled his obligation to the community. Attention was shifted away from money to the real purpose of the meeting. This according to the final speaker of the evening, the intermediary, was a meeting of followers of the Islamic faith (*dyulbe*) to fulfill their obligations. The question of money in his stated view was unimportant in comparison with the maintenance of good relations within the community.

Before this couple's marriage, the man had had difficulty finding a wife. He had been married once before, but that marriage ended in divorce. His father then prevailed on kinsmen of his major patrilineages to give their daughter to his son.[23] This case

23. This is an example of two men from genealogically unrelated minimal lineages acting as members of one major patrilineage.

provides a fine indication of the changes in marriage now taking place; the girl did not want to marry and, in fact, had spent some time in the city, which she preferred. The mother hoped her daughter would marry someone rich so the family would have more wealth.

The second case of divorce proceedings involved a marriage of long standing. The husband asked for the divorce. The wife came from a neighboring village, from which the founders of Hoore Tane had come. However, she did not live in the part of the village where the kinsmen of Hoore Tane lived. The husband accused the wife of having stolen money from him. She complained in turn about his bringing lovers to their home and giving them more gifts and wealth than he gave her. This is a frequent complaint of wives, aggravated in this case because they lived in the same house. Because the woman had borne five children, one of whom was still at her breast, divorce was not a simple procedure. The man had asked for the divorce, but his wife refused to accept it. The seriousness of such divorces is easily understood when we know that the children remain with the father and his lineage. If there is a divorce, the mother loses her children. The major patrilineage of the husband did not want the divorce because raising children without their real mother is considered very undesirable and cruel to the children. Pragmatically, they also felt that the husband could remain with her for another five or six years, at which time her sons could support her. However, the husband insisted, and sent his wife home to her mother.

The committee was called to regulate the affair because theft and two different villages were involved. In such a discussion an attempt is made to arrive at a decision acceptable to all concerned. All interested parties are permitted to speak. In the first meeting all the details were discussed, and a decision was reached that a divorce should not take place. However, during the week following that decision the husband insisted on obtaining a divorce because he claimed his wife had stolen from him again.

The second meeting began with a saying: "If you have gone

around the house, by the door you will enter" (*Ko taridaa suudowo ko dambugol naatirta*). Figuratively, this means that if you have gone around in a circle trying to do something, it is better to start over. This was an attempt to set the tone for the discussion. That is, it would be useless to restate all the disagreements and problems; rather, one should search for the door.

The events of the week were discussed. The wife spoke first. She noted that she did not have enough milk to feed her baby and that her husband did not provide money for her to buy milk. In order to obtain assistance she, who was staying with her mother, returned to her husband to get milk. During this visit she asked her husband to tell her whether he truly wanted a divorce or whether she could return. He didn't answer. She then asked him to take her to her mother's home, which would signify that he had divorced her. He refused. She then stayed the night, and he gave her soap to wash the sheets. The next day she decided to return to her mother's, and asked her husband's mother to take the baby because she had no milk. The mother refused. She then took the baby to the home of the former president of the committee to call a meeting to settle the question. He agreed, and she returned to her natal village.

The husband, who spoke next, said she lied. He always sent milk, or money for milk. He said he had not wanted her to spend the night, and that it was she who had demanded soap and some cloth to carry the baby. He said she also took a blanket. He refused to say whether he wanted a divorce; it was up to the elders to decide.

Thereupon an officer of the committee proposed a solution. He said that he was against a divorce. He wanted to pose questions, along a new line, to both individuals. He began by asking the wife if she would no longer steal. She replied by insulting her husband. He silenced her and asked her to answer the question. She answered affirmatively. In other words, she was asked to correct her faults, not to steal, not to insult her husband, and to obey him. Subsequently, the husband was questioned in the same way. He, however, was given more latitude in speaking his mind. He claimed it was his wife's wont to steal. He was asked whether he would take his wife back and treat her fairly as his wife. He said yes, but that she would steal again. However, he would take her back if that was what was decided.

After he finished, many elders spoke—both Fulbe and former serfs. They observed that it wasn't the husband alone who was at fault. They all expressed the opinion that the elders of both the husband's and the wife's major patrilineages had to accept the decision and see that it was followed. The girl's mother then asked to speak. She is a *tierno,* one of the very few women who is. She is a *tierno,* one of the very few women who is. She said that she wanted her daughter to remain always at Hollaande. She was willing to do whatever was necessary to see that her daughter stayed, and that there not be divorce.

Following the mother, the head of the husband's major patri- lineage spoke and maintained they would work to see that the marriage continued. He uttered an interesting sentence: "It is Allah alone (by death) who can divide a man and his wife after children have been born" (*ko Allah rek wawi sendube si bibbe hebama*).

The girl's father promised that she would not steal. From the discussion it was clear that the overriding consideration was the fate of the five children. It was pointed out by many that had there been no children, no one would have come to the meeting. The sense of the meeting was that both were at fault, but the marriage had to continue for the sake of the children, and that both had to change. The wife should no longer take from her husband, but he in turn should take more wives instead of lovers. He was too old and had too many children to continue in his irresponsible ways.

When there is a divorce, the bridewealth is always returned if there are no children. If there are children whether the bride- wealth is returned depends on who asks for the divorce. When a husband sends his wife away or renounces the marriage, no return is made. However, if a woman asks for a divorce, the bridewealth is returned. During the period of May 1966 to July 1967, there were two divorces. Although there is no quantifiable data to calculate a rate of divorce, except for one village, it appears the rate is quite low. Certainly the attempt to avoid divorce in the case in which there were five children testifies to its rarity.

FULBE-SERF MARRIAGE

There is a saying that clearly expresses the status of the serfs in the past in the eyes of their Fulbe masters: "It is at the mosque that a marriage of the Fulbe is tied [legitimated]. The serfs don't tie their marriages. They are like sheep. It is to Fulbe that their children belong" (*Ko ko dyulirde deugal habete fii fulbe beng. Fii haabe beng deugal habaataake, ko be tyiikuli. Ko pullo debbo ong dyei bibbe beng*). Thus, in the eyes of Allah serfs could not marry legitimately because they could not go to the mosque to "tie" their marriages.[24]

This was not the only way by which serf marriages were controlled by the Fulbe. The consent of the bride's master was required for marriage. Moreover, he received a substantial share of the bridewealth. There is still a small payment given to the Fulbe, vestige of their earlier and larger share. At present there are many former serfs who continue to ask their former masters to "tie" the marriage at the mosque.

The Fulbe took women from among the serfs as concubines and as wives. The children born to a concubine were serf and were returned to the serf village as serfs of the woman's owner.[25] In the case of marriage, the children became Fulbe and members of the patrilineage of their father. In order to be married legitimately the serf woman had to be freed and "made" Fulbe by the performance of *rimdingol*. The distinction between concubine and wife is hard to define. A woman could be a concubine for a

24. To "tie" a marriage means to present rope and kola at the mosque.
25. According to Islamic law, if the father and owner are the same the child is free. However, this was not followed.

few years, and then have children and be taken as a wife only later, or alternatively she might be returned to the serf village. When a master owned a serf, particularly if she had few kinsmen, little influence could be exerted on him to act one way or another. If a Fulbe married one of his own serfs, he avoided paying a large bridewealth, and he didn't lose her labor.

Marriage was complicated when the serf of a Fulbe who wanted to marry a serf was owned by another Fulbe. Permission had to be obtained from the serf's kinsmen, and from her master. Moreover, bridewealth had to be given to both parties, or, alternatively, during the late nineteenth century and early twentieth century, the serf could be bought. In any case, such a marriage would entail a large bridewealth, for a serf woman brought a good price because her owner also owned her children. Marriage with a serf of another owner was usually the man's second or later marriage.

If there were rivalry between a Fulbe and a serf over a woman (which could happen if she were exceptionally pretty), the Fulbe would usually win. If there were rivalry between two serfs and one of them had the same master as the woman, he would marry her.

There was general consensus among my informants that the chiefly lineage of the area took more serf women than did other Fulbe. If we look at the wives of the last chief of the *misside* Popodara before the French came, we find that of the seven wives who bore him children, three were serfs.[26] The chiefly lineage took wives from among their serfs to avoid affinal obligations and alliances with nonchiefly lineages. Moreover, marriage with their own serfs guaranteed that their wives would be politically loyal to them.

All Fulbe viewed marriage with a serf as having potentially desirable consequences: "The child of a union with a serf will be very strong" (*Bii tara ḳeldai tung*). An objection to marriage with serfs was the belief that the children born of a serf would

26. The limit of four wives appears to have been followed less during precolonial times. Of course, concubines did not count as legitimate wives.

dominate the Fulbe's other children. Quite often, on the other hand, the family of a serf woman would object to her marriage with a Fulbe on the basis that it would weaken her. The serfs viewed the Fulbe as quite lazy, a characteristic which would put too much of a burden on a wife. The real objection had to do with the loss of their daughter. The Fulbe did not maintain affinal responsibilities to serfs, and children of such a marriage rarely visited the village of their mother.

Currently there are two women from Hollaande married to Fulbe, both marriages having taken place prior to 1958. There is also one woman living in Hollaande who is divorced from her Fulbe husband. She was taken by force from her parents by the Fulbe, who was a kinsman of the *chef de canton*. In short, within the past ten years no marriages have taken place between a Fulbe and a woman from Hollaande, whereas between 1948 and 1958, there were three, and between 1925 and 1948 at least six.

There are two men in the village of Hollaande who have married Fulbe women. They do not live in the village, nor is it likely they ever will. Before they married they paid for the ceremony of *rimdingol* to be made free, in this context to become "Fulbe". Although there has been an increase in the number of marriages between former serfs and Fulbe women, all the examples I came across (and admittedly they weren't many) involved a man who had become "Fulbe." However, the ceremony of *rimdingol* is no longer performed, mainly because of the actions of the Guinean state. It remains to be seen whether as a result there will be an increase or decrease in marriages between Fulbe and former serfs.

The traditional social order, which led to such sayings as "A serf is like a chicken; the proprietors of chickens' eggs are not the chickens but the chickens' owners" (*Kado no wa'i gerto, ƙo pullo beingumakko dyei bibbe*), has ended. No longer can a master oblige a serf woman or her parents to accept him as her husband, although the former master's permission is asked and he receives a token part of the bridewealth. The decline of serf-dom has diminished the potential advantages of marrying former serf women. The reasons for Fulbe-serf marriages have ended along with serfdom and chieftainship.

Former-serf attitudes toward the Fulbe vary greatly; however, the older former serfs often show deference to them. For one marriage of a girl from Hollaande no money was sent to the girl's former master as token of his traditional share of the bridewealth. The major patrilineage of the girl decided to take his share of the money from that designated as the share of the father's sisters and brothers. They insisted that no marriage agreement would be right without the part of the Fulbe: "We will not give the girl before speaking to her Fulbe" (*Meng dyonnata dyiwo ong baawo hallidigal e pullo ong*). Many former serfs still follow the customs surviving from their period of serfdom, even though the underpinnings of the institution of marriage have changed.

The current period can be viewed as one of transition to greater control over marriage by the potential spouses both male and female, and to a more individualized form, particularly since that is the explicit policy of the Guinean state. Many of the keystones of the older system have ended, such as betrothal at birth, and the maternal uncle's promising his nephew one of his daughters as a wife. Although it will clearly be awhile before the age minimum of sixteen for the marriage of women will be accepted, women are now marrying later, and the practice of having a girl married prior to puberty, and living with her husband almost as his child until that time, is ending.

SUMMARY

Within the three Fulbe strata there has been a marked decline in the political and economic functions of the major and maximal patrilineages. This has led to the expression of the functions of the lineage primarily in a ceremonial context. However, the minimal lineage has retained much of its economic importance, because the head of a minimal lineage in a Fulbe village continues to redistribute both fields and garden land among the members. The former-serf strata has not seen a comparable decline in the importance of the major patrilineage, because the conditions of serfdom greatly restricted the functioning of kin groups in the first place. Elder former-serfs, who were formerly denied the prestige, influence, and authority due them, can now enjoy their role as elders of the major patrilineages. This has not stopped the trend toward the increased importance of the household, although the minimal-lineage head in a former serf village does not have the same economic leverage as his counterpart in a Fulbe village.

Despite the increased importance of the elders within the former-serf village and their increased control over such internal matters as inheritance and marriage, the major patrilineage does not assume any new economic or political roles. The economy hinges increasingly on the household, and the political process on the committee. However, former serfs now have much greater independence from their former masters. Fulbe control over their serfs was many-faceted. We have noted the economic basis of their relationship and how that relationship has been transformed. Changes in the social sphere have also occurred, but are less dramatic. These changes affect particularly inheritance and marriage. In the case of marriage we find the end of concubinage, former serf control over the choice of marriage partners with only the formal consent of the Fulbe required—a shell of the earlier practice, former serfs beginning to take Fulbe wives, and the end of marriage between Fulbe and former-serf women.

The independence of Guinea, with the intervention of the Democratic Party of Guinea in the countryside, has brought significant social change, which is slated to increase with the further insistence of the P.D.G. on a minimum age for the marriage of girls, women's consent before marriage, limits on bridewealth, and the end of polygyny. Already the P.D.G. has been responsible for the end of concubinage and the ceremony of *rimdingol,* whereby former serfs became "Fulbe."

Four

The Economy of the
Fouta-Djallon

The current economy of the Fouta-Djallon is a mixture of subsistence agriculture and a growing commercial sector. Animal husbandry is practiced, although cattle raising is not as dominant in the Fouta as it is in other Fulbe areas. Although the need for money for consumer goods and for the expenses of ceremonies is increasing, the growing of basic food crops is scarcely commercialized. From the point of view of the Fulbe peasants, money is unattainable from agriculture, and yet money has become a necessity. The result is a proliferation of the means by which people obtain money (other than by selling basic food crops) and a developing commercial sector of the economy.

We have described the impact of money and markets on village organization during the colonial period. In this chapter we shall be concerned with the economy of a village during the period from 1966 to 1967. The influence of the colonial period remains strong. Colonial rule destroyed the self-sufficiency of the rural population, and created a strong demand for European goods. Furthermore, it created a large reservoir of laborers, who needed money to pay the newly introduced taxes. This reservoir of labor has not decreased, because there is a continuing need for money and a lack of opportunity for earning it in the countryside. It is in this perspective that we must view the economy of Hollaande.

THE SUBSISTENCE ECONOMY

Women's Gardens

The women's garden is intensively, annually cultivated and is planned, cultivated, and maintained by women.[1] Moreover, women distribute the harvest. Each wife in a polygynous marriage has her own garden. However, although the woman works her garden (with the aid of her children), she does not own the land. Her husband, or another man, owns the land, and if a woman is divorced, she loses her rights to that land. The harvest from the garden feeds the woman, her children, and her husband. The ceremonial obligations of both the woman and her husband will also be met from the produce of the garden. If there is a surplus, the woman has the right to sell it at a market without the consent of her husband, because the produce is viewed as belonging to the woman by virtue of her labor.

The women's garden has become a critical source of food, at least since 1900. This conclusion is supported by a study of a series of villages composing the *misside* of Ndantari in the neighboring region of Pita done by the Mission Démographique de Guinée:

The total of women's gardens covered 21 hectares, which is nearly half of the area cultivated in fields. It is this fundamental observation which explains where the major part of the subsistence of these peasants comes from. *The calories furnished by women's gardens is much greater than that coming from the fields of fonio* [emphasis in original] (1955: 26).

1. The position of women in African society varies greatly. Contrast the position of women in the Fouta to the Nupe as described by Nadel:

The role which the women play in the agricultural production of the country lends itself to a simple formula. With very few exceptions the women do not perform any primary productive activity: they do no farm work; they do not help in cultivation except occasionally when assisting the men in the harvesting of cotton or beans or the digging out of cassava—the easiest crop of all. Their sphere of work is, first the "refining" of agricultural produce to make it marketable, and secondly, the marketing itself (1942: 252).

In short, the garden provides a greater part of the diet of the inhabitants of the Fouta-Djallon than does the grain harvested from the fields. The relative importance of the garden is due to three factors. First, there has been a decrease in the availability and fertility of fields, which is related to the second factor, the increase in population. Third, a husband's migration to find work elsewhere often leaves a woman and her family without a man (and therefore no fields). The family therefore has to make do on whatever money he sends them and on the harvest of the garden.

When the women's gardens were developed and why are unknown. Unfortunately, traditional Fulbe history was not concerned with the work of women. We do not know if the garden was an innovation of the Fulbe, or whether they adopted the practice from the Diallonke who inhabited the Fouta-Djallon prior to their arrival.[2] Jacques Richard-Molard has proposed an explanation for the origin of the *sunture*.

It is poverty which has pushed the Fulbe woman to work in the women's garden. By the ritual laziness of her husband, by the erosion of the fields, and by the default of the captives [serfs] in many modest families, it has become necessary to cultivate the women's garden in order to complement the production of the fields. The women's garden always keeps this complementary character but it is a vital supplement, which explains the care with which it is exploited (1944: 222).

It is evident that this theory is unsatisfactory, for poverty does not necessarily lead to such development. However, Richard-Molard was the first to point out the great importance of the women's gardens, and he goes on to note that the Fouta-Djallon, given its physical characteristics and its already advanced state of erosion, is overpopulated. "Over-population," or the high density of population, could be sustained only because of the women's gardens. He concludes his discussion of the gardens by stating:

2. It appears likely that the women's garden was adopted from another people. The word *sunture* is borrowed, and is not part of the vocabulary of other Fulbe groups outside of the Fouta-Djallon.

Pushed by necessity and constrained by conquest and victory, the Fulbe had to develop expert cultivation practices because they were so numerous and because the mountain mass had already been severely affected by the disastrous exploitation of earlier cultivators. These cultivation practices have perhaps made Fulbe women the most expert cultivators in Black Africa (1944: 226).

Richard-Molard was in the Fouta-Djallon in 1942. Since that time the importance of women's gardens has increased, not declined.

In the village of Hollaande the primary crops of the women's gardens are sweet manioc or cassava, taro, and maize. Crops of secondary importance are sweet potatoes, yams, peanuts, cotton, and small hot peppers. There are also several plants (for which I do not know the English equivalents) whose leaves are used in sauces. Within the compound, where the women's gardens are, are also many fruit trees. However, these fruit trees are not a part of the women's gardens, for they are not maintained by the women nor do they belong to the women. The fruit trees usually belong to the proprietor of the compound, who is always a man. When a woman plants a tree, the tree will be inherited by the person who inherits the land of her garden. The most common fruit trees are orange trees, mango trees, avocado trees, papaya trees, and kola trees.

Although I have described the *sunture* as the woman's garden, the husband plays an important role, for it is the obligation of every husband to provide land for his wife's garden. Formerly, the residents of Hollaande did not own the land on which they built their gardens and houses. The fact that the land was owned by the Fulbe was indicated by the payment of the *farilla* to the Fulbe proprietor of the land. The *farilla* was drawn only from the maize. The husband, who borrowed the land, was responsible for paying the *farilla,* not the wife who labored in the garden. Many women claimed ignorance of how much *farilla* was given from their harvest. Today, there is not a single household head in Hollaande who owns all of his compound. He may have bought some parts of it, or feel that he owns parts he has recently added, but all the men in the village must continue to pay *farilla* on maize. The payment of the *farilla* does not, however, mean that the proprietor of the land can repossess it if it is occupied. When put in these terms, the villagers were unanimous in their agreement that the Fulbe could no longer dispossess them. In short, the proprietorship of the compound land is passing from the Fulbe into the hands of the former serfs of Hollaande.

Women's gardens are cultivated annually. This is possible because of continual fertilization. During the long dry season all the "garbage" of a household and the manure of goats, sheep, and cattle are spread in the garden. The women are quite cognizant that the fertility of a garden depends on the extent of fertilization. All the women maintained that the older a garden—the longer it had been under continual cultivation—the greater its fertility. The tool used for cultivation is the ubiquitous *daba,* or hoe. The hoe is used for digging up roots, turning over the soil, and weeding.

The end of the previous year's agricultural cycle is marked by the harvesting of taro. Taro is immediately replanted, marking the beginning of the agricultural cycle. During the month prior to the coming of the first rains in May the women begin systematically hoeing-under all the remaining plants from the previous year. They soften and turn over the soil, adding additional organic material to it. As they do this, they remove all the taro not yet harvested and replant for the coming season.[3]

When the entire garden has been hoed, it is ready for the planting of maize. The women frequently do not finish this process by the time of the first rains, and the three weeks following are marked by a flurry of activity, the women spending ten to twelve hours a day working in their gardens. The timing for the plant-

3. There are two varieties of taro grown, *dyabere futa* and *dyabere goba.* The latter is said to be indigenous, and the former introduced from the south. In the case of the *dyabere futa* the "mother" taro is replanted each year for ten to twenty years, and the offshoots are eaten. In the case of *dyabere goba* the "mother" taro is eaten, and the offshoots are replanted.

ing of maize is crucial to the success of the crop, because the first rains are usually followed by a dry period of two weeks to a month before it rains more frequently. If the corn is planted too early, the kernels will dry up and die in the earth. If they are planted after there has been too much rain, the taro will already have begun to grow and its leaves will block the sunlight from the corn. If the timing has been right the maize will appear before the taro.[4]

The last of the basic crops to be planted is manioc. Stalks of manioc saved from the previous year are cut into small lengths and placed in little mounds. Of the various crops planted in the garden manioc requires the least amount of care and fertilization. Whereas corn and taro will not grow in newly expanded gardens, manioc will.[5]

The termination of planting in the garden does not mark any slack in work for the women. When the maize reaches approximately seven to twelve inches in height, the first weeding is done. When the maize attains the height of approximately two feet, the women commence the arduous process of covering their entire garden with leaves. This process takes from two to three weeks, depending on the size of the garden and on how many children a woman has to help her. The leaves are cut from the scrub in the hills near the village, which requires a walk of two to five kilometers. The leaves used in this process are known as *foyong* (a generic term not referring to any particular plant or leaf, but to any leaves used in this process). Jacques Richard-Molard has observed that the function of the freshly cut leaves covering the

4. A woman and her children plant maize by digging holes with the *daba*. Into the holes are dropped three or four kernels of maize. The holes are then recovered with earth. Because of the crucial importance of the timing of planting maize, all the maize is planted within one garden in two days. In the village as a whole it takes only five or six days for everyone to plant. Furthermore, because of the need to sow all the corn at one time, it is one of the few times when co-wives will aid each other as a matter of course.

5. The manioc takes approximately twenty to twenty-four months to mature in the region of Labe. Therefore the cuttings are planted in only one half of the garden at any one time.

garden is to preserve the warm humidity of the soil, without which taro will not grow well. Furthermore, it is an excellent method of protecting the soil, rich in organic material, from the hard rays of the sun, which otherwise would sterilize the manure (1944: 224). With the completion of this phase, work in the garden eases. The women then shift their attention to the fields.

The harvest comes at a time when food is at its scarcest and when many families are living primarily on taro. Thus it is a particularly joyous time. It begins with the maize harvest about three months after planting. Immediately after harvesting, preservation procedures are begun. Maize that is to be eaten for the rest of the year is left to dry on the stalks before being removed. However, families take maize off the stalks before this time to roast or boil. For a month before this the men of the family bring large pieces of wood to feed the fires that will dry the maize. The fires built by the men are constructed in one house in the compound, and the maize is left inside to dry for one to five days, depending on the size of the harvest. Maize, fire dried, can be kept for a full year. With the completion of drying the maize, the women return to their garden to weed and loosen the earth around the remaining crops.

By August or September the manioc planted a year and a half earlier is ready to be dug up. Manioc will keep in the earth, but once harvested will spoil rapidly. Therefore, only what will be consumed immediately is removed from the earth. The rest is left to be cut and dried after the end of the rainy season. Taro begins to mature at about the same time as manioc. Taro can be stored out of the ground in its original state much longer than can manioc, but it is nevertheless also cut and dried. Harvesting the taro takes place in two phases. The first harvesting is done when the taro leaves are dry—the sign it is ripe. This is done on a day-to-day basis depending on the needs of the family. The second harvest is systematic and takes place toward the end of the dry season. The woman begins at one part of her garden and works until the entire garden has been covered, systematically turning over the earth, removing the taro, and preparing her garden for the next planting cycle. This whole process requires about three to four months of work.

Extending a garden is the responsibility of the husband, who must first provide the land. In the past a villager of Hollaande had to ask the Fulbe proprietor of the land for his permission. During colonial times he might buy the land from him. Both these practices have nearly disappeared, as the former serfs now regard the compound land as almost their own. The second step is to enclose the proposed extension within a fence, again the work of the husband. With the completion of the fence, the wife takes charge. She clears the area, and then burns the dried vegetation. A new plot requires a great deal of manure. As the manure is gathered over a period of weeks it is mixed in with the earth. This work is done during the dry season, and with the first rains the plot is ready for its first planting. Manioc (and sometimes fonio) can be planted, but maize and taro will not grow due to the lack of sufficient nutrients. It is only after the third year that taro and maize will begin to grow, and even then not well. It generally takes six to ten years before a new garden begins to attain the productivity of the older gardens.

Gardening is essentially the work of the women, but there is one vital task the men perform, namely, building and maintaining the fence that surrounds the compound and the garden. Without a fence a garden would not last a day because of the great number of animals (goats, sheep, and cattle) which abound in the village. Finding a way to prevent each type of animal from entering poses its own particular problem. Cattle will knock down a fence if it is not strong enough. Goats and sheep will jump over a fence if it is not high enough. And, of course, termites continually eat the wood of a fence, aiding the rapid process of natural decay. The main problem in fence-building is the shortage of wood. To find the necessary wood requires a walk of five to eight kilometers one way. One load is enough for perhaps five feet of fence. For a fence of thirty yards (a small compound) eighteen trips are required. Furthermore, a fence will last without repair only three years. The shortage of wood has become so great that several men in Hollaande have taken to digging large ditches surrounding their compounds and making earth walls in which they plant sisal, whose thick growth and thorns will keep out animals. The advantage of ditches and earth walls is that they are relatively permanent in contrast with wood fences. The disadvantage of such a technique manifests itself when someone wants to expand his compound; the labor and time required to dig the ditches exceeds that of hauling wood for the fence.

There is one difference between former-serf villages and Fulbe villages with respect to the division of labor in the women's gardens. At Hollaande men occasionally aid their wives in the gardens during the peak work times of preparing the gardens after the first rains and planting the maize. Although this is not typical, it does indicate the critical importance of the women's gardens and the recognition by certain men of this fact. It is also no accident that the crop with which the men help is maize, for it is the most important crop in ceremonies.

Work in the garden is performed mainly by a woman with her unmarried daughters and uncircumcised sons. Each wife of a husband works her own garden without the aid of her co-wives, except at certain peak work times—the planting of corn and the bringing of leaves to cover the garden. A woman's daughters work as hard in the garden as she does herself. As a woman gets older, she can call on her married daughters for their assistance, or can ask for the help of an older grandchild for several days when she needs assistance. Of the characteristics thought by the men to make a good wife, the ability to maintain a productive garden was of great importance.

Work in the garden, in marked contrast to that in the fields, continues for the whole year. During the dry season a woman spends three to four hours a day harvesting taro, manioc, and hoeing the area. The rest of the day is spent cleaning, cutting, and drying the taro and manioc. This is also the time when manure is gathered from the surrounding fields (which become pasture during the dry season) to spread in the garden. The coming of the first rains marks the beginning of feverish activity that does not end until the woman has finished covering her garden with leaves. During this time a woman spends six to eight hours a day working in her garden. In general, a woman does not work in her garden when there are ceremonies, markets, or during peak work times in the fields (sowing, weeding, and harvesting).

The crops of the garden are not considered of equal value, which is reflected in their distribution. The maize harvest is destined primarily for ceremonial occasions and only secondarily for direct household consumption; the taro and manioc harvests serve an opposite purpose. Control of the distribution of the different crops varies accordingly. Maize is subject to greater control by the head of the household; and it is the husband who is directly responsible, and who actually gives the *farilla* from the maize. Decisions regarding the distribution of maize, and the balance between household consumption and ceremonial outlay, are made by both husband and wife. Moreover, there are instances when a husband stores a portion of the maize harvest for himself. The root crops (taro and manioc primarily, along with sweet potatoes) are the province of the woman who cultivates them. She controls the distribution and consumption of these crops. However, her decisions are based on "intuition." She does not make a quantitative assessment of her needs for the year.

As part of their control over distribution, women have the right to sell the surplus from their gardens at the market, and to keep for themselves the money they receive. However, the amount sold is small. Women sell taro and manioc by the small basket (*korung*) when dried, or in small bunches of five or six roots when whole.[6] To give an indication of the small quantity

6. The Fulbe have an indigenous system of measurement based on the *korung,* or *sari-ari,* and the *debeere.* These are both baskets manufactured locally by artisans of serf origin. The weight of one *korung* filled with fonio is approximately 1 kilogram, with rice, 1.5 kilograms, and there are approximately 4000 kernels of maize in one *sari-ari.*

of root crops sold, we might note that to start a garden, twenty-five baskets or more of taro (*debeere,* or 2000 *korung*) are required. Thus, a woman selling two *korung* of taro per week at the market—a large amount—would be selling very little in relation to her harvest.

Maize is sold at market by the women of Hollaande even less than taro and manioc, because it is a food required at all ceremonies. All household heads indicated that at some time during 1966 they had to buy maize at the market in order to meet their ceremonial obligations. It is the most highly preferred food from the garden. Combined with sour milk, it is the most desired food at ceremonies. Taro is said to have been the food of the serfs, because the serfs were more dependent on the harvest of the garden than were the Fulbe, who consumed a larger proportion of field crops. Taro is also connected with the lack of cattle, and therefore of milk, among the serfs. Taro, which grows particularly well at Hollaande, is the staple of their diet, although they do not like it much. Taro is the diet of the poor.

In summary, the garden has become the most important part of the subsistence agriculture of the villagers of Hollaande, and of others of the plains of the High Fouta. The garden, worked by the woman and her children, provides the starchy root staples taro, manioc, sweet potatoes (at Hollaande), yams (at other villages, but not at Hollaande), and maize. Peanuts and other plants required for sauces are also cultivated in it. The high productivity of the garden is due to fertilization with manure and garbage, as well as to the protective covering of leaves spread over the garden after the crops have begun to grow. The woman has control over the production, harvesting, and distribution of her garden. However, she has less control over maize than other crops because of its ceremonial importance and because it is required for *farilla.*

The Fields

We can hypothesize that in the eighteenth and nineteenth centuries the field crops fonio and rice provided the major part of the Fulbe diet.[7] We can also speculate that fields were never as important to the serfs as they were to the Fulbe because of the system of land ownership and labor requirements. The authors of the Guinean Demographic Mission were able to calculate the difference between the areas cultivated by a master and by a serf. Their chart, done in 1954 when serfs were still working for their masters, shows that the Fulbe were cultivating much more land than were the serfs. The authors state the the area of the compounds varied little,[8] and therefore the difference was due to the fact that the Fulbe cultivated more land in fields than did the serfs. My own conclusion is that the area varied little for each woman but that between households there was marked variation in the size of the *sunture* which depended almost entirely on the number of wives.

The fields have now lost their earlier importance in the area of what was formerly the *misside* of Popodara. The harvest of fonio now provides a smaller part of the Fulbe diet than it did in the past. However, fonio remains a preferred food and, if possible, the Fulbe like to have fonio (or rice) and sauce everyday. Moreover, since it is no longer possible to grow rice at Popodara, fonio is the only possible field crop.

Table 2, from the Guinean Demographic Mission Report (1955:

7. The Fulbe distinguish several varieties of fonio, depending on the time of maturation, the kind of soil in which it will grow, and the kind of grain it produces. The *fonye bolefonde* is the most common variety. Under normal conditions it takes six months to mature and grows well on the *ndantari*. Another variety, *fonye sirage,* is usually planted in the part of a garden that has been recently added or if the first planting of corn has failed, because it matures in three months (although its yield is lower). *Fonye konso donghol* and *fonye kuli* are planted on mountain sides (*kaadye*). The latter has a maturation time of three months and has large grains. The former matures in five months. Another variety, *fonye sagantang,* rare around Popodara, grows well on the *ndantari* but takes several months to mature. The villagers dislike it because of the long maturation time, which makes it more susceptible to being eaten by birds, monkeys, or domesticated animals.

8. According to the French Demographic Mission, "The surface area of each compound varies so little that it didn't seem useful to present a detailed division of these areas" (1951: 26).

27), indicates the difference of land use between Fulbe and serfs. The table indicates the average amount of *sunture* and field land measured in ares (both cultivated and uncultivated) held by each individual, by each active adult (those who actually work the land), and by each productive unit.

Table 2. DIFFERENCE IN AREA OF LAND HELD BY FULBE AND SERFS

Categories	Misside			Runde		
	I.	A.A.	P.	I.	A.A.	P.
Women's gardens	10	25	53	11	21	50
Fields cultivated	26	63	133	16	29	70
Fields uncultivated	48	116	247	22	41	100

I. = Individual
A.A. = Active Adult
P. = Productive Unit
Unit of measurement is the *are* = 100 square meters

The decline in the importance of fields has affected both former serfs and the Fulbe, although not equally. There are three reasons for this change. First, the fields are declining in fertility because not enough fallow time has been allowed. Second, it is increasingly difficult to obtain land for fields because of the increase in population and the erosion of good land. Third, many men, seeking to earn money, either migrate or engage in activities that preclude the cultivation of fields. The result is a greater dependence on the women's gardens. This generalization applies primarily to former serfs, who have less field land than the Fulbe, but it also applies to the poorer Fulbe.

In general, the Fulbe cultivate larger fields than do the former serfs, but field size varies greatly among both. Those who are wealthy tend to cultivate (or have cultivated for them) larger fields than do their poorer brethren. The Guinean Demographic Mission observed at the villages composing the *misside* of Ndantari that 50 percent of the total number of fields represented only 20 percent of the total area of all the fields, and that 50 percent of the land units worked (*exploitations*) represented only 17 percent of the total area (1955: 22).

Fonio and rice remain the two major field crops of the Fouta-Djallon. Around the turn of the century rice was cultivated on the mountainsides in the nearby environs of *misside* Popodara.[9] A field could be planted in rice only the first year, for the yield diminished so greatly by the second that it was not worth planting. Fonio was planted the second and sometimes the third year. Rice is still planted in many areas of the Fouta-Djallon, but rarely in the central plateau where the peasants maintain that the effort required for the extremely low yield renders rice-growing useless. Fonio is now the only field crop at Popodara.

There are basically three kinds of land in and around Popodara: *ndantari, hollaande,* and *kaadye*. Portères has described *ndantari* and *hollaande: ndantari*— ". . . is a permeable soil with a high content of sand. Often it is quite thin and in many areas of the Fouta it can be used only for cultivation of fonio, not for rice. On the fields left to restore fertility the vegetation is very weak, and is becoming weaker as less is now left for fallow." *hollaande*— ". . . is land without trees, without stones, less sandy and more clayey. It is hard and compact during the dry season but turns to mud and often is covered with water during the height of the rainy season." (1964: 156–57).

Portères does not discuss *kaadye* because it does not have a clearly defined meaning. In general usage around Popodara it refers to hillsides and mountainsides where the soil is filled with rocks (often the "rocks" are not real rocks but hardened laterite).

9. Although it has been a long time since mountain rice was cultivated in Popodara, there is another technique that was employed as recently as three years ago. It is known as *mukti*. The land required is *hollaande*, where water gathers during the rainy season. First the area is cleared of grass and brush, which is formed into little mounds where manure is put. Then the whole field is burned. Then the rice is placed in the mounds. The manure and burned grass and brush serve as fertilizer, and the lowness and nature of the soil of the *hollaande* retains enough water to permit the successful harvest of rice. It appears that this practice is no longer continued due to the expensiveness of rice seeds and the need for land for fonio, which yields a larger crop.

Such areas drain rapidly, remain relatively dry, and require more effort to cultivate. The villagers, however, feel the yield is better than on other types of soil. The predominance of *ndantari* and *hollaande,* which make up the plains, gives Popodara its particular character and makes it different from the areas where mountain (*kaadye*) and valley-bottom cultivation are predominant.

Depending on the nature of the land to be cultivated, there is a great difference in the amount of time required for preparation. In the case of cultivation on mountainsides, the clearing of the area requires much work and time. The cultivation of the plains (either *hollaande* or *ndantari*) does not require the same intensive effort for clearing, and even digging in the soil is easier because of its softer composition. However, all the villagers agree that the mountainsides yield more fonio, and that the Fulbe for the most part keep the good land for themselves.

Much of the cultivated land around Popodara is plains (*hollaande* or *ndantari,* the latter preferred for fonio cultivation). Because the *ndantari* is relatively stoneless and treeless, and because there were many cattle to serve as draft animals, the French introduced the plow. For their experiment the French used a *chef de canton* and those villagers who had fought in the French army. One of the first men in the area of Popodara to use a single-blade plow and oxen was a former soldier who had lived in a village one and a half kilometers from Hollaande. He bought the plow on credit from the French in 1926. The result of the introduction of the plow has been that wives of men who cultivate in that fashion have been freed from much work in the fields, because plowing is a man's work. In the village of Hollaande there were two men who owned and used oxen and plows. Another man lent his bull to a kinsman in a nearby village because he himself chose to cultivate on the mountainside, where it was not possible to use a plow.

Very few former serfs have ultimate titles of ownership to their fields. Fields are still owned by the Fulbe, and landless Fulbe are rare. In the village of Hollaande there was only one man who owned a field. He bought it during the colonial era with money earned from his service in the French army. He can cultivate this one field for three or four years in succession (it is *ndantari*), and then has to let it lie fallow for five years. During those five years he has to borrow land as do the rest of the villagers. A former serf's borrowing of land from a land proprietor is an individual matter. The head of a household goes to a land owner during the dry season to ask about borrowing a certain amount of land for the following cutivating season. Sometimes one land owner has only a little to lend and a villager must borrow land from more than one owner.

Although the borrowing of land is an individual matter, there are some considerations that make it desirable for men from the same village to cultivate in the same area. The major consideration is the necessity of constructing a fence around the fields to keep out the goats, sheep, and cattle, for, despite all precautions, it is not possible to insure that everyone's animals will return to his compound each night. Consequently, groups of men try to cultivate in the same area in order to cooperate in the building of a fence. In general, Hollaande usually divides into its two major patrilineages for selecting its field area. This is not always true, for many factors influence the decision of a household head as to where he will cultivate. Among these are whether he owns a plow and oxen, whether he is able (in terms of time and physical stamina) to clear away forest and cultivate a mountain field, or whether he prefers the easier clearing required of fields on the plains. At no time during the past years have all the households of Hollaande had their fields in one area.

During the first cultivating season I observed, there were two main field areas for Hollaande. The first was on a plain (*ndantari*) bordering the village; the second was a hillside above a large stream, a forty-five minute walk from the village. The land on the plain was obtained individually by the head of each household. The land on the plain on the hillside was owned by one individual, a Fulbe, who lent it to one man from Hollaande. He in turn divided it among members of the village. He gave his elder brother and his mother's brother first choice of the land. All members of his minimal lineage cultivated in that area. He also gave land to one of his wife's two elder brothers. The man who borrowed the land was responsible for collecting the *farilla* from all the cultivators and rendering it to the proprietor.

There is great variation in the size of fields, or in the amount of fonio that is grown. In general, wealth and age determine how much a man sows. The wealthier he is (which includes money income), the more fonio he will usually cultivate in comparison with others of the same age with less wealth. Although growing a small amount of fonio usually indicates the poverty of a household (which will eat little fonio during the year), there is now an increasing number of men with a steady money income who prefer to buy most of their fonio at the market and cultivate only a small amount. There was one man in Hollaande who considered himself a full-time merchant and did not cultivate any fields.

The following tabulation shows the variation in the amount of fonio cultivated by the household heads and their wives during the year 1966. In general, with the marked exception of household head number 7, the harvest was felt to be quite poor. The information was obtained as part of an economic survey. The results were not verified by actual measurement. Furthermore, as one can observe from the tabulation, many figures are missing because of the reluctance of individuals to give me information about their economic status. Some individuals were ashamed to let me know the extent of their poverty, particularly in relation to others in the village; and elders of the village thought it improper of me to ask for such information. In short, either it was thought to be none of my business, or I offended sensibilities by asking such questions. I therefore had to stop asking elders if they sold any of their fonio. The few answers, given reluctantly by the first three men I asked, were of course, no, because fonio is grown to be eaten or to be given as a gift, not to be sold at the market.

COMPARISON OF FONIO SOWED WITH
FONIO HARVESTED BY VILLAGERS OF HOLLAANDE
(Measured in *Korung*)

Household	Fonio Sowed	Fonio Harvested
1	15	88
2	88	600
3	20	0[a]
4	22	70
5	8	0[b]
6	32	195
7[c]	26	360
8	19	unknown
9	16	120
10[d]	0	0
11	23	88
12[e]	8	unknown
13[d]	0	0
14[f]	0	0
15	16	refused answer
16	35	120
17	15	refused answer
18[g]	refused answer	refused answer
19	10	80
20	24	240
21[h]	10	unknown
22	9	100
23	56	refused answer
24	40	refused answer
25	58	240
26	refused answer	refused answer
27	refused answer	refused answer

Household	Fonio Sowed	Fonio Harvested
28	25	refused answer
29	4	unknown
30	46	200
31	40[1]	150
32	49	160
33	40	320
34	25	refused answer
35	120	refused answer
36[j]	unknown	unknown
37[d]	unknown	unknown
38	24	160
39[k]	unknown	unknown
40[1]	36	unknown

[a.] Seeds were spoiled.
[b.] Worms ate seeds.
[c.] Includes harvest for household 8—head of household 7 was son of head of household 8 and did most of work because father was infirm.
[d.] Wage laborer.
[e.] Total was low because head of household was a merchant, rarely resident.
[f.] Merchant, resident at Hollaande, who bought grain at market.
[g.] Did state that he paid 15 measures of *farilla*, at least 150 measures of harvest.
[h.] He said it was a small amount without specifying.
[i.] Includes mother.
[j.] Did not ask—oldest man in village.
[k.] Recently married, just beginning fields.
[l.] Recently divorced, shared fields with his father.

In Hollaande the household head obtains fields for his wives, and perhaps his children. He sets aside the largest section for himself. He then divides the remaining area among his wives, and perhaps gives small areas to his unmarried children to prepare them for later life. The harvests from these different fields are kept separate. Each wife stores her part in her own house. The husband keeps his part in his house, to be given to his wives as the need arises. However, the household works together sowing, weeding, harvesting, and threshing. Clearing and plowing with oxen are the tasks of a man. The time at which the clearing of the area to be cultivated begins is highly variable, depending on the kind of terrain and the number of years it has lain fallow. Planting time is usually June. If it is the first time a hill or mountain slope is to be cultivated, the work begins three months before planting. If a similar terrain has lain fallow for ten to twelve years, clearing may take two months. If the area has been cultivated the year before, less clearing will be required. If the land is on *ndantari* and has been cultivated the year before, no clearing at all is required.

Slash and burn agriculture, by which a field was burned in preparation for planting, was once the dominant form of field cultivation, but it is no longer practiced at Popodara. The French began and the Guineans have continued a prohibition against the burning of fields in an attempt to stop the further erosion of the already heavily eroded Fouta. Thus the present mode of cultivation at Popodara is a modification of the slash and burn method, although the original practice continues in more remote areas. Today, the cut material is gathered together in one pile and burned. The work of clearing is performed by the head of the household and his male children. Married brothers of the same mother do not work together; each has to clear his own field. When a father is living and all his sons are married, the youngest one, or the one who has remained in the village, will continue to work with his father, their fields being contiguous.

After an area has been cleared, the earth is turned with either the hoe or the plow. The work group varies depending on whether the hoe or oxen and plow are used. Plowing is entirely men's work, performed by the household head and his male children or, if he is rich, by someone hired to do the plowing for him. When a hoe is used, the entire household works together. The initial hoeing is usually done by men and their sons because the wives and daughters are working in the gardens during this time. It is only after the completion of covering the gardens with leaves that the women can join their husbands in the fields. If the husband is absent and the wife cultivates a field, it will be on the plain and she will do the hoeing with her children.

A means does exist for either cultivating large areas or cultivating rapidly. This is the *kile,* the calling of kinsmen and affines to help accomplish a particular task. A *kile* can be large or small depending on the tasks to be performed and the resources of the person calling it, for he is required to provide food and entertainment for the participants. Sowing is not done until an entire area has been hoed and is then performed as rapidly as possible. In general, only the wealthy can afford a *kile;* the poor rely primarily on their household. Sowing is one of the few times when co-wives work together. During sowing the household works together, but it is only the head of the household who actually throws the seeds into the ground. At a *kile* a religious leader, rather than the household head, throws the seeds. On the plains plowing and sowing may take as little as ten days when an oxen and plow are used. On a mountainside, without a *kile,* it will take one to three months depending on the size of the field.

Within a few days after sowing the new shoots of fonio appear. The women return to the work in their gardens. However, they will have to return twice to the fields for the two weedings done prior to the harvest in November. The men have the laborious task of constructing fences to protect the fields from the goats, sheep, and cattle.[10] For those whose fields are on the plains, fence-building is particularly arduous as it involves walking several kilometers to find wood. Fencing is done yearly; villagers

10. The chiefs used to send their courtiers (*mbatulaabe*) into the fields to take any animals they found there. In fact, the courtiers often took the initiative themselves. In order for an owner to get an animal back he had to pay a fine. If he refused or couldn't pay the fine, the chief kept the animal.

Today fines are levied on the owners of animals found in the fields after they have been cultivated and after the fences are built. The fines are 1000 francs per day for cattle, and 500 for sheep and goats. The committee regulates these affairs.

do not think it is worth the effort to build a fence that will last longer because women and children take their firewood from the fences during the dry season.

Birds and monkeys pose a constant threat to the fields. With the appearance of the first grains on the fonio, precautions have to be taken to guard the fields from predators. The problem of crop-watching is more acute in the mountains where there are more monkeys than there are on the plains. Men who cultivate fields on the mountains and hillsides remain there all day to chase away animals and birds. Those whose fields are on the plains and nearer the village, go out relatively infrequently—once every three or four days—to observe their fields.

Harvest time is in November. The fonio is cut with a sickle (*wortowal*) and then gathered into bundles. These bundles are tied and stored in an area known as the *bugo*. This is done by the entire household, with the additional help of married daughters when necessary. A *kile* is also sometimes held, although it is usually smaller than those held for hoeing and sowing, and is comprised of the household head's minimal lineage and affines. Each person who has his own field has his own storage area. At this time the head of the household takes one of every ten bundles to be given as *farilla*. Following the removal of the *farilla,* the household separates the grain from the chaff by threshing with long sticks. If the household is particularly large, they may divide by sex into groups. After the chaff is removed by hand, the women sweep up the grain from the ground and place it in baskets.

Fonio is marketed even less in Hollaande than are the products of the garden. In fact, most people do not harvest enough fonio for their dietary and ceremonial needs during the year. Of the 33 household heads who planted fonio, 13 bought the seeds at the market. This is risky, because many seeds are likely to be spoiled, and it is very difficult to recognize the different kinds of fonio from the seeds. Moreover, to buy seeds is, in some imprecise way, acting against what many consider to be the ideal of not being dependent on the market for seeds. There were several individuals who stated with quite a bit of pride that they had never bought any fonio seeds at the market, and that they were using the fonio seeds given to them by their fathers. This is not to be taken literally; it means that the individual has never had to buy or borrow seeds from anyone else. He is, and has been, self-sufficient in fonio cultivation.

The village of Hollaande faced a land crisis in 1967. The two areas where the fields had been were no longer cultivable and no alternative areas were available. The other areas traditionally cultivated had not lain fallow long enough to be used again. There was no concerted action either at the village level or the lineage level to find a solution. Rather, each household head attempted to find a solution by himself.

In one case a man was able to borrow sufficient mountain land to share with his minimal lineage and the minimal lineage of his mother's brother. The oldest man in the village, this man's mother's brother, was given the best piece of land. However, the land was acquired late and was not considered ready for cultivation. When I left the village in the middle of July, the household had not yet finished clearing the land, whereas sowing is usually finished in June.

In other cases, if the household head had difficulty finding land for his wives, they went to their former masters to see if they could borrow land for themselves. Thus, in several instances women obtained land on their own, and in some cases they cultivated land four or five kilometers from the fields of their husbands.

One man, with a source of income, paid what was considered a large sum of money (2000 francs or $8.00) to borrow land from a merchant. He will also have to pay *farilla*. This was considered a dangerous precedent and one that bodes ill for the future for those who do not own land. Some men decided not to cultivate at all and left the village to seek work for wages. Two other men decided that the market price of fonio would be lower than that of peanuts the following year. They planted their small fields with peanuts and hoped to have enough money to provide their families with fonio bought at the market.

It is perhaps too early to speculate on the significance of this land crisis. However, it is clear that the problem of finding cultivable land for fields is increasing, for the number of years fields are left fallow is declining under the pressure of a growing population.

Cash-Crop Gardens

An appendage to the traditional women's gardens and the fields, the "jardin" is cultivated exclusively by men, particularly, although not exclusively, by former serfs. These gardens date from after the founding of markets and were generally meant to provide for the needs of the French in Labe. The departure of the French has not greatly changed the situation, because there is always a population of foreigners in Labe and an increasing number of officials who like such things as stringbeans, potatoes, tomatoes, lettuce, cabbage, and pineapples. Furthermore, the Guinean government buys tomatoes for the canning factory at Mamou.

The cash-crop gardens are planted near streams at the end of the rainy season and are cared for during the dry season. Crops are sold to traders who come to the local markets, or they are taken for sale to the large daily market in Labe. Thus, the gardens provide a source of income for men during the dry season.

Cash-crop gardens were of marginal importance to the economy of Hollaande, because there is no suitable area for them in or very near the village. There were only two men who planted them. One of these men had obtained land by a stream through a kinsman at a neighboring village. The other tried cultivating by a stream near Hollaande which was thought not to have enough water. Nor was the soil judged good enough for successful results. Judging from the lack of yield from the garden, that particular area is a poor location. Other former serf villages in the area with suitable land have more gardens.

The work of maintaining a garden is extremely arduous, for the garden must be watered each morning and evening with a watering can.[11] Along with watering there is also weeding, loosening of the soil, and intensive fertilization with manure.

Cattle-Herding

Other ethnographies of the Fulbe deal as much with cattle as they do with people. Stenning, for example, has chapter headings such as the "Fertility of Cattle and Women" and "Founding a Family and a Herd" (1959: 100, 147). Such an emphasis on cattle would be misleading in discussing the Fulbe of the Central Fouta. It would be doubly misleading for the former serfs.

The thrust of economic developments in the Fouta-Djallon has been away from cattle-herding. With increasing sedentarization, the Fulbe's day-by-day existence became increasingly less dependent on their cattle herds, and more dependent on their fields and gardens. As the institution of serfdom grew, wealth was more directly related to the number of serfs one owned than to the size of one's cattle herds. These developments were more pronounced in the central plateau area because of the high population density and restriction of grazing areas for cattle. Most transhumance ended during the colonial era. Today, cattle are brought back to the compound every night. Thus the possibility of finding good pasture has been severely limited.

Cattle are economically important as a store of wealth for times of crop failure or for ceremonial obligations (primarily marriage and death), as a source of milk and meat, as a source of manure for the gardens, and for plowing. Midway through

---

11. The rise of cash-crop gardens has led to increased specialization among blacksmiths. There were three blacksmiths in the area who made watering cans and almost nothing else.

my economic survey at Hollaande I became really aware of the importance of money in all spheres of life. Thus I added a question to the interviews about whether an individual preferred money or cattle. The responses were divided, with about half opting for money, and the other half for cattle. Those who preferred cattle cited the convertibility of cattle into money (the price of cattle was high then) and the necessity of having cattle for the fulfillment of certain religious obligations, the most important of which is the slaughtering of a cow or bull by the children or parents of an adult who has died. They also considered possession of cattle to be a mark of wealth more important than the possession of money. The attitudes of the Fulbe, with the exception of elders, have also changed. The number of men who are said to cry more at the death of a cow than a wife is decreasing.

The importance of fertilization for the productivity of the women's gardens has been noted. It is obviously much easier for those households who own cattle to gather manure. They can gather it from where the cows spend the night, whereas the women of households who do not own cattle must search the fields for droppings to bring to their gardens.

As with many cattle-keeping peoples, the Fulbe keep cattle more for their milk than for their meat. Milk is the most valued of all foods, necessary for all ceremonies except funerals. Milk is really only available during the rainy season when there is adequate pasture. During the dry season a cow provides barely enough milk for her calf, much less for humans. Milk is available at the market, but in limited quantities. It is almost always watered down.

Before colonial rule, cattle were not slaughtered simply for their meat. There were different kinds of occasions that called for the supplying of meat, such as marriages, births, or the coming of a chief. However, as part of the commercialization of other aspects of Fulbe life, cattle-keeping has also been partially commercialized. Only "partially," however, because cattle are not raised primarily to be sold, but rather to produce herds of cows. Bulls are sold far more frequently than cows, and are the backbone of the butchers' business. The cows they receive are those that have not borne calves for two or three seasons or are sick.

Although bulls have been used to pull plows only since the 1920s, some standardized practices have developed. Plowing is done only in the morning, never beyond noon, and rarely beyond 11 o'clock, so as not to overwork the bulls. They are not permitted to graze freely during the plowing season. Instead, food (including leaves of certain trees known to be liked, or thought to be good for cattle) is brought to the animals.

Within the village of Hollaande there are 72 head of cattle (Table 3). Of the 35 household heads listed on tax rolls 23 did not own any. Of the 72 head of cattle, one elderly woman and three men owned 31 of the total. In short, the distribution of cattle within the village was quite unequal.

At Hollaande, and in former-serf villages in general, the care of cattle falls more on women than it does in Fulbe villages. Women milk the cows, preferably in the morning, and the women, or their children, take them to grazing areas on fallow fields or bush near the village for the day. The cattle are left unguarded for the duration of the day until someone goes out to bring them back to the compound of the owner.

Until 1958 boys from the village watched the cattle during the day. When the office of *chef de canton* was abolished, the practice of seizing cattle that wandered into someone's cultivated fields or gardens ceased. Despite the system of fines now in force for allowing cattle to eat growing crops, no one watches them; people prefer to pay fines.

Sheep and goats are also kept. There were 35 or so goats and 20 sheep in the village. It was much harder to keep track of their exact numbers, because they were bought, sold, and sacrificed far more frequently than were cattle. They are kept for many of the same reasons as catle: as a store of wealth, as a necessary item in many ceremonial occasions, as a source of fertilizer, as a source of meat, and the goats as a source of milk.

Table 3. OWNERSHIP OF CATTLE IN HOLLAANDE.

Head of Cattle	Number of Household Heads	Total number of cattle
0	23	0
1	1	1
2	3	6
3	6	18
4	3	12
5	0	0
6	1	6
7	2	14
8	0	0
9	0	0
10	0	0
11	1	11
One old woman owned 4 cattle which she bought with money received when her son died in the French army:		4
		72

Cattle received as *tenge* (about 4 cows) have been counted as belonging to the household head.

Chickens are also kept by both men and women. They are used as a source of meat on ceremonial occasions and for honored guests. The eggs are traditionally not eaten, but used either to raise new chickens or to sell at the market. Roosters are sold at the market when small amounts of money are needed.

To balance the account of cattle-herding, which has been de-emphasized in this study partially because the focus is on former serfs who live in an area where cattle-raising is not a predominant activity, I shall relate how an elderly Fulbe (an *ngerianke*) acquired a herd. This particular gentleman would, by all accounts, have to be considered "traditional." He was over seventy years old, having been born prior to the French conquest in 1896. When his mother died, she left him one bull, an old cow, and a calf. At the death of an adult, a bovine has to be sacrificed. In order to assure the continuation of the herd, the man sacrificed the bull. He kept the old cow until the calf had matured and then slaughtered the cow to trade for fonio. With the fonio he bought another calf, a male. He kept him for three or four years and then took him to Kindia (a large town located in a non-Fulbe part of Guinea) where he sold him for 45 francs. On his return he used 6 francs to pay the annual tax for himself and his wife. With the remaining money he bought a one-year-old heifer for 30 francs. Now he had one heifer and one cow. That year he cultivated very large fields of rice in order to have a surplus to sell. He exchanged his rice for one heifer, one-and-a-half-years old, and one goat and a sheep. The sheep died and he decided to buy only goats thereafter. Goats multiply faster than do cattle, so after two years he had five goats to exchange for one baby bull, and nine goats for one young heifer. With the acquisition of these last two calves he stopped buying cattle; he reckoned that his herd would now grow on its own. However, the herd proved unstable. He lost seven head of cattle in one week to rinderpest, he lost eight to the French as "corvée," and he gave five to his daughter when she married. Other diseases killed six other members of his herd. When I visited him, he had six head left in a herd that had once been as large as thirty.

The proper care of his herd required much movement, the period of transhumance ranging from four to seven months. If the cattle were to be kept far from the village, he himself took the herd there until they were habituated to the new area. Afterwards his wives took turns watching the animals. If the pasture was close to the village, he would borrow a house or construct a hut nearby. In this case a wife would come each day to bring him his meals and milk the cows.

Transhumance stopped five years ago in the mountainous area fifty kilometers northeast of Labe where this man lived. Furthermore, the number of cattle in his village has greatly diminished. However, even during the years of transhumance only a few men were involved because only a few owned large herds. There is now only one man in the village who gives his cows to another to keep for him during the dry season.

Presently there are at least one and a half million head of cattle in the Republic of Guinea. More than half of these are in the Fouta-Djallon proper, with most of the rest being in the areas bordering the Fouta-Djallon. Nevertheless, most Guineans do not have enough meat to eat, and there are virtually no facilities to move milk out of the local areas where cattle are herded. But the government continues to seek solutions to provide more meat for the population and to preserve the cattle herds for future use. Thus, when in 1967 there was fear of an epidemic of bovine plague, the Office of Cattle (*Office du Bétail*) vaccinated most of the cattle in the area of Popodara and elsewhere. The government has also instituted a percentage of cattle which must be commercialized in each area each year. Unfortunately, owners of cattle view this forced commercialization more as a tax than a sale, because they receive only twenty-five to fifty percent of the market price for their cattle.

THE COMMERCIAL SECTOR OF THE ECONOMY

By *commercial* is meant exchange (whether of goods or labor) based on money. The commercialization of the Fouta-Djallon has been gradual and by no means complete. In particular, commercial agriculture has not developed as extensively as it has among the Gouro, the Hausa, or the Ashanti, who sell agricultural products to the world market. Nevertheless, economic self-sufficiency has ended in the Fouta-Djallon as a result of French colonial rule. Money has entered the fabric of village life and plays an increasingly important role. Money is needed for certain kinds of food. Many of the ingredients for sauces have to be purchased at the market. Because no one cultivates rice around Hollaande, it has to be bought at the market. The food needed for ceremonies—meat, milk, maize, and rice—is frequently purchased at the market. And, as we have noted, more than one-third of the household heads bought their fonio seed at the market. Money is needed for bridewealth, as well as for clothes.

There are presently three ways to earn money for those who continue to make the village their home: to migrate for relatively short periods for wage work; to seek wage work within the surrounding area while living in the village; and to use traditional or newly acquired skills to earn money in the countryside.

Migration

In the villages of the Fouta approximately twenty-five percent of the men between the ages of fifteen and thirty-five migrate for wage work. Migration cannot be characterized as seasonal. In earlier years, when large groups of men left to work in the peanut fields of Senegal, there was seasonal labor migration. Since the decline of work on the peanut plantations there is no definite pattern as to the time of year when the men leave. This is hardly surprising. As the garden has gained in importance over the field in the provenance of food, rainy season cultivation of the field is less essential for the maintenance of the household than before.

Formerly migration was a response to the French demand for taxes, or else a form of flight from forced labor or conscription into the French army. Currently money is needed for building a house, for buying tools, salt, kola, meat, cloth, and kerosene from the market, and for paying taxes.[12] No single explanation emerges as to why men now leave the village. Four different cases will exemplify the variable factors furthering or inhibiting migration.

The first case is that of a twenty-six year old man whose wife was pregnant with their first child and who wanted to leave to earn enough money to pay for building a new house. He had learned to tailor (one of the few former serfs in the area to have done so), but he found that the money he earned from his work was not sufficient to pay for building a house. However, as he was the eldest son of an elder, pressure not to leave was put on him by his father, and by the women who served as his mother after the divorce of his father and his real mother. His father gave him the money (he was an *ancien combatant* and therefore had a source of money) to help him build the house. His father also gave a great deal of his time to the construction of the house. The son stayed to help his father in the fields (his father had the largest fields in the village) and to be with his wife and their expected first child.

An older man thirty-five years old with two wives was unable to obtain land for fields. His two wives went to their former masters to obtain small plots for themselves. He was a blacksmith but did not receive very much work. In order to feed his family and have enough money for the year he left the village in the middle of the sowing of fonio to seek wage labor in Senegal. He had previously left the village three times to work. In this case, leaving had little attraction for him because he was a "traditional" person; that is, he liked the life of the village, participated in all the ceremonies, and was extremely close to his older uterine brother, whom he treated as his father.

Another man of the same age left the village to go to Dakar. He, however, had done wage work since he was thirteen years

12. All citizens are required to pay taxes. For peasants the amount is 1000 francs. Each individual over the age of fourteen is taxed, with the exception of the aged, the sick, and mothers with four children under fourteen.

old. He began working at the regional farm and learned the trade of "boy" (local usage for *servant*). He was gone from the village for as long as three years at a time without paying a visit. He returned to the village shortly after my arrival, having left his job with the Israeli Ambassador to Guinea. He did not stay long. He was used to life in the city and, as he told me, he simply did not like the hard work of life in the village.

This man's older brother had done wage work many times. However, in the early 1950s after his release from the French army he learned to be a mechanic for motorcycles, motorbikes, and bicycles. He plied his trade successfully and was the only former serf to build a store at the *carrefour* at Popodara. He tried commerce as well. However, for various reasons he lost money and had to give up his store and his trade. He packed up his tools and left to earn some money. He was not successful and returned to the village where he worked again awhile as a mechanic and tended to the affairs of his family. He left the village again several months later to attempt to earn the capital necessary to restart his store.

These four examples indicate the diversity of reasons why individuals decide to leave the village. Not all individuals return. There are two men who worked as laborers on the railroad for the French. They were able to receive further training. Both have now resided in Conakry, with their wives and children, for more than twenty years.

The reason given by most villagers for labor migration is the need of young men to accumulate enough wealth to pay bride-wealth and to start a household. However, more than fifty percent of the men who had left the village were married. On the other hand, there was not a single male between the ages of nineteen and twenty-five who had not left the village at some point to seek work. Suffice it to say that obtaining money for marriage has become the responsibility of the individual; and this necessitates some means for earning it.

153

Local Wage Labor

Most men and women over thirty-five, when asked what they wanted their husbands or sons to do, expressed a preference for their staying in the village if able to make the choice. Two sources of fulltime wage work for the men of Hollaande are available within walking distance of the village. One is a regional governmentally owned and operated farm about five kilometers away. The farm was founded by the French in the 1930s on land taken without compensation from the Ragnaabe and has employed wage labor since its inception. Almost every adult man in Hollaande has worked there at some time, even if only for a few weeks. Contact with the farm was not restricted only to labor. The neighboring villages were required, without renumeration, to supply the French daily with milk with which they made cheese and butter. Today the farm is run by a government civil servant, a gifted farmer whose specialty is the grafting of mangos.

During the time of this study, three men were working full-time at the farm, one of them as an assistant director. Full-time means from 7:30 to 3:30, the work day established by the government. All three had been working steadily at the farm for a number of years. In addition, the son of the assistant director, aged seventeen, began working at the farm. He was the eldest son, and his father therefore did everything possible to keep him in the village. Four other men also worked for the farm for shorter time periods during my stay.

The second source of employment is the plantation, the only foreign-owned corporate operation in the region of Labe. This is a French company that exports essence of orange to France to make perfume. During my stay this plantation expanded to within only four kilometers from Hollaande, thus creating a source of wage employment for the villagers. Work is hard and the pay is lower than at the government farm, but four men were working full-time there.

It must be remembered that the situation at Popodara is not

typical for the Fouta-Djallon as a whole. There are more opportunities for wage employment than in other parts of the Fouta because of the presence of the regional farm and the French plantation. However, although there is more wage labor available, the constitution of the labor force reflects earlier status differences. The workers are mostly former serfs. This results from at least two earlier conditions. We have already noted that during the precolonial period a Fulbe ideally concerned himself either with his cattle or with Islam, whereas the serfs did the necessary agricultural labor. Second, during the colonial period the French employed and taught many more former serfs than Fulbe about cash-crop gardening, that is, about European practices and crops. Needless to say, the French obtained much of this labor through force and coercion, but the heritage has remained.

While we have noted the expressed preference for remaining in the village over migration for wage work, we must consider who expressed the preference and what this meant in terms of the status of agricultural laborers. When the villagers were asked about whether it was necessary to leave the village to obtain money, they always pointed to one young man who had been working at the farm for several years. They used him as an example of what they thought was an ideal solution. He had a steady income, he lived with his family, helped his mother, and he had earned enough money to buy some cows and other items. However, he was considered an example by women and older men, not by the young. It is clear that the young have not adopted him as a model, for job opportunities have arisen at the farm or at the French plantation and they have either not applied or have worked there awhile and then left. They are reluctant to accept a life-style that will revolve around kin obligations and agricultural labor. In short many want alternatives to life in the village.

Many young people have left the village and returned because they weren't successful in the cities, but they will try again. Others have returned to the village to marry but leave again after their wives have become pregnant. Part of this pattern, aside from the attraction of the city, has to do with the status of agricultural labor. It is thought that those who have the ability, skill, or money will do something else to earn money. The young, of course, see themselves as having alternatives to unskilled agricultural labor and therefore leave to make their way.

Specialists

The third and largest group are those who combine agricultural labor and a specialty by which they can earn money. This is not to imply that those who are wage laborers and live in the village don't cultivate fields; they do, but less than others. Of the men residing permanently in the village only one man consistently did not cultivate any fields. By specialty is meant traditional serfs' crafts, traditional labor tasks done by former serfs for Fulbe (or rich former serfs), and new specialties having their origin in the colonial period. Prior to a discussion of labor specialization in Hollaande, we must comment on the division of labor between those of Fulbe and serf ancestry.

The division of labor between Fulbe and former serfs continues to be of significance. Crafts formerly done by serfs are still performed by their descendants. Crafts formerly reserved exclusively for the Fulbe are still performed by them. The continuing specialization resulting from the earlier status differences has social and economic consequences. Socially, earlier differences are still emphasized by the work that people do. One has only to ask for a blacksmith (*baillo*), and he knows he will be dealing with a former serf. If one wants to buy a hat, he has to buy it from a Fulbe and have a Fulbe embroider it. The perpetuation of the traditional division of labor helps preserve certain beliefs about the characteristics of each group. The descendants of serfs are seen as hard-working, performing tasks that are difficult but essentially nonintellectual. The reverse is said of the Fulbe.

Economically the two groups play different roles in the countryside. The Fulbe have had few possibilities outside of commerce to earn money in the countryside. They have not adopted any craft that was formerly the province of their serfs. They have rather sought to become merchants (selling kola, manufactured goods, etc.), and some have continued their crafts as embroiderers of hats and robes. One could hypothesize, although without the information necessary to verify it, that the Fulbe migrate in greater numbers in proportion to their population than do the former serfs. This hypothesis stems directly from the preceding analysis. Because they tend to avoid agricultural wage labor and have not adopted any new crafts, they have fewer ways to make money in the countryside although their need for money is no less than that of former serfs. We have already considered the commercialization of the traditional serf crafts. Here we are concerned with a brief discussion of the contemporary importance of crafts. Among the villagers of Hollaande (and, in general, among all former serfs) four kinds of craftsmen dominate in terms of both their numbers and their economic significance. These are blacksmiths, cloth-weavers, leather-workers, and basket-weavers. There are other crafts, but they involve fewer people and are either relatively easy—for example, rope makers—or so specialized—for example, circumcisers—that they are less commercialized. These crafts can be referred to as "traditional," because they were performed prior to colonial rule. This is not to imply that the items produced or the way in which exchange takes place have remained unchanged.

Blacksmiths combine several specialties under one rubric; they are carpenters and jewelers as well as blacksmiths proper. At Hollaande there were three blacksmiths. Two were sons of the same blacksmith, and the third was apprenticed to a blacksmith in a village twenty kilometers away. One man made metal pots and watering cans; another made tools and furniture; and the third made the posts, doors, and frames for houses. All three repaired and sharpened tools. Almost all of their work was done on command and paid for in cash. Among the three, the one who made watering cans and pots went to the market to sell his wares. The others went to the market to obtain scrap metal or other items they needed. Most of their orders were received at their homes, not at the market.

Blacksmiths play an essential role in the local economy. They continue to make almost all the tools used by the peasants for cultivation: the hoe (*daba* or *keri*), the axe, the adze, the machete, and knives. They also make such things as doors, posts, frames for houses, beds, and chairs. In short, both the economic necessities and amenities are still provided largely by indigenous manufacture.

The greatest change for blacksmiths has been the abandonment of iron-smelting. This took place gradually as the blacksmiths turned to European scrap iron for their work. One other point might be mentioned concerning the future of the blacksmiths. When I was in the village, there was not a single apprentice blacksmith. However, one of the blacksmiths intended to apprentice his oldest son, who, at the moment was only five years old.

Cloth-weavers are also always serfs. Formerly only indigenously grown cotton was used. However, the yield from such cotton has not been enough to supply the weavers' growing need. Prior to French rule Fulbe clothing was relatively simple and standardized, consisting of large robes dyed blue and white for the men and skirts for the women. The importation of European colored thread permitted the elaboration of styles and patterns for both men and women.

Most cloth is woven to be sold. There are three ways it is sold: on command to purchasers choosing beforehand the colors, patterns, and price; at the market to purchasers buying for themselves; and at the market to merchants buying from individual weavers for resale in the cities. The weavers work at home on a modified traditional loom wider than the traditional one. There was only one weaver at Hollaande who sold cloth at the market. There were several men who could weave, but they did so only occasionally for the needs of their households.

It should be pointed out that most clothing now is not woven, but is made from imported cotton or, increasingly, from cotton made in Guinean textile mills. Cloth is bought by the meter and a tailor is employed to make the clothing. Woven clothing is worn mainly for formal occasions.

Leather-workers now principally make sandals. Formerly sandals were only one item in the repertoire of leather craftsmen, who also made sheaths for swords and knives, saddles for horses, and leather covers for hand-written Korans and other religious works.[13] These are rarely made now. Despite the decline in the number of traditional leather goods made, there are presently more leather-workers than before. Following World War II new patterns and styles were developed quite unlike the traditional Fulbe sandal. Fulbe sandals are known and marketed throughout Guinea. At Hollaande there were no leather-workers, although two boys had been apprenticed by their fathers to leather-workers in a nearby village. In 1920 there were only two or three leather-workers in this village, while now half the adult men who stayed in the village are leather-workers.

Basket-weaving is the least prestigious and least preferred craft, and chances for commercial success are small. Basket-weavers make the various basket containers used for measuring, storing, and carrying grain and other food. They sold their goods at the three nearby markets. At Hollaande there were four basket-weavers, all of whom had learned the trade from their father.

Aside from basic agricultural labor and specialized crafts, the serfs formerly performed many other tasks for their masters as part of their economic obligations to them. Among these were building and maintaining fences, constructing and maintaining houses, roofing houses, and gathering firewood. After the ending of agricultural-labor obligations many former serfs continued to perform much of the same work that they used to for the Fulbe, but the economic basis of such work has been altered. This has given the former serfs another way of earning money, although it remains sporadic because the work is seasonal. It is now per-

13. Handwritten Korans are very rarely made now. Most Korans sold in the Fouta are printed in North Africa.

formed especially by those without crafts. At Hollaande over forty-five men (including everyone who had been circumcized) had worked in this capacity for money within the year. Almost all of the work was done for Fulbe.[14]

Among those engaged in new specialties and the professions,[15] the most important group are the merchants, people who buy goods at one price for resale at a higher price. As we have seen, merchants were not found in precolonial Fulbe society. The two words used for "merchant" are both non-Fulfulde: *ndyula* and *commercant*. Although there are words for "to buy," *soodugol,* and "to sell," *yeeyugol,* neither forms the noun for "merchant," as so often happens in Fulfulde (for example, *sannyugol,* "to weave," and *sannyowo,* "weaver.")

In the village of Hollaande there were six male merchants. These merchants dealt principally in kerosene, buying it at Labe and reselling it at a higher price at the market and in the village. They dealt with manufactured items—shoes, sandals, cigarettes, flashlights, matches, and paper—also bought from wholesalers in Labe. Of all the occupations in the countryside commerce is the most preferred, for it holds out the promise of great financial reward and high status. For the former serfs it has been an important source of mobility. Almost all the boys in the village engaged in some kind of commerce, whether selling kola at the market or, during the week, in the village, or selling blackmarket items for their older brothers. In their eyes, the world of the merchant was a desirable one.

To be a merchant takes a great deal of time. For the villagers of Hollaande there were three weekly markets (at Popodara, Kountoubel, and Tyaangol Buri) where merchants sold their goods. In addition they had to go to Labe at least once a week to

14. House-building, roofing, and fence building done within the village of Hollaande was usually performed by those most skilled. However, in the village context labor was often donated, or else gifts (including money) were given, but with no fixed price agreed on beforehand.

15. We are excluding those introduced by the state, such as teaching, nursing and administration.

maintain their stock of goods. Among the six merchants of Hollaande only one did not cultivate any fields. The fact that he did no cultivation was unusual. He was the wealthiest merchant in the village, but there were far wealthier merchants in the surrounding villages who continued to cultivate or who employed others to cultivate their fields. The typical pattern even for merchants continues to be combining a specialty with the cultivation of fields.

Butchers are essentially a specialized form of merchant. Like merchants, butchers arose after the advent of colonial rule. There is no Fulfulde word for "butcher," but only for the actions of skinning and chopping-up an animal.

The main places of activity for butchers are the weekly markets. It is there that butchers bring their live animals to be slaughtered and cut up for meat. Butchers are licensed by the Guinean government and pay a tax. Cattle are inspected by a veterinarian to insure that diseases do not make them unfit for human consumption.

One man of Hollaande was a butcher. Another served as his paid assistant; he skinned and chopped up the meat. For the market of Popodara as a whole there were eight butchers. Although both former serfs and Fulbe now serve as butchers, there remain differences which reflect the earlier status differences. The proper slaughter of any animal is accompanied by a particular phrase, which must be uttered by a Fulbe. This has to be performed at the market as well. At Popodara a Ragnaadyo performs the act, as the Ragnaabe are said to have brought cows to the area.

Another new trade is that of tailor. Tailors, more than weavers, are the primary clothesmakers. Clothing and fashions have become important in the villages, particularly for the young men and women, and as the demand for clothes has risen, so has the number of tailors. Tailors arose with the importation of European cloth and, later, the sewing machine. Tailors were formerly exclusively Fulbe, perhaps because the closest traditional task was embroidery, an exclusively Fulbe craft. However, increasing numbers of former serfs have become tailors. Within Hollaande there were three tailors. Their place of work was in a store at the *carrefour* at Popodara. Tailoring, like all other specialties, is learned through apprenticeship. The first tailor of Hollaande was taught by a Fulbe. He in turn has taught the two others.

THE MARKET

This discussion of the markets of the Fouta-Djallon does not pretend to be exhaustive, but attempts rather to indicate the major features of the markets and, in particular, the importance of the market for the village of Hollaande. We have already discussed the over-all significance of the introduction of markets to the Fouta-Djallon.

Every resident of Hollaande, as well as all the inhabitants of the general area, participates in and benefits from the market.[16] Despite the religious proclivities of most of the Fulbe, it has replaced the mosque as the highlight of the week. For the women, particularly, who rarely, if ever, go to the mosque, market day has become virtually a holiday. On market day the usual daily work is done only during the morning hours. By midafternoon almost all the inhabitants of Hollaande are found at the market.

The market place of Popodara is located on the top of a hill that borders on the village of Hollaande. The market place has no permanent structure, but the more prominent merchants each

16. The only individuals who didn't go to the market were elderly religious leaders. The origin of their distaste for market was unclear to me, for typically they were elders who did go in the past. They explained their present reluctance to attend the market by referring to the fights that sometimes take place. They did not want to fight, which they would have to do if a kinsmen of theirs were involved. Others cited the fact that the market, by its very nature, produces a situation where the proper relations of respect cannot be followed. Thus, one would be embarrassed to see an in-law at the market where proper respect cannot be shown. In general, the squatting and avoidance behavior while giving salutation to an in-law is observed while one is going to the market, but not at the market itself.

year build several lean-tos of stick and thatch to shade themselves from the sun or rain. Everyone else sits in the open, their wares displayed on the ground in front of them. A second market, subsidiary to the major one, is held at the *carrefour* of Popodara. Here the sandal-makers and cloth-weavers bring their products in the morning to sell to merchants.

The market is held every Thursday. It attracts people coming on foot from within a radius of ten kilometers and people come on bicycles or in trucks from as far away as fifty kilometers. The market begins early, around ten o'clock in the morning, with the arrival of the first truck from Labe, and ends with their departure toward five o'clock. After five the market becomes a young people's center for socializing and searching for lovers.

Prior to independence the supervision of markets was in the hands of the French *chefs de canton,* who appointed marshalls to oversee the activities, collect the usage fees, and maintain order. In no way was a market identified with, or controlled by, a particular individual or chief. Today the region of Labe is directly responsible for the market at Popodara, and the regional government appoints two men to collect the various market taxes.

The market at Popodara has long been one of the largest weekly markets in the Fouta-Djallon. It is said to be the largest market in the region of Labe, with the exception of the daily market in Labe. This information was provided by merchants, who should know. Trying to count the number of people at the market at any one time proved impossible, because there were four different routes to the market which were always full of people going in both directions. There were probably between 750 and 1250 people selling on a given market day.

The market can be divided into several different areas of activity. One area, the small cloth and sandal market at the *carrefour* has already been mentioned. Significantly, this is the only part of the market that fits into the Western notion of wholesale-retail. There the producers sell their good to wholesalers, who will then retail the goods at other markets throughout

Guinea. However, to describe the major market in terms such as *wholesale* and *retail* have only very limited usefulness.

The main selling pattern at the market is that of merchants from the regional center of Labe who come to Popodara to sell manufactured goods such as cloth, clothes, flashlights, batteries, cigarettes, matches, and sneakers. Within this group are the general merchants who sell a variety of manufactured goods, and those who sell one or two particular items, like salt, kola or *nebang kari* (a cooking oil made from leaves found in other regions of Guinea). In addition to the Labe merchants are the merchants who live in the local area. They may specialize in one item—kerosene, kola, or cigarettes—or sell a wide range of available consumer goods. In terms of what they sell they cannot be distinguished from the merchants who are based in the city of Labe. There was one general merchant from Hollaande who sold the whole gamut of relatively inexpensive manufactured items, two men who specialized in kerosene, and two young men who pooled their resources to sell kerosene and whatever else they could, depending on their available money.

Another important category of sellers are craftsmen who bring their own wares to the market. The major ones are the cloth-weavers, tailors, blacksmiths, sandal-makers and basket-weavers. In addition there are Fulbe makers of raffia covers and hat embroidery, Diallonke pot-makers, and Diakanke tobacco-growers.[17] The Diakanke live quite far from Popodara (about 100 km. to the northwest), and the Diallonke live in one small village about twenty kilometers away.

A third, and numerically the largest, group at the market are the women. It is interesting that women, who in precolonial times were not involved in the long distance trade, have become

17. There are some Diallonke who have continued to live in the Fouta. The Diakanke entered the Fouta late and are found in Mali, Guinea, Sierra Leone, and Senegal. Both peoples have remained relatively unstudied until the recent survey in Kedougou, Senegal, which borders the Fouta-Djallon (Smith: 1965).

numerically dominant (both as buyers and sellers) at the market place. We can divide the women into four categories. First are the merchant (*ndyula*) women from the regional capital who come to the market to buy primarily agricultural products to resell at the daily market in Labe. They buy such products as mangoes, oranges, chickens, eggs, and avocados. They are distinguishable from the local women by their fine dress, and are a major source of income for the local women. The second group are those women from the local villages who buy at the outlying markets to sell at Popodara or to the merchant women from Labe. These women buy primarily peanuts, rice, winnowers, maize, and tomatoes from the market at Tyaangol Buri to resell at a higher price at Popodara. Peanuts, which sold for 50 francs a small basket unshelled at Tyaangol Buri could be resold at Popodara for 60 francs. At the village of Hollaande there were four women who went frequently (at least once a month) to Tyaangol Buri. Of these women only one was relatively wealthy. She could buy a sack of peanuts (at a cost of 5500 francs), or a sack of rice, and when salt became scarce she bought a sack of salt. Otherwise the women bought in much smaller quantities. The third group, the largest number of women, sell small amounts of the produce from their own gardens or sometimes their husband's craft products. The wives of basket-makers always sell baskets; this, however, is the exception, not the rule. The fourth group are the women who come from the surrounding villages at the outlying markets to resell the goods at Popodara. They sell both their own and bought items at higher prices in Popodara than they could have asked at their local market.

Women sell goods at the market to obtain money. They need money to buy the ingredients for sauces, for kola, for "medicines" (protection against sorcerers and spirits), for clothing, and, if they earn much money, to pay their own taxes. Moreover, market day is a welcome break in their hard and continuous work.

The last two areas of activity of the market are the meat market where beef (and sometimes the meat of goats and sheep) is sold and the live-animal market, which is set slightly apart from the rest of the market.

There were six licensed butchers at the market. The richest of them slaughtered on the average two cows per week at Popodara and one a week at another market. The butchers bought most of their animals at Tyaangol Buri, a market about 55 kilometers from Popodara. Tyaangol Buri is well known for its excellent and abundant cattle. The cattle are brought by guards to the Tuesday market at Kountoubele and arrive at Popodara on Wednesday where the butchers pick up the animals they have chosen.

Goats, sheep, and cattle are sold in an area slightly distant from the rest of the market. This is entirely the province of men. Even if a woman sells one of her animals, or buys one, the actual sale has to be handled by a man. There are two kinds of buyers and sellers in the animal markets: merchants who are selling and buying for profit, and those who are buying or selling individually for ceremonial or specific economic needs. The merchants are most often butchers who make the rounds of the various markets to get the best possible animals for the lowest possible price. The other merchants who buy and sell animals, primarily goats and sheep (because individuals who buy cattle to begin or supplement their own herds rarely do so at the market), keep and guard them until they find a buyer who will pay a price greater than the original purchase price.

The other animal buyers and sellers are those with specific needs. For example, if a childbirth is expected and the father does not have a proper goat to be slaughtered, he will make the rounds of the market. Similarly, if one is expecting a death, or if a death has occurred, the father or eldest brother will have to buy a cow if he does not already own one.

All negotiations concerning animals are handled through intermediaries. Both the buyer and the seller call upon someone (and he can be a stranger) to discuss the price. The seller sets a very high asking price, the buyer a very low purchase price. Both have set ideas of the minimum or maximum price they will accept. If they agree, after bargaining, on some intermediate price, the purchase is concluded. The money is paid right on the spot, along with kola and a little money to the intermediary who assisted. At this time a receipt form, provided by the regional government, is signed by the seller and handed to the buyer.

All sellers of animals, whether they are merchants or are selling for personal reasons, have to demonstrate ownership to the regional market officials before a transaction can be carried out. The regional government issues a combined form indicating ownership and permission to sell, which is gotten before market day. A variety of signs of ownership are accepted as proof by the authorities. Among these can be a receipt of purchase, a brand (branding was begun during the colonial period), or the testimony of a trusted witness. All animal sellers also have to pay a 500-francs market tax for each animal sold.

The major buying groups at the market in Popodara are merchants, both men and women. The women deal primarily in agricultural produce. The men deal in certain kinds of produce, but also in such things as cloth, sandals, cow hides, sheep, and skins. They come mainly from around Labe to buy goods to resell at the daily market in Labe, or to sell in turn to those women who sell daily at Labe. The merchants come on the first trucks from Labe in the early morning and immediately make a tour of the market to find out the prices and goods available. They then buy and go home as early as possible. They usually do not have direct personal ties with the sellers but buy on the basis of price and quality. The men who come from Labe specialize in two or three particular items. Thus when hot peppers are ripe, for example, a special area is set up where it is sold to the merchants. They establish a set price per kilo for the day, depending on the quantity available. Once the price has been set, they do not bargain.

Even though Fulbe agricultural production is oriented toward private consumption, many items they need for daily life and ceremonies can be supplied only by the market. The degree of the peasants' dependence on the market does not reach that, for instance, of the Yoruba,[18] but it is nevertheless significant economically and socially. The basic market items necessary for the daily household diet are peanuts, peppers, salt, and cooking oil. Peanuts are used for the preferred sauce. The presence or absence of peanuts marks the difference in diet between relatively rich and poor villagers. The amount of peanuts grown in Hollaande does not meet the villagers' needs. Other ingredients for sauces which are bought at the market are hot peppers and *oddgi* (for which there is no adequate translation). The latter is relatively cheap, the former expensive. Again, both items are grown in Hollaande but not enough for the needs of the villagers. Salt is also regarded as essential. It can only be bought with money. Depending on the supply, the price ranged from 50 francs to 300 francs per kilo.

As kola is both a household and a ceremonial item, so is rice. Rice is the preferred food. There is a marked tendency for those who are richer to buy a higher proportion of their food from the market, and they will buy rice. The price of rice was relatively high and most people thus ate it only at ceremonial occasions.[19]

Another item required for ceremonies is sour milk (*kosang*), which can be justly thought of as the national dish of the Fulbe. Within each village there are relatively few individuals who have lactating cows. Thus when there is a ceremony, and it is obligatory to provide sour milk (for at least the elders), it has to be bought. During the dry season when there are even fewer lactating cows, obtaining milk poses a particular problem; individuals often have to travel 50 or 60 kilometers to obtain it. Meat is also a greatly desired item, both for household consumption and ceremonies. Its cost is high (300 francs a kilo), and the frequency of consumption depends on wealth.

18. Gloria Marshall has demonstrated that the Yoruba buy at least 90 percent of their food at the market (1964).

19. The women of Hollaande bought both rice and peanuts at other markets to resell at Popodara for a higher price, usually about 5 francs per kilo or basket.

There are several ways the state attempts to control transactions at the market place. These are generally aimed at seeing that standard weights and measures are used, that prices of certain items distributed by the state are controlled, that contraband items are not sold, and that the market runs smoothly and fairly with those who attend paying the appropriate taxes and charges.

Every market is under the authority of a *commandant d'arrondissement,* an official (or two, as was the case at Popodara) who is chosen from the population by the regional government to supervise the market and to collect the market taxes. At every market each seller of foodstuffs had to pay 25 francs, each animal-seller 500 francs, and each merchant with a *tabal* (table) 500 francs. The region receives the money collected, and the collector receives 10 percent of what he collects. This is an important source of revenue for the two local market officials, both of whom reside at Hollaande. The most frequent disputes at the market are over the payment of the 25 francs; women particularly often attempt to avoid payment. Often soldiers, and more recently members of the People's Militia, also supervise the market.

The People's Militia are unpaid political personnel responsible for the continuing vigilance and militance of the population. They are members also of the national youth organization. They have been particularly concerned with two abuses: nonstandard measures, and transactions taking place on the routes leading to market. There are members of the Militia in the villages, but those who supervise the market at Popodara come from Labe. They make a tour of each market, measuring produce very carefully to see that the various indigenous measures are exact. A common trick, employed by many merchants, both men and women, is to use a smaller than normal *korung* for selling and a larger than normal one for buying.

Women often try to avoid paying the 25-francs tax by selling on the path to market. This is illegal and is punished by the Militia. The state's regulations are usually followed, but the few instances when they are not followed provide an interesting framework in which to view the relation of the population to the market and their identification of their interests with those of the merchants. One of the items fixed in price by the region is meat. Meat is sold only by the kilo, and one cannot ask for the part one wants, with the exception of kidneys and liver. The price for any cut of meat was 250 francs a kilo. At the same time in Labe it was 200 francs a kilo for meat with bones and 300 francs a kilo without bones. The price remained constant for almost one year. Then the region declared that meat was 200 francs a kilo. There were a couple of weeks when hardly any cows were slaughtered, and there were long discussions between the regional officials and the butchers. The butchers maintained they were willing to reduce the price of meat only if the price of cattle were lowered. The officials maintained the butchers were making more than enough money.

Up until this point there had been frequent complaints from the population that the price of meat was much too high and that it was only the rich who could afford meat. One would have expected they would side with the officials. However, it did not turn out that way. For a few weeks, when officials came out to the markets, people paid 200 francs a kilo for meat. As soon as they left, meat was sold at 250 francs a kilo and no one refused to buy. Soon afterward the price of meat went up to 300 francs a kilo, without any appreciable increase in the price of cattle. Some said the price was due to the dry season and that when the rains came, it would again be lowered to 250. It never was.

A similar process happened with kerosene. Almost everyone uses kersosene lamps, either storm-lantern types, or home-made ones made with wicks and tin cans. Kerosene is imported primarily from Eastern Bloc countries, and every so often there is a shortage due to delays in arrival. During these times the price rises. Ordinarily the price is higher in the rural markets, a fact attributable to higher transportation costs. Kerosene is sold by merchants who buy relatively large quantities at Labe (about 200 liters—one drum, or perhaps two) and resell it at the markets and villages.

Soon after I came to Hollaande the price of kerosene rose from 60 to 75 francs a liter. When asked why, the merchants responded that they thought they could get the higher price even though the wholesale price had not risen. Soon afterward there started a series of kerosene shortages, and the government attempted to control its distribution and sale. Often the merchants obtained it on the black market and sold it outside of the markets at 125 francs a liter. During this time it could not be sold at the market because the People's Militia knew that the origin of all kerosene being sold at the time had to be from the black market.

During this shortage the merchants of the area surrounding Popodara found a source willing to sell them several drums. However, someone informed on them and they were arrested. Upon questioning they refused to give the price at which they had really bought the kerosene, maintaining they had paid the official price, which was one-third less. They did so in order to protect their future source of supply and their reputations as honorable merchants, at least in the eyes of the merchant community. They were not imprisoned, but were chastised verbally and ordered to sell all their kerosene at the government-fixed price, 50 francs a liter, whereas they had bought it illegally at 60 francs a liter and were planning to sell it at 125 francs a liter.

The local committee sold the illegally-bought kerosene at Labe for two days and gave that money to the merchants involved. Many people turned out to buy the kerosene at the fixed price. However, no sooner had that supply run out than the merchants were back buying the kerosene and selling it at 125 francs. Soon afterwards it could be legally sold at the market for 110 francs.

These incidents reflect something of the nature of the peasantry in the Fouta. They are revealed as quite passive in the light of state intervention in their favor. They did not force or pressure either the merchants or butchers to sell their merchandise at the lower fixed government prices, which was favorable to the population as a whole. The peasants viewed prices as beyond their control, and they viewed with skepticism the government's attempts to control prices. The reasons for the peasants' behavior and attitude appear to be related to their lack of faith in the ability of the government to look after their interest in the market situation, and to the potential conflict between their desire for low prices and the necessity to maintain good tics with their kinsmen who are merchants. Ties with merchants are quite important in time of scarcity, and money is regarded as having a "life" of its own not subject to human control, despite the best of intentions. The degree of penetration of the money economy is exemplified by the fact that the peasants view the exorbitant prices charged them (even by their kinsmen) with equanimity.

Five

The Political Organization

The traditional serf village was not an independent or politically autonomous community. The former serfs of Hollaande now have greater control over several key institutions, but they remain nonautonomous, although in a new way. In precolonial times political power resided primarily in the chiefly lineages. During colonial times it resided in the French and their appointed officials, who may or may not have been legitimate chiefs during the precolonial era. One of the most important and fascinating events in Guinean history was the abolishment of chieftainship, treated well in an article by Jean Suret-Canale (1966).

Today political power resides in an independent national government. The organizational base of the national political party, *Parti Démocratique de Guinée,* are the *comités du base* (base committees), the key political units in the countryside. The committee has replaced all former local political institutions. In the countryside a cluster of villages forms a committee. In the cities and towns a committee is a neighborhood. The organization of the committee does not follow the lines of the older *missides.* Thus, although the village of Hollaande was formerly a part of the *misside* of Popodara, it is not a part of the committee of Popodara. There are four other villages within the committee of Hollaande that were not part of the *misside* of Popodara. Population, rather than the number of villages, is the determining factor in the composition of a committee. The committee of Hollaande consists of eleven villages with a total population of 1,700, whereas one village of 2,000 would form a committee. The populations of the committees range from 500 to 2,000.

The most important feature of the committee system for the former serfs is that their villages are politically equal to Fulbe villages. The political subordination of former serfs to their Fulbe masters has thus been eliminated. Fulbe and former serf villages are found within the same committees, where they have to deal with each other as equals.

Of the villages that make up the committee of Hollaande, there are four Fulbe villages, two of which are Khalduyanke, and two Ragnaabe. The other seven are former-serf villages. Therefore, the former serfs are in the majority. Although the earlier distinctions are not supposed to affect the election of officials of the committee, quite clearly one of the most significant aspects of the committee is that those who were politically subordinate now have the opportunity to redress the situation. The former serfs of the committee of Hollaande had done just that. When the committee was first formed, they elected a former serf to be president, and the Fulbe have not succeeded in replacing him with a Fulbe. It is important to note, however, that within the context of the work of the committee, earlier social distinctions are not observed. Thus, at cooperative labor projects both former serf and Fulbe work side by side, and it is the officers of the committee who direct the work.

When a committee is comprised of one village, it will be either entirely former serfs or entirely Fulbe. However, because of the nature of settlement in the Fouta, most committees are a mixture of both social categories. Moreover, the domination of one group by the other is limited by the ideology and practices of the P.D.G., which ignores the earlier social distinctions, and the local practice of having one committee officer from almost every village in the committee area.

Every adult who pays dues to the P.D.G. (which are separate from taxes) becomes a member of a committee. Youths become members of the local branch of the J.R.D.A. (*la Jeunesse de la Révolution Démocratique africaine*). Age is the sole criterion of membership in either group. Each group has its own membership and its own leaders, although each is part of the national party. Originally a third group, women's committees, were organized, but they lacked sufficient independent functions to continue in existence. Women now belong either to the *comité du base* or the J.R.D.A. In the Republic of Guinea there are now 10,250 *comités du base* and 10,250 *comités de jeune* (Touré, Volume XVI n.d.).[1]

All members of the P.D.G. vote for the ten officers of their committee; adults for officers of the *comités du base,* youths for officers of the *comités de jeune.* According to national law, which is rigorously followed, at least two of the offices in both groups must be held by women. Committee elections are held whenever a national election is called. Whereas national elections are held only every few years, *renouvellement* of the committee officers takes place yearly.

Renouvellement is a process by which all political officials are subject to review and recall depending on the wishes of the population. It is also a mechanism by which disagreement with the current leadership can be voiced annually. The entire political leadership of the P.D.G., from the committee to the secretary general of the national party, is renewed in this fashion. Moreover, if an office becomes vacant, or if an individual decides he no longer wants to be an officer, there are frequent opportunities to make the necessary change. The *renouvellement* is also viewed as an important source of contact, information, and advice between the base and the higher echelons of the party.

In order to understand *renouvellement* of the committees, we need to mention the other regional political bodies. The com-

1. There has been an increase in the number of committees in Guinea. At the time of the formation of committees there were 4500. This number increased to 7164 by 1962, and to 10,250 by 1964. The reason for the increase was to decon-centrate and decentralize political power. For further details see Henry De Decker (1967) and Jean Suret-Canale (1970).

mittees of a given area are grouped in "sections." Each section in turn has ten officers for the adult group and ten for the youth group. These officers (*comités directeurs*) are elected by the members of the *comités du base* and renewed by the committee officers. The head of a section is known as the *secrétaire général du section*. The sections are in turn grouped into the four provinces of Guinea under the political direction of the *Bureau Fédéral*, which in turn is under the *Bureau Politique Nationale*.

The Republic of Guinea has both an administrative and a political structure.[2] The lowest level of the administrative hierarchy is the *commandant d'arrondissement*, the administrative equivalent of the political section. Administrative officials are appointed rather than popularly elected as are those in the *démocratie populaire*. Above the *commandants d'arrondissement* are the governors of the regions, who in turn belong to the *Bureau Fédéral*.

Political officers at each level are renewed by all those who elected them. This is done at a meeting run by the officials of the next highest political level. Thus, to renew the officers of the *comité du base* and the J.R.D.A., all committee members meet with the *comités directeurs* and the *commandants d'arrondissement*.[3]

The most important offices are president of the *comité du base* and secretary general of the J.R.D.A. They both act as committee representatives of their respective age groups to the regional authorities, bringing complaints, problems, and requests to them. In turn, these two officers relay information, requests, and deci-

2. These two structures inter-relate, thus maintaining cooperation, communication, and common direction. The point of the dual system is "If the political authority goes from the base to the summit, the administrative authority goes from the summit to the base. This confers upon our state its popular character and assures the political preeminence of our party which is, in fact, the rigorous translation of the wishes of the people in the activities of the state" (Touré Vol. II: 374).

3. Upon my arrival in the Fouta-Djallon I accompanied a group of political officials who were in the process of the *renouvellement* of the committees. They also used this opportunity to discuss with the population such questions as the position of women.

sions from the regional (and national) officials to the villages within their committee.

Typically, neither a former chief nor a former *manga* serves as an officer of a committee. They have been discredited in the eyes of the population because of their cooperation with the *chefs de canton* and the colonial authorities. Descendants of former political figures have no inherent advantages in obtaining committee offices. Rather, the people most likely to be elected are those who can read and write French, who have knowledge of the policy, programs, and operation of the P.D.G., and who are judged to have the skills necessary for dealing with village problems.

Although an officer of the J.R.D.A. or *comité du base* represents his committee as a whole, committee members often desire to have an officer from each of the villages within the committee. This stems in part from the organization that existed following the abolishment of the *chef de canton* at the beginning of independence, when each village selected a *maire* (mayor). In addition, communication and organization are greatly facilitated when each village has an acting "head." In most cases this individual is also an officer of his committee. When there are more villages than positions, as was the case in the committee of Hollaande, some villages had a *de facto* head who was not an officer.

In a recent statement, Ahmed Sekou Touré described the functions of the committees:

Committee members meet regularly twice a month. During these meetings the committee takes decisions of local interest conforming to the words of the Party, diffuses the information emanating from the sections and discusses all the affairs relevant to the competence of the village or of the neighborhood (Touré, Vol. XVI, n.d.: 370).

The committee, particularly its officers, serves as the communication and information link between the villagers and the political leaders of the *section* and the administrative officials of the *arrondissement*. Its activities are manifold, including many of those formerly carried out by other institutions. Included in the committee's work are: the organization of cooperative work projects, collection of taxes, distribution of goods from the state, organization of receptions for visiting dignitaries, and dispensing justice in inter- and intra-village disputes, divorce, and theft.

The committee is financially independent. The funds necessary for carrying out its functions come from a percentage of the tax receipts of the population comprising the committee. The percentage is decided by each region. The committee either maintains a general fund for the use of its officers, or divides the money among the officers who are then responsible for meeting any needs that might arise.

As an example of some of the specific functions of the committees, the committee of Hollaande served as a focus for the distribution of items that otherwise might have appeared at overly high prices. When the Guinean textile factory began operation at Conakry and only a limited supply of cloth was available, the committee saw to it that villagers had an equal opportunity to buy the cloth at state set prices. The committee of Hollaande was given a quota of cloth by the regional administrative officials. The cloth was divided by the president among the different villages. Each officer then received requests from household heads and distributed the cloth so that everyone's request was fairly met.

National projects, such as the attempt to increase the production of cotton, reach the committees in the form of specific projects that need to be undertaken. At Hollaande, the committee had been asked to cultivate cotton. A plot of land was chosen in one of the villages, and seed was provided by the regional officials. During the growing season, the land was prepared, a fence was built, and cotton was sowed and weeded by various members of the member villages under the direction of the committee's officers. I left before the harvest, which was to go to the regional officials and then to Conakry. Another example of the committee meeting a national need had to do with the sale of tomatoes which were required by the Guinean canning factory at Mamou. The committee of Hollaande organized the sale of tomatoes so that they did not appear on the open market but were purchased only by the regional officials acting for the canning factory.

Receptions were organized at Labe during the period of my study for, among others, the king of Saudi Arabia, Under Secretary of State Katzenbach, and members of the consortium of FRIA (an international aluminum corporation). Large attendance at such receptions is considered important to developing an awareness of, and identification with, the national concerns of Guinea.

Our discussion up to now has focused on the adult committees. We turn now to the J.R.D.A., a new and significant institution for youths.[4] It provides a means to express their needs and to organize their own activities. It should be clear that this organization and its independence from elders marks a decisive departure from the traditional socio-political organization, which was dominated by elders.

The J.R.D.A. is composed of young men and women under twenty-five years of age, according to Guinean Law. However, the Fulbe have reinterpreted this to mean anyone who has not given up the ways of the young, that is, has not yet assumed his full religious obligations. Individuals in their thirties are occasionally in this category. The J.R.D.A. has its own leadership and is independent from the adult committees. At elections and at the *renouvellement,* the two groups each select their own leadership.

The committees are responsible for such tasks as collecting taxes and fairly distributing goods, whereas the J.R.D.A. serves as the

4. Ahmed Sekou Touré states that the J.R.D.A. was organized because "the Democratic Party of Guinea, conscious of the anarchic state in which the youth organization found itself and of the quasi-total isolation of rural youths, decided during the congress of March 23, 1959, to gather all Guinean youths in the same organization and to give them the maximum means to permit their full activity and development" (Vol. 12: 64). His account states that the J.R.D.A. was structured so that the inherent problems of the young and the action of Guinean youth would be politically directed toward the development of Guinea and her revolution. The P.D.G. was formed in 1947.

mechanism for relations among youth in a political, social, and ideological sense. Disputes or thefts among the young are dealt with by the J.R.D.A. Balls, soccer games, and marching in reception parades are also organized by the J.R.D.A. In addition, the J.R.D.A. provides ideological education for its members.

The following five cases are examples of how intra- and intervillage conflicts are dealt with. Three cases illustrate actions of the *comité du base* and the J.R.D.A., and two illustrate action of alternative institutions. There were no crimes of violence, with one possible exception, in the committee of Hollaande or in any neighboring committee during my stay or shortly before. Petty theft was the most common crime.

The first example indicates the relations between youths, the J.R.D.A., and elders. A radio and a pair of shoes were stolen from the unlocked house of a young man in Binde Pellung. While the theft was taking place, most of the youths of the village were together, spending the evening talking and visiting the way they normally did. Upon discovery of the theft, the young man immediately told his brothers, who immediately set about learning the whereabouts of all the young men in the village at the time of the theft. (They had assumed from the beginning the thief was neither an adult nor a woman). By dawn they had accounted for all but one of the young men in the village. He, of course, became the prime suspect. The victim and his brothers then went to tell the secretary general of the J.R.D.A., who was a resident of Hollaande. The secretary general decided to hold an enquiry (*tefugol*) as it seemed likely the suspect could be persuaded to confess.

During the day the suspect was found and informally questioned. When asked about his movements the night before, he first said he had been in another village, but he couldn't specify whom he had seen there. Upon further questioning he gave two different stories of where he had been and whom he had met. At this point the head of the J.R.D.A. decided to convene the members of the J.R.D.A. to confront the suspect with those individuals he said he had been with the night before. All the members of the J.R.D.A. of Hollaande attended; no one from the other villages of the committee of Hollaande were present. The two officers of the J.R.D.A. for the committee as a whole directed the meeting.

The confrontation indicated that the suspect had been lying. At this point the secretary general asked to speak to the suspect privately. He begged (*toragol*) the suspect to return the radio and the shoes. He pointed out that the affair so far was only a matter for kinsmen (*musibbe*) to settle, but that if the items were not returned, it would become an affair for the police (the nearest police station was at the regional capital, Labe). The suspect at this point confessed privately to the secretary general. The two of them then left to get the stolen items, which had been hidden in a cave in a nearby village.

It was not until after the stolen objects had been returned that the elders of the village were officially told of the theft, although they had known about it earlier through the children. The father of the thief, the member of the committee for Hollaande and his older brother, and the father of the youth from whom the radio had been stolen then gathered, and the secretary general retold, in great detail, all the events of the past evening and day. The elders thanked the young people. They referred to the thief as a *guddyo* (which implies habituation) and a *bondo* (someone who is rotten or no good). His own father was just as strong in denouncing him as everyone else. The secretary general then recommended, following the decision of the members of the J.R.D.A. and the youth who owned the radio, that the affair be closed, because the objects were returned. The only one who could further pursue the case, the victim of the theft, did not wish to do so. The elders agreed, but asked to speak to the elders of the major patrilineage of the thief (only his father had been directly told so far) before closing the affair completely.

The elders of the thief's major patrilineage were called in order by age and status, and the events of the past day were re-explained. However, in the meantime, the thief disappeared, for on learning of his thievery, a woman who had given him some bed sheets to be embroidered demanded that they be returned. It was learned that he had not had them embroidered, but had resold them to someone in a neighboring village. The thief went to the neighboring village in an attempt to get back the sheets, but he failed, and so did not return. The youths of J.R.D.A. ultimately found him, and when he refused to return, they told him that if he did not go voluntarily, they would use force. With this threat, the thief returned. The individual who had bought the sheets from the thief said he would bring them to Hollaande the next day.

The second day of the affair, another meeting was held to settle the question of the sheets. Again the entire J.R.D.A. of the village was there, plus the woman whose sheets had been sold and the youth who had bought the sheets. The thief asked the secretary general and the buyer of the sheets to accompany him to his mother's house, where she would give them the price of the sheets (approximately 2500 francs, or $10.00). The secretary general refused to go, for if all three went, the mother would be able to ask that she not have to pay because she had no money. The secretary general noted that in such a case he would not be able to refuse her, because he was married to her older brother's daughter. The buyer of the sheets also refused to go, because he said he had come for his money, not to walk around. The woman insisted that she receive the sheets immediately. However, the buyer refused, saying that he could not let them go without the money. Moreover, he could wait only three days before he would keep them permanently, for he had bought the sheets on good faith, and it was only his good will letting him part with what he had bought. After much discussion, the condition of the buyer was accepted, and that of the woman rejected. The decision was that the thief had to find the money.

At this juncture the officer of the committee for Hollaande arrived and took direction of the meeting. He mocked the young people who steal to have money to give to their lovers and everyone laughed. However, he praised the youths of the village for their diligence in apprehending the thief and for the manner in which they had conducted themselves (one of the rare times I heard praise for the young). He then addressed himself to the question of who is responsible for a thief, He stated that it is neither the mother nor the father—only the thief himself. In this case the parents were neither responsible for the actions of their child, nor responsible for making retribution to the aggrieved parties. (However, in the next example it will be seen that parents can be held financially responsible, if their child is not circumcised.) The officer then asked the thief to give him the money for the sheets. The thief attempted to have the secretary general of the J.R.D.A. speak for him, but he refused. The thief was thus forced to state in front of everyone that he had no money, and that his father had told him his mother would give him the money before dawn of the next day. The officer then observed that if it were up to him, he would have the thief put in prison. He then asked what the punishment of the thief was to be. The youth who owned the radio and shoes declined to speak and asked that the secretary general speak for him. The secretary general said there was to be no punishment. For the J.R.D.A. and the individual concerned, the affair was ended. Punishment, if there was to be any, would come from Allah.

The head of the thief's major patrilineage then spoke.[5] He noted that two years ago some of his cows had been stolen. Many had asked that an inquiry be held, but he had refused. Allah knew the thief, and that sufficed. He then asked only that a particular prayer (*salaatu*) be read which would reveal the identity of the thief. He stated that he was not responsible for thieves, not even if that thief were his own son. This was certainly proved by this case, as the father of the thief had never stolen anything in his entire life, not even an orange.

The meeting was concluded by the officer of the adult committee. He said the thief maintained he had returned to the village

5. He was also the thief's mother's brother (*kau*). This role, however, was subordinate to the other he held.

because he had fallen sick in Freetown. This wasn't true; he had stolen in Freetown, and had been put in prison. He had returned to Conakry, where he had again stolen. The thief had a bad character, for he watched his father work without helping him, feigning illness. Everyone now ought to pay attention to him since his character had been revealed. However, the real judgement, the real punishment, was that of Allah.

This story exemplifies several points about the present social and political organization of a former serf village. The inquiry was carried out by the thief's peers—the J.R.D.A. Had he been an adult, it would have been carried out by the adult committee. The inquiry was performed by the new political organization, not by the youth's major patrilineage. In short, the proper mechanism, as viewed by the villagers, is no longer the kin group, but the J.R.D.A. This, however, does not mean the kin groups are of no importance in such cases. The limits of the J.R.D.A. were clear. They felt they could not punish a thief. Their task was to discover the identity of the thief, but once he was discovered, their responsibility ended. They make a recommendation about punishment to an adult committee, which may or may not be heeded. In this case, their recommendation that no further action be taken was agreed to by the elders. The J.R.D.A. acted independently in the first stages, but once the identity of the thief was known, they called on the adult committee and the thief's close kinsmen to pursue the matter. They in turn called on the elders of the thief's major patrilineage, for it was the latter who could punish him.

The last point to note is that the major patrilineage declined to act against the thief. The statement by the head of the patrilineage that no one was responsible for the thief, that only Allah may punish or judge, is particularly interesting. The head of the patrilineage of Hoore Tane is also a religious leader. During the precolonial period religious leaders, who were also political leaders, did make judgements of this kind, and did punish individuals. A theft for example, might have been punished by cutting off one of the thief's hands, or by another less drastic measure. Under the French, individuals who inflicted punishment on an accused became liable themselves to punishment by the French. Now, punishment is either a matter for a restricted kin group, or for the judicial and police authorities, who are located in the regional capitals.

In this case the villagers rejected the alternative of bringing the thief to the regional capital, where, if punishment were decided on, it would be out of the hands of the villagers. Punishment was also rejected by the head of the patrilineage. In short, the latter maintained that he was too preoccupied with religion to be bothered with such concerns as judgement. This is an expression of the apoliticization of Islam in the countryside; Islamic leaders rely on the sanctions of Allah, not on those of men, to punish wrongdoers. During the period of colonization and independence the political sphere of Islam in the Fouta has been greatly restricted.

The second example is concerned with a theft involving an uncircumcised boy from Hollaande and a Fulbe boy from a neighboring village. The latter's father had been the master of a few people of Hollaande, but not of the individuals concerned. Further, the Fulbe was also a member of the former chiefly lineage. During the week of a reception at Labe for some visiting dignitaries, 10,000 francs ($40.00) and a dress and a blouse were stolen from the house of a young mother. At first she was puzzled as to who could have stolen the items. Only after several days did she recollect that a boy had been present while she went to get some money, and that he therefore knew where her hiding place was. She accused him, and asked the J.R.D.A. to have a meeting. At the same time other boys returning from the reception remarked on how much money the accused had spent while in the regional capital. It was also noted that a friend of the accused also spent a great deal of money.

The two boys were thereupon called before the J.R.D.A. and interrogated. When confronted by those who had seen them spend money in Labe, they admitted their guilt and enumerated the ways they had spent the stolen money—which included 2500 francs for beer. Once the two boys had admitted their guilt, the secretary general stated that the job of the J.R.D.A. was ended. Having discovered the culprits, all they could do was bring them to the person against whom the crime has been committed. The secretary general noted that whereas other committees might use whipping and other kinds of punishments, this was not permitted by the government, and he would not do so. He argued that the job of the J.R.D.A. was to determine who had committed a crime and, where possible, to recover the stolen items. In this case it was not possible to recover the money, so they brought the guilty parties to the husband of the aggrieved. The accomplice, a Fulbe boy, was permitted to return to his father.

For three evenings in succession the elders of the village of Hollaande met in an attempt to resolve the question. One problem was that the Fulbe boy's father would not come to the village, although many messengers had been sent requesting that he attend. It was pointed out that the Fulbe boy had never admitted taking the money, but only that he had been present during the theft and had later spent some of the money. Whether or not he had actually stolen the money rested on the accusation of the other boy. The father of the latter kept asking that he be told how much he should pay. The husband of the woman refused to state a sum, insisting that it was for the fathers of the two circumcised boys to agree on. The third night, the husband declared that he was going to the Fulbe village in the morning to take the two boys to the police in Labe and have them put in prison. This threat produced results. Both fathers, through an intermediary, agreed on the equal guilt of their respective sons, and each consented to pay 5000 francs immediately. However, because both boys refused to admit they had stolen the clothes, even under the threat of going to Labe, this matter was dropped.

The case was made more interesting due to the relationship between the father and son from Hollaande. The father asserted that he had not spoken to his son in three years, even though the boy was still quite young (about fourteen). In his view his son was no good (*bondo*), and he, therefore, would have nothing to do with him. Further, he had no control over his son. Only a month before the son had taken 2000 francs from him. However, although the father had practically disowned his son, he still had to redress the wrongs. The father, in retaliation, has refused to have his son circumcised.

In this second case the limits of the J.R.D.A. are again clear. They could not force a settlement, because the money had already been spent. It was left to the fathers of the boys to reach an agreement with the victim, on threat of intervention by the authorities at Labe. The father of the boy from Hollaande did not need such a threat to convince him to pay. He was willing to make a settlement in order to maintain his standing and his kin relations within the village. On the other hand, it was necessary to threaten the Fulbe father with the police—outside intervention—to induce him to pay.

The third example illustrates that the way disputes are handled depends partially on the relationships between the involved parties; that is, whether they involve intra-village relationships, inter-village relationships, or, as in this case, unknown individuals. In the following incident, the committee called on the regional authorities to resolve the problem. Two strangers arrived in the village of Popodara, carrying articles that made them suspect. As is their right, certain members of the J.R.D.A. asked the men to enter a store to be searched. The two strangers fled, but were soon captured. Each had a sack that contained salt and rope, the standard equipment of cattle thieves. The salt is used to attract the animal; the rope to lead it away. As soon as these items were discovered, a messenger was sent to Labe to summon the head of the police, who arrived shortly thereafter to arrest the two men. He congratulated the population on their vigilance, and informed them that the two men were wanted for cattle thievery.

The social functions of the elders have been discussed. At Hollaande six men were considered to be elders. However, only two of these men played decisive political roles within the village. Both of these men were the eldest of the two major patrilineages. Their accession to these positions was based essentially on age, but both were also remarkably strong and active. Neither was descended directly from the previous head of his lineage. In Binde Pellung there was no conflict over who should serve as head of the patrilineage. Perhaps this was due to the fact that one of the sons of the former head was serving as president of the committee and therefore already had an important political position. Thus the eldest was quite readily accepted as head of his major patrilineage.

In Hoore Tane there was disagreement between the son of the deceased *manga* (the head of the serf village during the colonial period, who was designated by the *chef de canton*) and the eldest member of the major patrilineage. The former maintained he was the real head of the lineage, as he was the eldest son of the former head of the major patrilineage, whereas the acting head of the lineage, although its oldest member, was descended from a captive. His grandfather and grandmother had been brought as captives to the village.

The explanation given by the son of the *manga* as to why he himself was not the head was that a younger man should not speak disrespectfully to, or argue with, an elder. Furthermore, it would be embarrassing if there existed a great inequality in age between the heads of the two lineages within Hollaande. The son of the *manga* was in his late forties, whereas the head of the other major patrilineage was in his seventies. The acting head of Hoore Tane was sixty-five and the villagers accepted him as the real head because of his age and ability. The conflict emerged as the result of the different origins of the minimal lineages of Hoore Tane. As we observed when analyzing the genealogy, there are three different ancestors for Hoore Tane, two of whom came as captives after the village had been founded by the third.

We shall now consider the way the elders of the village handled a dispute between two members of the same major patrilineage. Four dogs had killed a sheep belonging to K.G. He asked that the elders of the village meet to decide on a course of action. He clearly wanted compensation for his loss, as it was the only sheep he owned. Of the four dogs involved, one belonged to an elder brother of K.G. (same father, but different mother), and another belonged to an elderly woman of the same major lineage as K.G. The other two dogs apparently did not have owners. N.D., the elder brother of K.G., argued that the dog belonging to him did not attack sheep, but must have done so only in the company of the other dogs. The head of the major patrilineage of Binde Pellung promptly replied that if there are a group of thieves, and only one is caught, he has to pay nonetheless. N.D. then pointed out that the woman concerned did not have any money. The same elder again interrupted and asked K.G. if he wanted money. K.G. replied that the judgement, the form of compensation, was the concern of the elders. He was voicing no opinion, and would accept gladly any decision of the elders, even if it meant nothing for him. The son of the old *manga* then spoke and argued that the owners of the two dogs had to buy another sheep for K.G. The eldest quickly disagreed, pointing out that between members of the same major patrilineage, concessions had to be made. He then proposed that 4,000 francs be given to K.G. A few of the younger men present interjected to observe that 4000 francs was not enough to buy a sheep. The supervisor of the market, who was also the president of the committee and a resident of Hollaande, said that 4000 francs could buy a sheep. The others disagreed, but the eldest villager again interjected to say that 4000 francs was just. He added that the sum of money to be paid was to be made up equally by the two dog owners. K.G. expressed his thanks to the elders for their consideration of the matter and for reaching a settlement. He gave them each a kola.

Although an incident of dogs killing a sheep is rather un-interesting, dramatic examples of conflict are difficult to obtain, for violence is at a minimum and crimes are rare, usually taking the form of petty thievery. Nevertheless, there are several important features to discuss in this case.

First, the dispute concerned two brothers who had different mothers. Had this same incident taken place between brothers of the same mother, nothing would have been said. Further, had the dogs belonged to a member of another village, the committee would have had to decide the form of compensation.

Second, because all of the parties involved were members of the same major lineage, the decision was left to those of Binde Pellung. To have had the elders of Hoore Tane make the decision could have caused bad feelings among members of the same major lineage. In this instance, the village acted almost as one major lineage. The assistance of Binde Pellung was always called on because the eldest member of the village, and the president of the committee, resided at Binde Pellung.

Third, because all of the parties involved were of the same major patrilineage, and the same village, the appropriate way to handle the problem was by referring it to a council of elders, not the formal non-kin body—the committee. On the other hand, when a problem involves youths of the same village, the J.R.D.A. is activated—a clear sign of the difference in generations. However, adults (as opposed to elders, who are more conservative) bring inter-village disputes to the committee. We have already discussed a divorce case between a man of Hollaande and a woman of a different village which was taken before the committee of Hollaande. In preindependence days a divorce case similar to this would have been handled by the major lineages of the man and woman and their respective Fulbe master.

A third alternative to settling conflict through the patrilineage or the committee is to refer it to the religious leaders of the mosque. Although the political role of religious leaders has declined considerably since they can no longer apply legal sanction, they can and do use their relationship to the supernatural in handling certain types of problems. To illustrate this, let us examine an instance in which a house in the village burned down. The villagers believed it to be arson.[6] One might have expected either the committee or the religious political authorities to be informed and an inquiry held. Instead, the individual whose house had burned, while clearly concerned over who had destroyed his house, maintained that the punishment for such an act should be left in the hands of Allah. He asked that the prayer *salaatu* be read at the time of the reroofing of his house. The *salaatu* was led by the *almamy* and religious leaders of the mosque of Popodara, as well as by the former *chef de canton*. Reading the *salaatu* is said to cause the revelation of the identity of the individual who performed the act, or else cause him to become mad.

The burning of the house was an extraordinary event, and it deeply upset the villagers. Quite clearly arson is a serious crime. If the fire actually was set deliberately, this was the only attempt at murder during my stay. Despite the importance of learning who was responsible, no inquiry was held, and no political officials were informed. Rather, it became a matter for Allah and the religious leaders. It is interesting to note that in this case, because of the gravity of the incident, the *almamy* and the other religious leaders of the mosque came to the site of the fire. The reading of the *salaatu* in the compound of the burned house was also not typical; the normal procedure is to read *salaatu* at the mosque.

6. There are many houses destroyed by fire in the Fouta. Almost all fires are accidents started from cooking fires, or fires kept burning all night to provide warmth. In this case it was believed the fire had been set deliberately, because it started on the straw roof at around 5 a.m.

Six

Ideology

Both Fulbe and former serfs view life as the unfolding of a plan made by Allah. Allah decides the destiny of each individual. Life is to be accepted as it comes, and passivity and resignation in the face of life are virtues. An illustration can be found in the poem, "A propos de l' impôt," in which the point of view of the poet is that the Fulbe should pay taxes and not oppose the French. The reason proposed was that those who pay taxes in this world will receive in the next, and those who are the collectors will pay in the next world by going to Hell.[1]

In this chapter we shall be concerned only minimally with the Fulbe side of Islam, concentrating instead on what was observed in a former serf village. The focus of the chapter is the growing adoption of Fulbe practices and beliefs by the former serfs and the continuing Fulbe ritual domination over their former serfs.

The inhabitants of the Fouta-Djallon have long been known for their religiosity and education, although the following description could not be applied to the serfs:

Most surprising of all, to those previously unaware of the civilizing influence of Islam, the Fulani of Futa Jallon revealed themselves as a literate people, their chief men possessing books on divinity and law, their children taught to read in the schools which were maintained in almost every town (Watt and Winterbottom 1803: 272).

1. Author and date of poem unknown (Sow 1966 : 119).

The study of religion, education, and ideology in a serf village provides a very different picture from the one described by early explorers. Access to religious status was denied to serfs. It was their masters who, in ways to be described, interposed themselves between the serfs and Allah. In short, Islam was used to justify and support the institution of serfdom. The non-Islamic practices of the serfs served to validate this subordination.

However, with the decline of serfdom major changes took place in the ideological realm. The major differences in ritual between the Fulbe and their former serfs are ending. Thus there are no significant differences between the present-day ceremonies of Fulbe and former serfs. According to informants, however, Fulbe and serf ceremonies forty years ago were very different.[2]

THE LIFE-CYCLE

The life-cycle and its ceremonies constitute what can be called the traditional Fulbe way of life in the Fouta-Djallon, or more precisely those aspects of Fulbe life which have changed least since colonialism. The ceremonies accompanying changes in the life-cycle embody "Fulbeness." Islam also serves to reinforce the traditional way, but is not exclusive to the Fulbe, although all ceremonies are viewed by the Fulbe as part of Islam.

An individual's place in the life-cycle is an important (although not by any means the sole) determinant of his rights and privileges. Statuses based on membership in particular descent groups are declining in significance. Statuses connected to life-cycle stages remain. Men and women go through similar stages

2. Unfortunately, the former serfs were reluctant, and in many instances refused, to discuss these questions because they were ashamed of their earlier practices. In particular, they viewed as pagan such practices as men dancing at the circumcision of boys, even though this has ended only with the past fifteen years. For an excellent description of an area where such dancing at circumcision continues, see Dupire (1963 : 222–298). However, the ceremony in the Fouta was quite different due to differences in cultural influences from surrounding peoples.

of the life-cycle, but these are not entirely equivalent, either in terms of age, status, or responsibilities. Women have an inferior status to men from an ideological, religious, and social point of view throughout their life. For both sexes, one's status increases as one gets older.

Babyhood. From birth until two and one-half to three years, an infant is breast fed, and all his whims are catered to. He remains a continual center of attention and he has no responsibilities. The period of breast-feeding is three years for boys, and two and one-half for girls. Thus, even in the earliest stage of life, a difference in sex roles exists. As a child approaches the age of weaning, the mother's breasts are used less for food and more for comfort.

Weaning. The transition between babyhood and childhood is marked by the two to four week period during which a child is abruptly weaned. Typically, the child is cared for by his maternal grandparents, away from his mother during this difficult time.

Childhood. Childhood is divided into two stages. The first lasts from ages three to six, the second from six to circumcision or clitoridectomy. The first part of childhood is marked by the beginning of association with one's age-mates and the gradual decline of continual supervision by one's mother. By the time a child reaches six years of age he spends a good part of his time in play with his age-mates, usually out of his mother's immediate presence (although not out of the presence of other adults of the village.) During this period the child is still not considered capable of taking on responsibilities, but is expected to begin learning how to share and take turns with his age-mates and to not fight with older siblings. The life of boys and girls is very similar during this period, although girls are kept under closer supervision by their mothers.

At the age of six or seven children are considered ready to begin learning and to gradually take on the essential responsibilities and skills of Fulbe life. From this point on sexual differences become marked, girls having considerably less freedom and free time. Children spend their free time with age-mates of their own sex, except during moonlit nights when they sing and dance together. Boys work hardest during hoeing and harvest time. During the several months of the dry season they spend most of their time with their age-mates in search of excitement and games. There is evidence, moreover, that this life is freer now than it used to be. Formerly, in serf villages boys were apprenticed to craftsmen at around eight years of age, whereas few of the boys are now apprenticed. In Fulbe villages boys no longer serve as herdsmen for their father's or paternal uncle's herds. The greatest area of new freedom for former serfs' boys (and girls) however, comes from the ending of labor obligations to Fulbe masters and the *chef de canton*. Girls work during all seasons helping their mothers in their various economic tasks. They are free at night and during holidays to play with their age-mates.

Clitoridectomy. Unmarried girls in general are referred to as *dyiwo,* which means "girl" and "virgin." The latter becomes very important after the clitoridectomy, and attempts are made to see that she stays virgin until her marriage. In earlier times girls were betrothed after their clitoridectomy and went to live with their new husband's family until their first menstruation, after which time they became true wives. This custom is just recently ending. From her clitoridectomy to marriage, a girl's responsibilities increase as she learns all the skills necessary to be a good wife; preparing food, gardening, and, theoretically, obedience. She generally works as hard as her mother at the various economic tasks, but usually has evenings free to visit with her age-mates.

Circumcision. Prior to colonial rule the ceremony of circumcision marked a dramatic and sharply defined change in status from childhood to adulthood.[3] Since at least 1900 there has been a tendency for the age at which a boy is circumcised to decrease. The result has been a longer period of transition to adulthood, since few men marry before the age of twenty-five.

Young men are in a changing position in Fulbe society. On the

3. The fact that many circumcised boys are not sexually mature is recognized. A true *suka* is someone who can also ejaculate (*hellifaadyo*).

one hand, they consider themselves dominated and restricted by their elders. On the other hand, they are beginning their lives in a new and changing society, and it is often to them that the elders have to turn for advice and financial support. In general, young men balance reliance on their elders with autonomy in the J.R.D.A. Decisions for the village as a whole are made by the elders. The expression of their status in the eyes of the elders can be seen at all ceremonies. Young men and older boys, although the most numerous of any group in the village, receive relatively the smallest portions of food. In the context of the ceremonies they are referred to as *seewobe beng*, literally "those on the side." Young men consistently complain of the lack of adequate portions for them at ceremonies, a complaint which has a great deal of justification, for most adults receive as much as a full meal at the ceremonies, whereas young men usually receive only two or three fistfuls of food.

In precolonial times, as now, allowances were made for the restlessness and "irresponsibility" of the young. In the relatively strict Islamic society of the Fulbe it was the young who could go to the moonlit dances at serf or Diakanke villages. There were also violin and flute players, and those who told funny stories (*nyamakala*). The traditional story-telling and music have now been replaced by the "High Life" and "balls" organized by the J.R.D.A. Moreover, the young were and are not expected to meet all their religious obligations.

Although young men are not expected to carry out many responsibilities, they do work a good part of the time. Particularly, during the cultivating season and at a *kile* they make up the core of the household work group. Many have trades or skills—as barbers, petty merchants, or fence or house-builders—by which they gain some money around the village. As they reach marriageable age, it becomes necessary to seek work that will enable them to earn enough money to set up a household and pay for the ceremony. A large number leave the village for cities in Guinea and surrounding countries for this purpose.

Adult women. Young women enter adulthood sooner and more abruptly than their male age-mates. Typically, women marry shortly after puberty, although there is a growing tendency toward marriage at fifteen or sixteen. If a girl marries out of her natal village, the break from childhood to adulthood is even more abrupt, for she is then no longer with her age-mates. Those in her new village who are of the same age never replace the friends of childhood. Pregnancy occurs generally (no statistics were collected) within one to one and one-half years after the couple begins cohabiting. The birth of the first child marks the full entrance of a woman into adulthood. From this time until she enters the next stage of life, a woman works continuously, in fact many more hours than her male age-mate.

An adult woman's status is generally inferior to her male age-mate's in terms of authority and rights. However, there are signs of some movement in the direction of increased autonomy for women. Although a woman has always had control over the distribution of crops raised in her garden, her opportunity to sell a surplus at the market gives her increased economic independence. This surplus is usually very small, although for women who are called *commercants,* the profit derived from market trade enables them to buy a modest amount of clothes and other items independently of their husbands. One reaction to this monetary "wealth" of women is represented by the husband of a successful *commercant,* who felt that his wife should start paying her own taxes. Not surprisingly she refused, saying that taxes were the responsibility of a husband.

As seems to be true in many societies, the fidelity of wives to husbands is said to have been much greater in the past. Complaints of increased adultery have at least two bases in reality: the result of the labor migration of young men who leave their wives in villages, and the restrictions on the actions of an aggrieved husband and his kinsmen against his wife and her lover. By national law some of the officials of the committees and of the J.R.D.A. are required to be women. While women in the countryside still play only a nominal role in this capacity, urban women are increasingly active politically, and hold increasing political authority.

Adult men. Young men are not considered adults until after they have had children. Marriage itself does not suffice. Even after the first two children a young married man is apt to find himself still eating from the plates of youths at ceremonies, although assuming full economic responsibility for his family. There are certain circumstances which determine the time a man establishes a household. When a boy's mother dies, he is usually forced to marry at an early age because of the reluctance of a woman (usually another wife of his father's) to continue caring for him. Both of the two youngest married men in Hollaande had lost their mothers; one through death, the other through divorce. Later attainment of adult status results primarily from the inability to obtain the financial resources necessary for setting up a household. A man is not considered fully adult until he has renounced cigarettes, the search for lovers, and other frivolities, and meets all his religious obligations. This stage usually is not achieved until a man reaches age thirty or thirty-five or later. Adulthood for men means full participation in all aspects of life. Adults are expected to maintain their kin and ceremonial and religious obligations, and are held responsible if they do not.

LIFE-CYCLE CEREMONIES

The major ceremonies in the life-cycle of an individual are the naming ceremony (*denabo*), clitoridectomy for girls (*koriko*), circumcision for boys (*fidyo*)—which is becoming more linked to the completion of reading the Koran, marriage (*peera*)—which we have already discussed, and the funeral (*faatunde*).

Underlying all ceremonies is an ideology of reciprocity. This means that everyone expects to receive back at the ceremony approximately what he has brought or contributed. The specific individual and household for whom the ceremony is undertaken, however, do not fall within this category. Although they will receive many gifts, it will not compensate for the sums of money dispensed. The father who buys and sacrifices an animal, who buys much of the food and kola, will not be recompensed for the value of the items. However, he will view these expenditures as obligations toward his child; he will be recompensed by his child in the future. This is to be differentiated from the clear expectations of the major patrilineages and the matrilateral kindreds that the food and gifts they receive will be essentially what they contributed. Ill-feeling will easily develop if it is thought that one side or the other did not contribute their share. Moreover, reciprocity cannot be understood simply in terms of what one contributes economically. Obligations also have to be met in terms of personal appearances and interest in the affairs of one's kin groups. For example, there was one man in Hollaande, a merchant who economically met his share, but who rarely came to the ceremonies. When his wife gave birth, very few men came to the naming ceremony, whereas a full number of women attended the women's afternoon part of the ceremony, because the merchant's wife participated fully.

Ceremonial obligations—attendance and economic support— conflict with the search for money. Merchants who make the rounds of the markets will not attend ceremonies on market days. Ceremonies that fall on market day at Popodara show a much lower attendance than those held any other day. It is not only the men who are affected; women similarly are affected. Thus, one day before a circumcision and *alluwal,* the mother of the boy did not have the assistance of her close kinsmen for preparation because they were at the market.

However, it is not simply that the Fulbe sees a conflict between demands of work and demands of attendance of ceremonies. They are coming to view the expenses incurred through ceremonies as burdensome and in conflict with their own and their children's needs. The result seems to be a decrease in the scale and lavishness of ceremonies, particularly marriage. Other ceremonies, such as the one held when someone attains the status of *tierno,* have remained the same in size and importance. The outcome seems clear. Ceremonies will continue, for even in cities among full-time employees the ceremonies marking the different life-stages are held. However, as the support for such ceremonies falls more and more upon individual households, and as reciprocity diminishes both in ideology and practice, the attendance, size, and wealth involved at the life-cycle ceremonies will decrease.

We will now discuss the naming ceremony, circumcision, clitoridectomy, and funeral ceremonies.

Naming ceremony. On the eighth day after the birth of a child, the Fulbe hold a naming ceremony. The completion of the ceremony marks the acceptance by the major patrilineage of a new member.[4] The major responsibility for planning the ceremony—notifying the appropriate individuals, obtaining an animal to be slaughtered, obtaining and preparing food—falls on the father and his brothers (the father's minimal lineage). The major participants in the ceremony are the major patrilineage of the father and child, the matrilateral kindred of the child, and the Fulbe of both the mother and the father.

The most significant part of the ceremony in the morning is the actual giving of the name to the newborn child. Formerly one could almost tell whether someone was serf or Fulbe simply from the individual's name. Certain names were characteristic of serfs: for men, Sara, Dyang, Sabala, Talatou, Dyuma, Saini, Seini, Manson, Fode, Yero; and for women, Sira, Kumba, Penda, Dyiba. Fulbe names are taken more from Islam and the Koran. Some examples are Mamadu, Mamudu, Alpha Oumar, Ibrahima, and Boubakar. There were a few names in common, principally Ahmadu and Oury (derived from *wurugol,* "to live," given to help insure the life of a child). In recent years more and more former serfs are naming their children with what were Fulbe names.

4. If the child dies prior to the *denabo,* it is buried as rapidly as possible in the woman's garden, not in the cemetery.

The name is given with the slaughtering of an animal, which in Hollaande is a goat. When all the necessary parties have arrived, the elder of the major patrilineage asks the Fulbe of the father to slaughter the sacrificial animal. The goat is held by the villagers while the Fulbe utters the phrase necessary to spill the blood of an animal and then announces three times the name of the new child. It is the Fulbe of the father, therefore, who before the eyes of Allah gives the name to the infant, although the actual name of the child is chosen by the parents. Once the animal's throat has been cut, and the name stated, the child becomes a member of the patrilineage of its father.

In all but two of the naming ceremonies I attended, the Fulbe did come. On one of these two occasions, after a long wait, a *karamoko* from Hollaande slaughtered the animal, reluctantly and only with the decision of the elders of the village. When questioned whether they thought they could do without the presence of the Fulbe, their answer was no. The continued performance of the naming ceremony by a Fulbe constituted the perpetuation, at least ideologically, of the notion that a child "belongs" to his Fulbe. The Fulbe who came to the village to perform the act were often young and less learned than the elders of the village. This indicated the continued acceptance of the ideological inequality between Fulbe and former serfs, at least in the ceremonial sphere.

The Fulbe of the father usually comes with a small delegation of his patrilineage, who, like all others, bring a gift of money. Typically they sit apart following formal salutations, until the sacrifice of the goat. They then go into a separate house and are given their portion of food. They do not stay long after eating (some elderly Fulbe refuse to eat in a former-serf village), leaving upon receiving their portion of meat and kola.

The items distributed at a naming ceremony are the meat of the slaughtered animal, money, kola, rope, and other food. The father is responsible for acquiring a goat, and for providing kola to the major patrilineage, matrilateral kindred, and Fulbe of the child.

He also has to provide at least three mats employed to carry the meat and kola to the matrilateral kindred and Fulbe of his child. His major patrilineage provides rope and some mats, and each individual who attends contributes money. Within the village of Hollaande each married adult man gave about 50 francs ($.20). If he were particularly close—a brother or age-mate—he gave 100 to 200 francs. Money is not given directly to the father, but to the head of the minimal lineage, who in turn gives it to one of the elders of the major patrilineage. Everyone who attends the ceremony receives kola. The Fulbe receive their portion first, then the delegation from the matrilateral kindred. The remaining kola is divided afterward among the elders and the heads of each minimal lineage, who redivide the kola among all the members. Kola is given separately to the younger brothers and sisters of the mother (*kenang*). The money is collected and counted. One portion is set aside for the matrilateral kindred of the child, and another for the Fulbe of the child. The remainder is either given to the father to help him defray his expenses or is redistributed among his major patrilineage.

The meat of the goat is divided in five ways: one-quarter to the mother; one-half to the matrilateral kindred; a leg to the Fulbe of the mother; a large piece to the Fulbe of the father; and the rest to the major patrilineage of the child.

A typical list of items distributed at a naming ceremony is as follows: 45 kola brought by the father; 12 mats, six given by the father, one given by each of his three older brothers, two by the head of his minimal lineage, and one by his affines; 20 cords of rope brought by five different members of his major patrilineage; and 4000 francs from all those attending. These were divided as follows: 9 mats, 15 cords, 1000 francs and meat to the matrilateral kindred; 3 mats, 5 cords, 500 francs, and meat to the Fulbe of the mother; and kola equally divided to all those attending the ceremony.

All major ceremonies among the Fulbe involve the preparation and eating of food. For a naming ceremony the father is responsible for providing the food, and preparation is the task of the baby's mother, her co-wives, her sisters, and her mother. The Fulbe are fed first, then the representatives of the matrilateral kindred. The rest of the food is divided among the various age-groups within the village, who eat together. The elders receive couscous with sour milk, (*latyiri ƙaba e ƙosang*) the preferred food. If no milk is available, the elders are given rice and peanut sauce. The rest are usually given fonio or rice and peanut sauce.

After eating, two delegations are constituted to bring the name of the child to the child's matrilateral kindred and to his Fulbe. The delegations usually consist of seven men to the matrilateral kindred and three men to the Fulbe. The eldest person in each delegation is appointed to act as head, who presents formal greetings and their share of the ceremony goods. The father of the newborn child never goes, nor does the father of the mother receive the delegation.

When the parents of the mother live in another village, the bringing of the name (*nabugol inde*) is treated seriously. A delegation is chosen which represents seven of the eight minimal lineages of Hollaande. The labor of those individuals is lost for the day because quite often it may be an hour's walk to the mother's natal village. When the delegation arrives at the village, the most respectful forms of salutation are employed. Following the salutations, the matrilateral kindred of the child provides the delegation with a large bowl of food, which is eaten prior to any announcement of the ceremony that has just taken place. Only upon completion of eating does the delegation thank the child's matrilateral kindred for their hospitality and present their share of the ceremony. When the mother comes from Hollaande, the villagers, not without humor, have to choose among themselves who is to be the matrilateral kindred and who is to be the major patrilineage. If relations are strained, sending a delegation is taken more seriously. Bringing the name to the child's Fulbe is done rapidly with little more than formal communication. No one from the Fulbe's patrilineage gathers to greet the visiting men. The Fulbe simply presents a plate of food, and then hears the announcement of the birth of the child and its name. In one case, a delegation found upon arrival that no food had been prepared. This was viewed as an insult, although clearly ties between the mother and her Fulbe had lapsed as a function of distance (the villages were 15 kilometers apart). It appears likely that the next time the woman has a baby, the name will not be brought to her Fulbe unless he attempts to reestablish ties in the intervening period.

Although there are two major patrilineages within Hollaande, the entire village is always present at, or at least invited to, every ceremony. Because of the kin ties that relate various members of the village to one another—either through the male or female lines or through residential proximity (*kautal*)—the village operates as if it were one lineage in many situations. This presents an interesting circumstance for role analysis. Given the limited population, it is quite clear that any one individual can play different roles in any ceremony. The head of the lineage might be, for example, intimately involved both with the major patrilineage and matrilateral kindred. And, in fact, this happens. If both parents are from Hollaande, following the slaughtering, naming, and eating, a delegation has to be taken from within the village to act as the matrilateral kindred. The men chosen to be the matrilateral kindred then leave the area only slightly before the representatives of the patrilineage proceed to the compound of the mother's father. Those men who had just before been talking as members of the same major patrilineage then face each other as members of the patrilineage and matrilateral kindred, respectively. The same procedure as described above is followed—and food is always given, as is the ceremonial share due the matrilateral kindred. The only difference occurs following the presentation of the name and ceremonial share. All the men of both groups sit together to then redistribute the share of the matrilateral kindred. When such a situation arises, it is not infrequent that someone who has given 50 francs in the morning will receive 50 francs in the afternoon as a result of the redistribution of the money given to the matrilateral kindred.

In all Fulbe ceremonies there is segregation between men and women. The women's part of the naming ceremony takes place in the late afternoon at the house of the mother. The critical act of the ceremony is shaving the baby's head. However, there are instances when due to suspicion of sorcerers, or perhaps a *karamoko's* warning that it is a bad day to shave a baby's head, shaving can be put off until another day, when those who have access to the baby can be controlled.

For the women the mood of the ceremony is set by whether the child is a boy or a girl. Solemnity and seriousness mark the birth of a boy, joking and horseplay the birth of a girl. A strong preference is expressed for sons. The women who attend the ceremony bring gifts of dried taro or manioc, or about 25 francs. The amount of dried food given is roughly equivalent to 25 francs worth at market price. The gifts are given to the mother.

The father's responsibility to the women is to procure food for his sisters (*nyiiri yaiye*), and a plate of food for those who shave the baby's head (*nyiiri femboobe*). Food is prepared by the mother, her mother, co-wives, and sisters and by the father's sisters and brothers' wives. Food is divided by the child's paternal aunts who are helped by the elder women of the child's major patrilineage. A plate is first given to the wives of the mother's Fulbe, next to the old women of the matrilateral kindred and major patrilineage, and then to the rest of the women present.

Those attending the shaving are the women of the patrilineage of the child, the most important members of which are the father's sisters. The women's ceremony is directed and carried out by the father's sisters, the eldest "true" sister being in charge. Women who have married members of the child's patrilineage also attend and are treated as members of that group. Women of the child's matrilateral kindred also attend. However, the maternal grandmother does not come.

The wife of the Fulbe of the mother (and therefore the child) attends the afternoon ceremony, although her role is not nearly as important as that of the Fulbe of the father. The baby's head is shaved by several individuals, each one taking her turn. These are primarily members of the child's patrilineage, his father's sisters. While the baby's head is shaved, a representative of the matrilateral kindred holds him. The father's sisters take the shaved hair from the baby and hide it to prevent a sorcerer from doing harm to the newborn child. After the baby's head is shaved, he is carried three times around the house by his father's sisters. If the newborn is a boy, the women carry him around with a machete and basket; if a girl, with a hoe and a basket. As the women carry the child and the basket, old women in the house throw corn and dried taro into the basket. This is followed by the division and eating of the food. Finally, the father gives money to his oldest sister, which she then distributes to the rest of the father's sisters (in its classificatory sense).

Circumcision. As in other African societies circumcision in the Fouta-Djallon marks the transition from childhood to adulthood. The circumcision ceremony has also become deeply involved with Islam, having been joined with an Islamic ceremony marking the completion of reading the Koran. This integration was true in the past only for Fulbe boys. Circumcision of serf boys and clitoridectomy of both Fulbe and serf girls remained unconnected with any Islamic ceremonies. Now, with the former serfs able to participate in Islamic education far more than was traditionally possible, the religious difference between the circumcision ceremony of Fulbe and former serf boys is rapidly diminishing.

A simple circumcision (without the inclusion of any Islamic rite) is call *fidyo*. The ceremony that marks both circumcision and the completion of the Koran is called *alluwal*.[5] The circum-

5. The word *alluwal* has two meanings: the plank of wood used for writing the Koran and other religious works; and the ceremony marking the completion of reading or translating the Koran. Any time one finishes reading the Koran, an *alluwal* is held. In the case of a boy it is thought to be of great significance, because it marks the first time he has done so.

ciser (*baredyeli*) of both Fulbe and serf boys was always a serf, and continues to be a former serf. The circumciser symbolizes the non-Islamic elements of a circumcision, for he is also considered a sorcerer. The circumciser also led the *fidyo,* but the leader of an *alluwal* is always a Fulbe and a *tierno*. In former years the roles of circumciser and *tierno* were irreconcilable. The latter was concerned with Islam and the ways of Allah, the former with sorcery and connections with spirits. The circumciser is still often referred to as a chief of sorcerers. Yet at Hollaande, the circumciser has also become a *tierno*. In short, he has reconciled what had formerly been opposite positions. However, because of his former serf origin he cannot lead an *alluwal*.

Circumcision ceremonies epitomized the differences between the religious Fulbe and their serfs. Previously, the nights before and after a serf's *fidyo* were marked by the dancing of serf men, a practice regarded as non-Islamic and forbidden to Fulbe men. The former serfs have adopted the Fulbe view that such dancing is non-Islamic and prevents them from being properly religious. Dancing at circumcisions is therefore forbidden. One of the reasons why women are only rarely viewed as being properly religious is that they dance to the drummer (*dyeliba*). At one circumcision, the matrilateral kindred of one of the boys, who lived in a faraway village, came to Hollaande beating a drum. They were promptly told that the ceremony was an *alluwal* and that there was to be no singing or dancing. Former serfs strive to hold *alluwals* for their sons, even though this ceremony entwines them more with the Fulbe than would a *fidyo*. Although former serf children may have former serf teachers, it is rare that the teacher of a boy who has terminated the Koran is a former serf. The teacher is a significant member of the *alluwal,* as it is he who gets the major portion of the slaughtered cow. Further, only a Fulbe can lead the *alluwal* and slaughter the animal.

The Fulbe of a circumcised boy usually contributes a large plate of food and assists in the ceremonial dressing of the boy just prior to the actual circumcision. Traditionally, the formal consent of the child's Fulbe was required for circumcision. Today in many instances his formal consent is still asked for, and in all cases he is told of the decision before the ceremony takes place.

The major and minimal lineage of the child bear the brunt of the expenses for the ceremony. The matrilateral kindred of the boy shower him with gifts (*laba*). This is composed of grains, dried taro, manioc, and money. His mother's brothers give him money (550 francs at Hollaande) and large roosters.

The period of healing is set at about six weeks. During this time the boys are not permitted to work or to pray, and they live in their own houses, continually looked after by an older brother. The wounds are cared for by the circumciser. In the case of Fulbe this period of healing may be passed either in their natal village, or in the village of the circumciser. There is a small ceremony that marks the end of the healing period.

Although circumcision remains the most important dividing line between childhood and adulthood, boys are now circumcised at an earlier age. Hence the transition to adulthood is less abrupt, and in most cases the boys are not sexually mature. Nevertheless, newly circumcised boys are expected to start meeting some of their religious obligations, in particular, fasting for the entire month of Ramadan and to begin preparation for building their own little houses. Their new adult status is symbolized by the fact that when they want to enter the house of an adult male they must say *Asssalam Alaikum* and not answer unless the person responds *Alaikum Salam*. This particular practice is referred to at most circumcision ceremonies.

Clitoridectomy. As circumcision marks the transition from childhood to the preparatory period of adulthood for boys, clitoridectomy signals a girl's period of preparation as wife, mother, and economic producer. The clitoridectomy of both Fulbe and former serf girls, in contrast to circumcision, remains one of the few rituals that still has no connection with Islamic ritual or ideology.

Serf women in the past, and former serfs now, perform the

clitoridectomy. They are also called *baredyeli* and, like their male counterparts, are believed to be sorcerers. It is interesting that whereas the female *baredyeli* continues to wear a special dress of red with a belt of bells for the ceremony, the male circumciser has eliminated everything but a red handkerchief.

The most important part of the clitoridectomy ceremony takes place not at the time of the actual clitoridectomy but three weeks later. The operation itself is done at twilight in the compound of the *baredyeli,* with the girl's paternal aunts attending. The circumcised girl then goes to her paternal grandmother's where she stays for three weeks. During this time she is not required to do any work. A Fulbe girl goes to the home of an older former serf woman rather than to her grandmother's.

The *koriko* is the ceremony that takes place when a girl is healed. The ritual indicates the non-Islamic character of the clitoridectomy ceremony. The ceremony takes place at a stream near the village and at the paternal grandparent's compound. The ceremony at the water involves acts to protect the girl from the actions of sorcerers and to secure her fertility. There are a number of different songs attached to different parts of the ritual at the stream. The words to these songs are non-Fulfulde. The second part of the ceremony at the grandmother's compound involves the women of the girl's major patrilineage and matrilateral kindred. Gifts are given while the women sing and dance around her. The mother and the *baredyeli* are also given small gifts. As with the boy's ceremony, ceremonial plates of food are distributed to the different groups of participants.

Funerals. The ceremony at the death of an individual reflects the Islamic nature of the burial, the role of the Fulbe for the former serfs, and the relations and relative importance of the kin groups as indicated by their different obligations.

According to Trimingham (1959), death rites and mourning customs vary less from pure Islamic practice than does any other sphere of Islam in Africa. Trimingham states that the distinctive elements are:

ritual washing with prayer, incensing, specified types of grave clothes, and use of a stretcher, separation of the sexes; speed between death and burial; graves of specific form and orientation; ritual funeral prayer; mourners' participation in carrying corpses, repetition of phrases, throwing earth on grave; widow's ritual mourning, washing seclusion period and purification; and ceremonial gathering offering and feasting (1959: 178).

All of these are elements of funerals in the Fouta-Djallon.

When a person is gravely ill, members of his patrilineage and his affines gather to pay their respects to his family and to see him if possible. When he dies, the elders of his patrilineage stay together at his house (or the house of the husband if a women dies, or the house of the father if an unmarried person dies). There they assign the various tasks to be performed prior to burial. These include digging the grave by members of the village, something the serfs did for the Fulbe; cutting and bringing wood to be placed in the grave, a task for young men; acquisition of food for the *tyobbal,* the ritual dish eaten on all Islamic ceremonial occasions; [6] acquisition of a mat on which the corpse is placed, usually given by the major patrilineage; acquisition of white cloth necessary for the ceremonial dress (*kasange*); notification of the rest of the matrilateral kindred, patrilineage, all brothers and sisters, the Fulbe of the deceased, and any other possible members of the *bolonda;* acquisition of an animal, or animals, to be sacrificed. In the case of a married woman, animals are given both by her affines and by her major patrilineage.

The body remains in the house until interment. Incense is placed in the house. The corpse (once a person dies, he is not referred to by name but as *fure,* or "corpse") is washed, dressed, and placed on the ground by its closest kinsmen. At the same time those men who are attending the funeral gather at the traditional gathering place close by the cemetery outside the village. The women gather and remain in the compound of the deceased, but separate from the men. No women attend the burial

6. It is made of rice, honey (or sugar), and sometimes fonio and corn.

ceremony, but they do pray in the compound. Many of those going to the funeral pass by where the elders of the patrilineage are seated to pay condolences, and then go on to the cemetery.

When all preparations are complete, and all the necessary parties have arrived, the body is placed on a mat and carried by close kinsmen—representatives of both the patrilineage and the matrilateral kindred. The body is placed in front and to the east of the gathered assemblage. The prayer must be led by a Fulbe, never by a former serf. As soon as the prayer is completed, the body is carried as rapidly as possible to the grave, where members of the matrilateral kindred, patrilineage, and affines, and the Fulbe of the individual (also the Fulbe of the father if a child) place the body deftly into the grave. Wood is then placed on top, and everyone attending throws earth onto the grave.[7] Everyone immediately washes his hands before thanks is given to Allah (*duagol*). With the completion of the *duagol*, the *tyobbal* is distributed to all those who attended, by maximal lineage if they are Fulbe and by village if they are former serfs. The sacrificial animal is slaughtered and the meat distributed. If the deceased is a child, no animal is slaughtered.

All those who attend the ceremony, aside from very close kinsmen, give a little money, which is redistributed among those who have given the most for the funeral.

ISLAM IN THE VILLAGE

Having outlined the life-cycle and its attendant ceremonies, we have a perspective on the importance of Islam in all aspects of Fulbe society. Every Fulbe considers himself a Muslim.[8] However,

7. Normally graves are unmarked, but in the case of celebrated political or religious leaders their place of burial may be marked by a little house without a door, or now with a tiny cement house without windows (*maisonnette*).

8. The Fulbe of the Fouta now consider themselves to belong to the Tijaniyya sect, which involves learning the *wirdu*, a litany recited after the first and fifth daily prayers. However, this is to be distinguished from a political hierarchy.

the knowledge and practice of Islam varies greatly, not only between individuals, but between former serfs and Fulbe and between men and women.

The mosque is recognized by all as the center of religious activity, and the *almamy* as the religious head of the area. This recognition is given public expression by the two mass prayers marking the end of Ramadan and Tabaski, and by the work and gifts given by everyone in the *misside* to the mosque and the *almamy*.

Although the mosque had equal religious significance for both Fulbe and serfs, serfs did not—and former serfs do not now—participate very much in the affairs of the mosque. Today the mosque is still run by those of Fulbe origin, brought up during the era of serfdom and maintaining traditional attitudes toward serfs. Illustrative of these attitudes was one of the elders of the mosque, a deeply religious man who, while maintaining that the life of an ant and of a man were equal before Allah (meaning that man should have a very good reason for taking the life of another living creature), would not attend any ceremony in a former serf village, including the investiture of a *tierno*.

The *almamy* of the mosque is always a Fulbe. Most of the inhabitants of Hollaande viewed him as an object of fear and veneration, which is very different from the Fulbe attitude toward

---

Formerly, all the Fulbe belonged to the Qadriya, but Tijaniyyism from the Maghreb has replaced it.

A still more peculiarly African but a much more recent order is that of the Tijaniya, founded about 1195/1781 by an ex-Khalwati disciple Ahmad al Tijani (d. 1230/1815), at Fez. This order considerably simplified the ritual and laid greater stress directly on good intention and deeds, a fact which has contributed to its rapid success at proselytization and has also given it, at times, a more militant outlook. It makes no separation between the spiritual and the temporal. Whereas in Algeria it has been on good terms with the French colonial administrations, it has resisted actively the foreign domination in Morocco. From Morocco it spread in French West Africa during the 13th/19th century, propagated by Muhammad ibn Mukhtar (d. 1245/1830), and was carried into French Guinea by al-Hajj Umar Tall killed (1270/1854) in fighting (Fazlur Rahman 1968: 197).

him. The Fulbe of Popodara have far more contact with him, in his position as *almamy* as well as in non-religious contexts.[9]

At Popodara the mosque is located on the top of a hill in the middle of the town, just across from the house of the former *chef de canton*. The physical organization of the mosque is in itself revealing of the social organization of the Fulbe and the place of the former serfs. At every mosque there are four doors. The door facing east is used only by the *almamy* and the muezzin (*saali*). At Popodara the other three doors are divided among the maximal patrilineages of the area. The west door is for the Khalduyaabe, the south door for the Seleyaabe, and the north door for the Ragnaabe. The former serfs enter through the door of the maximal patrilineage of their former masters. These divisions are still respected.

Very few men from Hollaande attended the mosque on a regular basis, and this is true of former serfs in general. Most serf men were found performing their normal work on Friday, when Fulbe gather at the mosque to pray. Only one man from Hollaande participated actively at the mosque, while two or three others went occasionally. Interestingly, the most religious and devout men at Hollaande preferred to attend the mosque at Koula, a religious center about fifteen kilometers from Popodara, rather than the mosque at Popodara. Former serfs performed many menial tasks around the mosque which others did not. There are also limits to the religious leadership a former serf can exercise, no matter how deserving he may be in terms of education and piety. In a mixed group of Fulbe and former serfs, the former always lead the prayer.

An example of menial tasks performed by former serfs around the mosque was furnished one Friday afternoon when I went to the mosque. I observed four men from Hollaande working on the roof of a house of the former *chef de canton*. They did not enter

9. There is an interesting trend now of villagers (Fulbe, not former serfs) building their own mosques, selecting their *almamy* from among themselves, and no longer attending prayers at the other mosque.

the mosque, nor did they pray with the others despite their proximity. Such an incident exemplified the separation of the villagers from the mosque. However, there have been changes. Formerly, if serfs had requests to make at the mosque, they would do so through their masters; today they do so for themselves.

Women's participation at the mosque is limited, whether they be former serfs or Fulbe. Women are not allowed inside the mosque. A small house has been built for them on the west side of the mosque so that they are behind the men when both pray. However, Fulbe women are less involved in the tasks of cleaning than the former serf women. As do their male counterparts, the women perform many of the work functions necessary for the maintenance of the mosque.

Young people (up to age 40), Fulbe and former serfs, do not as a rule go to the mosque. The extent and degree of religious practice depends on the age and sex of the individual involved, but it is not expected that young men will be properly religious. It is believed that those who are very pious and devout before their time will die young. It is expected, however, that the young learn the prayers and their religious obligations. The Fulfulde word *tuubugol,* "to repent," expresses the act of a man between the ages of 30 and 40 who gives up his vices—smoking, taking lovers, and drinking alcohol—and becomes religious, attending to his obligations both as a Muslim and a full adult within Fulbe society.

Villagers or patrilineages do not pray together daily except under extraordinary circumstances.[10] The five daily prayers are

10. Every village (and often every section of a village) has a place for prayer, which is used only on special occasions. It is referred to as *ngeru* (the same word for the stone area in a compound, which similarly serves as a place of prayer). Within the village of Hollaande there were three stone areas, which were used by the village as a whole. The most important of these was the one under a very large tree. This particular tree was important for the people of Hollaande because it is maintained that there is a spirit (*dyinna*) who lives in the tree, and that although he is good to children (the children climb and play in the tree all the time), anyone who cut off a branch of the tree would die. The second place of prayer and meeting is located by the same kind of tree, but that tree is spiritless. The third area is by the cemetery and is used for assembly and prayer at burials.

performed individually. However, as in all Islamic societies, the hours of prayer are marked by the call of a muezzin. At the *misside* the muezzin calls from a small tower, but in the surrounding villages one man serves as the muezzin for a village. This is true even in the former serf villages. The role of muezzin in the former serf village has served until recently as the main way to obtain recognition for knowledge and piety.

The Fulbe make a distinction between obligatory acts and recommended acts (between *farilla* and *sunna*). The obligations of a practicing Muslim, whether a Fulbe or former serf, are the five daily prayers, the fast during the month of Ramadan, and the giving of alms.[11] The pilgrimage cannot be considered obligatory on the same level as the others, because very few actually undertake the trip. Among the recommended acts are fasting during the month of Raadyibi, going to the mosque every Friday, slaughtering a sheep or goat at Tabaski, helping to support the mosque, and helping in some way with the fields of the *almamy* of the mosque.

The focus of Islam is on meeting one's religious obligations. All life and death are the will of Allah. It is He who decides whether a person goes to Heaven or Hell. Exactly when this decision is made and its irreversibility are subjects of controversy. One elder of Hollaande, a *tierno,* who had been familiar with the French, considered life as a system of credit. Whatever one gave in this world would be returned in the next world. In short, there is a direct relation between one's good works and actions in this world and his fate in the next world. If one doesn't pray now, he will pray later; if one steals here, he will pay later; if one gives here, he will receive in the next world. However, there were other villagers, although few in number, who maintained that a final decision was made within the first forty days of birth as to whether one was to go to Paradise or not. The general view is that after the last person to leave the graveside is three steps away, two angels sit on the shoulders of the deceased and begin to

---

11. Alms-giving takes two forms in the Fouta: the *muudo,* giving a number of measures of grain following the end of Ramadan, and giving ten percent of the harvest, known as *farilla.*

question him about his life. If he is going to Paradise, he is questioned for forty days; otherwise for sixty days. It is said there is a huge hammer that drives a deceased person to Hell, and when this hammer is driving someone down he screams. The screams are heard only by goats and sheep who paw at the grave.

Part of this belief system emphasizes the individuality of one's religious responsibility. Before Allah, a man stands alone. No one can help another in his religion. No one can pray for or meet any religious obligations of another. One could speculate that the individuality of Islam complements the individuality of Fulbe lives. Fulbe men need no company to meet their religious obligations.

Islam is well integrated with Fulbe society. Kin obligations and status differences are expressed in a religious as well as a social way. There is little separation between what might be called the secular and the sacred spheres of Fulbe life. In the specific context of the naming ceremony it is not possible to distinguish the obligation to slaughter a goat as being a social or a religious act. On the one hand the naming ceremony is viewed as required by Islam, and on the other, it is the means by which patrilineages recognize new members.

In discussing four religious ceremonies, three points will be distinguished: the intertwining of kin obligations and Islam; the continuing Fulbe ritual dominance over former serfs; and the integration of Islam with the earlier non-Islamic practices. The four ceremonies described are Ramadan (the fast month), Tabaski (the slaughtering of sheep), Dyom Bente, (New Year), and the *sadaka*. Although *sadaka* refers to any sacrifice, it refers specifically to the village-wide gatherings called during the year to insure a successful harvest.

Ramadan. As in most parts of the Islamic world, the month of fast is characterized by an outpouring of religiosity and by strong pressures on all to fast. Only women in an advanced state of pregnancy, women who have just given birth, and those who are sick are exempt from the obligations of the month of Ramadan.

In a village anyone who does not fast without legitimate reason will be subject to ridicule. Fasting is adhered to so completely that in Hollaande three men who were seriously ill during Ramadan not only maintained the fast, but did not take medicine between sunrise and sunset.

The month of Ramadan is the only time during the year when there is daily communal eating. Each minimal lineage (there were eight at Hollaande) gathers at sunset for prayer and then the meal. Men of the minimal lineage eat with each other, while their wives eat together in an adjoining compound. In villages where the minimal lineages are small, the major patrilineages eat together. In either case eating together is an expression of closeness, and the Ramadan has become a vehicle for reemphasizing kin ties.

During Ramadan there is a particularly long prayer said at the time of the evening prayer. In most villages, including Hollaande, this prayer is recited by the most learned men of the village with the entire village in attendance. This daily gathering by the entire village, men, women, and children, takes place only during the month of Ramadan.

Ramadan does not go by without continuous comment on the difficulty of fasting. The fast is also a subject of continual conversation, as though everyone, particularly the younger men and women, were demonstrating their seriousness and religiosity.

Ramadan ends when the new moon is seen.[12] The fast is broken that morning and there is then a mass prayer, known as *iidi* (*al-id* in Arabic), involving all individuals of a *misside*. In the *misside* of Popodara the prayer is held in a large field, for the number of people that come cannot fit into the mosque. The *almamy* leads the prayer and then gives a message to the members of the mosque. At the *iidi* I attended he reminded everyone that they had to give at least two measures of grain to a religious per-

12. During my stay the new moon was not seen. The Guinean radio station announced it had been seen in Senegal and that the fast would therefore end the next day.

son or else their fasting would be worthless in the eyes of Allah. He then observed that improvements were being undertaken at the mosque and more money was needed in order to complete them; 10,500 francs (approximately $40) was collected on the spot. At the end of his talk he led everyone—Fulbe and former serfs —to the mosque, where the men stayed for almost two hours singing religious chants. In this context Fulbe–former serf differences are not of great importance, except insofar as those who direct prayer and who make up the cortege of the *almamy* are all Fulbe. Of greater importance is the unification of all the members in a common ceremony at the end of Ramadan. At the end of Ramadan the youth hold dances, which are not held all during the month, the adults and elders bring gifts to their affines, and those former serfs who retain close ties with their masters bring gifts to their Fulbe. All spend the days visiting their kinsmen.

Tabaski. Tabaski (*al-id al kabir* in Arabic, *dyulde donking* in Fulfulde) lasts for two days. On the morning of the first day each minimal lineage eats a morning meal together. The members then disperse for ablution and to dress for the mass prayer that is held in the same field as that used at Ramadan. The same prayer as that for the ending of Ramadan is recited by the *almamy*. He also uses the gathering to give a religious message. After the prayer all those attending escort the *almamy* to the mosque and then to his compound while singing religious chants. The *almamy,* attended by other important personages, slaughters a sheep. The former *chef de canton,* who while chief slaughtered several goats and sheep which were distributed to his followers, now slaughters two sheep while attended by his kinsmen and a few of his former serfs. The rest of the day at Hollaande is celebrated by a cessation of work.

Others who slaughter an animal do so the next day. The sacrifice of a goat or sheep is recommended (*sunna*). At Hollaande five animals were slaughtered; all but one were goats. Three elder men and two elder women did so; both women were widows, and their sons supplied the animals.

Fulbe who want to offer a sacrifice perform the act themselves. Former serfs still must have their former masters perform the act for them. The Fulbe slits the animal's throat while the former serf holds his hand. In short, the Fulbe acts as intermediary between the former serfs and Allah, a continuing recognition that former serfs are not the religious equals of Fulbe. The serfs, however, are not the only ones denied the right to slaughter an animal by themselves. Women cannot do so. A Fulbe woman holds the hand of her husband, and a former serf woman holds the hand of her former master.

The division of the meat of a slaughtered animal differs from other ceremonial occasions. The liver and heart of the animal are grilled by an elder over a fire and are eaten by all. Care is taken to make sure that everyone receives a morsel. The rest of the animal is then divided. A large share goes to the Fulbe of the owner, at least an equal share is set aside for the owner's household, and the rest is divided among the assembled men of the village to grill and eat on the spot.

The New Year. The holiday celebrating the New Year (the first day of the month *Dyom Bente*) appears less connected with Islam than the other holidays. *Dyom Bente* is celebrated for two days. The evening before, age-mate groups of boys and girls go from house to house singing. It is interesting that the traditional Fulbe songs sung by the boys (*rabbingol*) are being replaced by Islamic religious chants (*dyaragol*). The girls' traditional songs (*sorrugol*), on the other hand, have remained unchanged. The next morning everyone goes to the stream, where they bathe and put on new clothes. The men then go the cemetery where prayers are said for the "corpses" (in Fulfulde, *dyangangol fureedyi ding*). This is the only time of the year when prayers are said for the dead or when the cemetery is visited. This aspect of the ceremony appears to stem from pre-Islamic times. It is performed by both Fulbe and the former serfs.

The rest of the day is spent in visiting kinsmen, affines, and— if one is a former serf—one's Fulbe. There is a phrase that refers to this period of intensive visiting on *Dyom Bente: dyokkere en-*

dang. Gifts are brought on this occasion to one's affines and Fulbe.

The Village Sacrifice. In the Fouta *sadaka* means a "sacrifice" that can be performed by anyone, at any time, for any reason.[13] For example, if something is stolen from a house, a religious leader (*karamoko*) may suggest that the owner offer a sacrifice of three white objects to anyone (the most appropriate sacrifice being kola), which would cause the unmasking of the thief. *Sadaka* also refers to a ceremony held three times a year by the village as a whole, the purpose of which is to pray for plentiful rains, no destructive winds, and a bountiful harvest.

Decisions about the time to hold village sacrifices are announced to the villagers by the religious leaders at the mosque. All the villages whose members pray at the same mosque on Friday hold their sacrifices on the same day. Today there are no differences between the Fulbe and former serf ceremonies. The sacrifice is carried out by the village as a whole, acting as a single unit. There is no ambiguity as to who is the ceremonial head of the village; it is the eldest male (unless, of course, he cannot perform the tasks required).

The ceremony itself is simple. Each household head decides what food his wives will prepare. The entire village gathers for the ceremony. At Hollaande the prayer site is called (*ngeru*). The men arrive first, bringing dried corn, peanuts, fonio, kola, and taro, which constitute the sacrifice. At the last sacrifice I attended

13. It has been noted by Trimingham (1959) that *sadaqa* in Arabic refers to alms-giving, whereas in Fulfulde its best translation is "sacrifice." Trimingham goes on to observe that the word *sadaqa* has played a great role in "desacralizing the sacrifice." In animist religion "sacrifice is an offering to a divinity to please, propitiate, and sustain its energy, and when consumed by the worshippers, constitutes a form of communion. Acceptance of Islam leads to a complete desacralizing of such ideas, for Islam has no idea of sacrifice in the African sense" (ibid.:74). While it is interesting and important to observe what happens to Islamic words and ideas in Africa, it does not explain the change. To say that Islam has no idea of sacrifice in the African sense does not explain why sacrifice continues in the Fouta and why *sadaka* is the word and concept employed for such practices.

a goat was also slaughtered to make the sacrifice "extra strong." This is unusual and was due to a series of misfortunes in the village—the lack of cultivable land, the burning down of one of the houses in the village, and several serious illnesses that were said to have been caused by malevolent spirits. The sacrificial animal is consumed, each member of the village receiving a part. The produce, however, is not eaten, but is symbolically thrown away following the completion of the ceremony.

Once the village has gathered, the eldest male of the village recites a particular prayer (*fatiha*), and then all give thanks to Allah. The food is then eaten and all remain together to perform the prayer at sunset. The women also participate in the prayers but stand behind the men, where they can barely hear the leader.

ISLAMIC EDUCATION

Many observers have noted both the intensive and extensive nature of Islamic education in the Fouta-Djallon. In the past, however, religious education, beyond the bare minimum required for prayers, was only for the Fulbe. Former serfs now participate to a degree impossible fifty years ago.

All children, both boys and girls, are required to begin their Koranic education around the age of six. Typically, parents find a master (*karamoko*) to initiate them into reading Arabic letters. Koranic school is held five days a week for about two hours. The first stage of Koranic education begins with the first letter and is therefore known as the *Ba* stage. During this stage all the letters are taught. Then come the *sigi,* when the child learns the various signs. This is followed by the third step, the *findituro,* when the child begins to read words and phrases. At no point in this process is a child taught the meaning of what he is reading. With the beginning of reading the Koran (*dyangugol dyande*) there is a little ceremony in which the *karamoko,* in front of assembled kinsmen, teaches the child the first sentence of the Koran.

Once a child begins the Koran, he is expected to read until he finishes it. The process is arduous. The *karamoko* (or an older student) writes a section of the Koran on a plank of wood (*alluwal*), which is supplied by the student. After a passage is written for the student he is expected to go home and learn it. In Hollaande the children gathered almost every evening at a small house, built especially for the purpose, to practice and recite their work in front of the *karamoko* of the village. At another village I visited kerosene was much scarcer, and the children gathered in little groups after sundown to read by the light of a fire. After a child can read these passages perfectly, they are erased and the succeeding passages are written. Depending on the ability and conscientiousness of a student, reading the Koran takes from one to four years. It is quite rare for a girl to finish reading the Koran. Girls usually stop after their clitoridectomy, somewhere in stage three.

In return for the education of their child, parents periodically give gifts to their child's *karamoko*. The child cuts and brings firewood to his religious teacher once a week. The greatest gift for the *karamoko* is saved until the student completes the Koran and is circumcised. The linking of Islam with circumcision can be seen clearly in the number of times that a child can read the Koran prior to his circumcision without the *alluwal* ceremony that marks the completion of reading the Koran being performed. The three boys who were circumcised during my stay were fourteen years of age and had read (and therefore recopied) the Koran at least twice. Two boys just a year and a half younger than these had already read the Koran three times. Yet the *alluwal* ceremony was not held until the boys were circumcised.

The education of children does not stop with the completion of the Koran. There are many other books to be studied. Whether a child continues depends on his inclinations and the pressure of his family. When a child reaches the age of sixteen or seventeen his Islamic studies often cease entirely, to be taken up again when he becomes much older.

Islamic education is theoretically unceasing. Those individuals who wish to continue their studies do so by attaching themselves to a master, depending on their level and ability. The most common form of continued study is the translation of the Koran into Fulfulde. This process is known as *tafsir* (according to Trimingham (1958: 78) it is a Wolof term meaning "commentary"). The completion of translating the Koran into Fulfulde entitles the scholar to the title of *tierno,* and it is marked by a ceremony also called an *alluwal*. Becoming a *tierno* is a long and difficult process. Formerly, the time and expense devoted to such a commitment was impossible for the serfs. Without religious leaders, the serfs had no effective voice at the mosque.

The difference in Islamic education was important in maintaining the difference between Fulbe and serf. Formerly serfs were given no more than a minimal education, sufficient for them to recite prayers, and a supplementary knowledge of Arabic letters and words. Therefore, few adult former serfs can read Arabic even now. There were three older men in the village, however, who had attained the status of *tierno* since 1958. In addition, and interestingly indicative of the greater emphasis beginning to be placed on Koranic education for women, one woman became a *tierno* during my stay in Hollaande. That she was not given equal status, however, was indicated by the fact that whereas a cow was slaughtered at the *alluwal* for each of the three men, only a goat was slaughtered for her.

With the opportunity for Koranic education, former serfs, even those who are themselves illiterate insist that their children study. One of the most serious infractions a child (particularly a boy) can commit is to skip Koranic school. It is one of the few things a child is beaten for. At Hollaande only two boys did not attend Koranic school: the father of one had died and he therefore had to help his mother; the other was a very rebellious, disobedient child considered "ruined" by the village. Even though former serf men have attained the status of *tierno,* former Fulbe-serf distinctions usually still supersede in religious situations.

223

SORCERY

Ideological changes within the former-serf village, set in motion
by the legal and economic end of serfdom, are particularly obvious in the area of sorcery. The distinction between witchcraft
and sorcery, used so frequently in the African literature, is not
employed here. It is quite possible that such a distinction would
have been appropriate in the past. However, I have adopted the
usage of the Fulbe themselves in referring to all those who now
use spirits for either good or evil as sorcerers. Although sorcery
was traditionally associated with the serfs, the increasing Islamization of the former serfs is weakening both the belief in and the
practice of sorcery. Rather, there appears to be a growing depersonalization of the forces that cause harm in the form of spirits
(dyinna, from the Arabic jinn) that are clearly associated with
Islamic belief. A nonhuman world exists for the Fulbe which is
basically a dangerous place for humans. The most threatening
part of that world are the potential actions of the spirits.[14] French-
speaking Fulbe use the word *diable* to translate *dyinna*, which is
misleading, because there are many different kinds of spirits. In
the area of Hollaande it is believed that three kinds of spirits
exist: *dyuldi*, the Muslims; *keferi*, the heathens; and *ngotte*, little
spirits. This classification itself reflects the integration of Islamic
and non-Islamic beliefs.[15] Only heathens and little spirits cause
trouble for human beings, mainly in the form of illness, although
the *ngotte* also do little things that frighten or cause annoyance,
but for which no medicine is required. For example, a *ngotte* will
scare babies by pulling at their arms and legs. This, of course, explains those times when babies cry for no apparent reason. The

14. Trimingham argues that Islam brought the word *jinn* to Africa as a
"synonym for spirits in general or depersonalized spirit agencies without necessarily displacing old terminology" (1959: 55).

15. This classification appears to be of recent origin and does not coincide with
the number and diversity of spirits which existed earlier.

only example of a spirit specifically helping someone directly is in a folk-tale that resembles a fairy tale with a good spirit of a spring helping a poor, disliked daughter to obtain wealth and happiness. *Dyinna* do help men, by helping them to identify sorcerers. Although those spirits who aid such work do not completely fit into one of the above classifications, they tend to be regarded as the "heathen spirits."

The spirits exist in many different forms and in many different places. They are said to live in certain large trees, in large termite hills, in certain spots on the land (which are not to be cultivated), and by all springs from which drinking water is drawn. There are also spirits in unknown places in the bush (*burure*). It becomes known through time whether the spirit who lives in a particular spot is reputed to be a Muslim, heathen, or *ngotte*. Thus it is said that a good spirit lives in the large tree (*kurahi*) in the village because the children climb and play there without being harmed. But it is also maintained that if someone were to cut a limb from the tree, he would immediately die as a result of the anger of the spirits.

Dusk is considered the time of day when the spirits are most likely to do harm. There are certain special phrases that many individuals read if they expect to be out at dusk. These prayers are said to keep the spirits away.

The circumstances surrounding the reroofing of a mosque deserve to be described, as they illustrate the integration of Islam with the notion of spirits. A spirit is said to live in the top of the straw roof of a mosque. (It is interesting that this spirit is not one of the three kinds of spirits described above.) When the roof is repaired or replaced, the top of the roof has to be taken off and placed on the ground while the work is done. The time the top is on the ground is dangerous, because spirits are free and may strike someone. It was claimed at Popodara that who would die depended on which side of the mosque the top of the roof was placed. This is connected with the location of the two dominant maximal patrilineages, the Seleyaabe who live to the east and south of the mosque, and the Ragnaabe who live to the west. This belief has led to an actual physical struggle between the two maximal lineages and their serfs. Informants maintained that a general brawl erupted every time reroofing took place (every three or four years) and that it involved all the men of one maximal lineage and their serfs ranged against the other. The chiefly lineage did not take part. No weapons were used in the fighting.

However, now the spirit has been driven out according to some informants or given a permanent home according to others. This has resulted not from any action on the part of the Fulbe, but rather as a consequence of technological innovations. It has become prestigious to build mosques of cement with aluminium roofs. This, of course, has ended the necessity for frequent reroofing, and the fights have become phenomena of the past.

The distinction between sorcerers and spirits is illustrated in Fulbe beliefs about illness. Illness is attributed to three causes. First, there is illness with no known cause (*ko naunai tung*)—such as measles, smallpox, or chicken pox. Second, there is illness caused by a spirit (*ko dyinna*)—illness without specific symptoms or swelling and infection without known injury. Third, there is illness caused by a sorcerer (*ko nyane*). Almost all illnesses and deaths of children are associated with the actions of a sorcerer. There has been a change in concept of the role of sorcery in death, particularly among men. This point will be discussed later in the chapter.

Only specialists can discern whether the cause of an illness is a spirit or a sorcerer. Two kinds of specialists existed in traditional society: the *mbiledyo,* who used non-Islamic means to discover and cure illness, and the *karamoko,* the religious leaders whose powers were thought to stem from Islam.

The word for sorcerer (both male and female) is *nyanedyo* or *nyane.* "To do sorcery" is *nyaamugol;* it carries the primary meaning "to eat." A sorcerer kills someone or makes him ill by "eating" his victim. Most informants were reluctant to describe how a sorcerer actually acts on a victim. One elderly, very knowl-

226

edgeable religious leader gave this account: A sorcerer eats a victim by sucking his blood, each breath extracting blood from him. The sorcerer then leaves the location of the victim and either fries or roasts the blood. As the sorcerer eats the blood the victim falls ill. This was just one technique among several.

Sorcery has always been associated with serfs more than with Fulbe. Both the Fulbe and the former serfs maintain that sorcerers are most likely descendants of captives. Although there are fewer sorcerers in Fulbe villages, most villages have at least one. Sorcerers in Fulbe villages are almost always women, whereas in serf villages they are both sexes. The Fulbe continue to frighten their children from going into former serf villages by warning them of the sorcerers that live there. Moreover, because Fulbe children are always coming into contact with former serfs, they need to be protected from the actions of sorcerers.

There are many different explanations for why a person is a sorcerer, including inheritance from a parent (from a mother in the case of Fulbe, from either parent in the case of serfs), but women beyond child-bearing age are the most likely suspects. The term for a woman who has never had any children (*maamaare*) is a synonym for *sorcerer*. Those who perform circumcision and clitoridectomy are also considered sorcerers. At Hollaande women who have married into the village are more likely to be considered sorcerers than women who were born and married in the village.

Estimates of the number and identity of sorcerers at Hollaande varied greatly depending on who the informant was. Informants from one major patrilineage always estimated a greater incidence of sorcerers in the other patrilineages than in his own. Outsiders claimed more sorcerers for Hollaande than the villagers themselves perceived. Moreover, Fulbe saw more sorcerers within the village of Hollaande than did residents of surrounding former serf villages. Because there are no longer any direct and public accusations, it was not possible to estimate reliably the actual number of sorcerers.

The manifestation of sorcery is most often connected with the illnesses of children. All children, whether they be the son of an Islamic scholar (*tierno*) or the son of a *mbiledyo* (someone who discovers sorcerers), are susceptible to the actions of sorcerers. One interesting way in which sorcerers were said to use their power in the past, and which is now disappearing, is connected with the consumption of meat, which is more widespread in recent times. Eating meat in public risked the envy of a passer-by, who might employ sorcery. Children dared not eat meat in front of elders, because these would employ sorcery against the privileged young. Sorcerers are also said to keep women from conceiving, and to prevent the attainment of other goals as well.

Direct accusations of sorcery have ended, at least in Hollaande. Prior to independence, disputes still occasionally gave rise to accusations of sorcery. Accusations were dealt with by elders of a village or by a *mbiledyo*. The *mbiledyo* cured individuals from the effects of sorcery, neutralized the potential actions of a sorcerer, and also identified sorcerers. These functions are also performed by the religious leaders. The *mbiledyo,* however, was always a serf, or a non-Fulbe, primarily Malinke.

An informant reported that ten years ago he came upon a large group of men and women, Fulbe and serfs, gathered in a field between two villages. Directing the group was a *mbiledyo* (who is still living, is very wealthy, but no longer practices his craft in the same manner). The *mbiledyo* and his two apprentices offered a potion for everyone to drink. Anyone who did not drink the potion was immediately suspected of being a sorcerer. The potion was supposed to affect only those who were sorcerers. Anyone who became drunk or lost consciousness was a sorcerer. About fifteen people fell to the ground and began speaking in delirium. Those who showed no reaction to the potion received another potion with which to wash their faces, which enabled them to see the sorcerer's pot (*payande nyande*). This pot was the symbol of sorcerers' activities. In it the fingernails, hair, and other parts of the bodies of their victims are to be found. Everyone looked around for the pot until the *mbiledyo* pointed toward the top of a very tall tree. He then fired his gun at the top of the tree, causing the pot to leave its resting place. Everyone then chased the pot until they came to a stream. At the stream the *mbiledyo* said he saw the pot in the water. He then dived into the stream and pulled out an object. (My informant did not know whether it was a pot or an animal. The latter appears more likely, because one of the abilities of sorcerers is to transform themselves or objects). Inside was a collection of bits of fingers, hair, nails, rings, and jewelry—some of which was identified as having belonged to recently deceased individuals. In order to release these objects the *mbiledyo* "slit the throat" of the pot, which killed the sorcerer. Following this act everyone returned to the village where plates of food and gifts were presented to the *mbiledyo.*

The ceremony described above is no longer performed—at least it has not been performed for the past five years in the area of Popodara. The dramatic seeing, following, and slaughtering of the sorcerer's pot appears to be a phenomenon of the past. The *mbiledyo,* however, continues to perform his role, although in a more limited fashion. The *mbiledyo* gives general advice to individuals on how to avoid sorcerers or to achieve success in life. I had the opportunity to observe an *mbiledyo* at a former serf village five kilometers from Hollaande. For an hour and a half before the actual ceremony began there was singing and dancing. The *mbiledyo* first called a young girl from the audience to come up to him, and asked to whom she belonged. The girl's father came forward and gave the *mbiledyo* money. The *mbiledyo* gave his advice, which was that the girl had to have a ring made for her to avoid the sorcerers, and that the mother has to pass a fistful of food around her head three times and then give it to a dog. He gave this advice because the girl got sick often. The *mbiledyo* then called out a name and asked that person to come forward. Three times no one came forward. The person finally did identify himself, and was told to carry a few grains of fonio, rice, and corn to a stream and throw them into the water as a sacrifice (*sadaka*). That evening the *mbiledyo* stipulated an appropriate sacrifice for each individual he spoke to for safeguarding against the actions of sorcerers (always unnamed and unknown.) The only reference to particular, potentially dangerous individuals was made to a young man who was told that two people in his village could make him fail in his life. These were two people whom he loved and thought of as friends but who were really his enemies. Further, they were members of his major patrilineage. The required sacrifice in this case was to take a whole white kola and throw half of it to the east, the other to the west, then take some very clean water and throw part of it to the east, the rest to the west.

In earlier days several kinds of action against suspected or proven sorcerers were available. In the case of the potion ordeal described earlier, people assumed to be sorcerers because of their reaction to the potion were simply shamed. No greater retribution was asked of them. However, informants maintained that in earlier years if someone were caught walking about nude at night, or if a person with whom he argued fell ill, he was suspected of being a sorcerer and was either beaten or had to give a sacrifice. The last time a *mbiledyo* was invited to Hollaande he stayed two weeks. Toward the end of his stay, the villagers came together to hear him. He said that within the village there was a young man with a very large head who was a sorcerer. Everyone in the village knew who this was, as there had been earlier suspicion. Interestingly, the young man named had been born in another village. Hollaande was the natal village of his mother (who had died), and he was living there with his maternal grandmother, who had married the son of a captive.

ISLAM AND SORCERY

The religious leaders (referred to as *karamoko* and *tierno*) serve a variety of functions other than formal religious instruction. Due in part to their knowledge of Islam and long contact with the Koran, the religious leaders are seen as integral parts of the way of Islam; their power is thought to derive from Islam and not from world of spirits and sorcerers. From an analytic point of view much of what they do appears no different from what is done by sorcerers, but from the point of view of the people they are seen, and treated, as very different.

Religious leaders can use their power to do good or evil. Certain religious leaders can perform *kortugol*. *Kortugol* involves reciting certain verses (which were not told to me and are known to only a few) and then pointing a finger toward the place where a person to be struck down is thought to be. The main reasons for employing *kortugol* are to take vengeance on an enemy or to kill someone who is stronger. Among the Fulbe it is said there are very few who are powerful enough to perform *kortugol*. At the same time it is something that former serfs are not supposed to be able to do. I could not obtain the name of any serf who had the ability to do *kortugol*. *Kortugol* is considered to be the way of Islam, even though it is clearly magic. It is not thought of in the same way as sorcery, the way of spirits and heathens. And yet sorcery and Islam, Allah and spirits are blended into one system, with differences in practice associated with difference in social status.

One of the more important functions of the religious leaders is to make medicine against sorcerers. Children wear around their waists and necks leather amulets containing Arabic writings that are written by religious leaders, primarily to protect them against sorcery, but also to make them strong, to make them succeed in what they undertake and to protect them against the harmful actions of others besides sorcerers. To ward off danger from spirits, children are washed with water that has been used to wash Koranic verses off wooden planks (*alluwal*). This practice is called *nasi*. Both *nasi* and amulets are used against spirits, in which case different verses are used.

When an individual falls ill, he might call a religious leader, whose principal weapon is a variety of Arabic phrases he has learned from a teacher. However, he might call an *mbiledyo* rather than a religious leader. It is here that the roles of *mbiledyo* and religious leader conflict. They compete in their ability to prevent sorcerers from harming people and to cure them once they have become ill. Their roles also conflict in matters other than curing. Both the religious leader and the *mbiledyo* are said to be able to foretell the future; however, as in the case of sorcery, the basis of their ability is supposedly different. The *mbiledyo* has contact with the world of spirits, and it is the spirits who aid him to cure, to prevent illness, and to foresee the future. In contrast, the religious leader in a vague and undefined way, derives his ability from the way of Islam, although not directly from Allah.

In the past there may have been significant differences in the definitions of the sources of power to do good or evil, whether spirits or sorcery. At present, however, the distinction between spirit power and sorcery is disappearing (*nyane e dyinna ko gootung*). This means that the distinction between the use of spirits for good or evil purposes is disappearing also. Use of spirit power is now sufficient to bring a man into suspicion of practicing sorcery. It is important once more to recall that individuals suspected of using sorcery are likely to be former serfs.

There appears to be growing recognition among both Fulbe and former serfs of a contradiction between belief in an all-powerful Allah and belief in sorcerers. This was stated in many conversations, especially those that touched on disease and death. An old former serf expressed it this way. "It is only Allah who gives us days. Before, whoever had a child, the child would be cut down. The Goodness of Allah, and those of Koula [a religious center] have stopped that now. Here. [the death of children] has diminished. But there are many areas where [it still continues]." [16] The old man went on to say that no children's deaths in the past five years were attributable to sorcery, and that "whenever death

16. *Ko Allah tung okkimeng balde. Hari hebado wo be tolaimo. Barke Allah e be Kula beng dung attyi dyooni. Do'o no butti dyooni. Kono serari nding haa.*

comes, it comes from Allah." Decisions are therefore attributed solely to Allah: "Someone can be angry with you, but to kill, only Allah [can do that]." [17]

Awareness of the basic contradiction between belief in sorcery and in all-powerful Allah is not the same for all members of the population; in general it is men who are most bothered by it. Women hold very strongly to their belief in sorcery and still attribute almost all children's deaths and illness to the actions of sorcerers. Women tend to seek out an *mbiledyo* for advice on how to protect their children and themselves, whereas men are satisfied with the recommendations of a religious leader.

The need to reconcile their beliefs is felt differently by Fulbe and former serfs, Fulbe men tend to deny their acceptance of the existence of sorcery by saying that it was only serfs who were involved with sorcery. They claim that spirits and sorcerers are the same thing (*Dyinnu e nyune ko goolung*). Because of the increasing Islamization of former serf men as religious education and postitions become open to them, and because of their greater involvement with sorcery in the past, former serf men are most directly affected by the need to reconsider earlier beliefs. They comprise the part of the population that is most rapidly changing its belief system.

One incident illustrates how former serf men are attempting to bring sorcery under control and how former serf women remain closer to earlier beliefs about sorcerers. Not long before my arrival at Hollaande, the elders of the village had reached a decision to bar all *mbiledyo* from the village. When a fire destroyed one of the houses in the village, one of the elders of a major patrilineage publicly forbade the women of the village, who had gathered together with the men at the site of the burned house, from consulting a *mbiledyo* about the identity and reasons of the person who had set the fire.

In a sense, the former serfs' declining belief in sorcery as the cause of illness, death, and other misfortunes increases Fulbe

17. *Godo no waawi monanaademaa, kono warugol ngol ko Allah tung.*

ideological dominance over them. Although greater numbers of former serfs are becoming *karamoko* and *tierno,* the inhabitants of the former serf villages still remain dependent on religious leaders for protection against sorcerers and spirits. Knowledge about medicines used against sorcerers and spirits is learned through an apprenticeship system from elder Fulbe *karamoko* and *tierno*. These have not yet accepted many former serfs as students in such matters. However, as more former serfs become religious leaders, they will undoubtedly become more independent.

In addition to ideological pressures on traditional ideas about sorcery, political forces have also played a part in the growing rejection of belief in sorcery. Direct accusations and retribution against suspected or proven sorcerers have ended. The Fulbe attribute this to the French, whose judicial system did not recognize the actions of sorcerers or the punishments meted out to them, which had ranged from simple shaming to severe beatings. The French viewed such actions as crimes and punished those who carried them out. Thus the Fulbe were prevented from dealing with sorcerers in their traditional way, that is, holding them responsible for their acts of sorcery.

The Guinean government has also taken a position against considering people to be sorcerers. The role of the *mbiledyo* is discredited by the P.D.G. However, political controls inhibiting the punishment of sorcerers, coupled with a continued belief in sorcery leaves one impotent to do battle against them. This may have led to the increasing unification of the idea of sorcery and spirits, or, in other words, to a growing depersonalization of the forces of evil.

There are probably other influences contributing to the changing attitude toward sorcery. The introduction by the Guinean government of hospitals and clinics into the countryside since independence presents the possibility for alternative explanations for illness and its cure. Villagers, particularly young men, commented on the decrease in the death rate of children. They claimed that the age-mate groups of young men were the largest Hollaande had ever known.

Sorcery still poses a serious dilemma for those youths attempting to break with their traditional ideological system. Boys between the ages of ten and fifteen spoke continuously of sorcerers and their fear of them. Initially such concern could be interpreted as reflecting a situation in which sorcerers continued to have their earlier ideological importance. Upon reflection it would appear the contrary is true. Such continual verbalization does not reflect a stable condition but a changing one. The youths were grappling with a declining, but nevertheless dangerous, institution.

Young men have more difficulty than anyone in reconciling traditional beliefs with the tremendous changes their society is undergoing. One of my close friends, who continually questioned the beliefs and attitudes of traditional society, and who consistently maintained that all *mbiledyo* were liars, nevertheless related two incidents that indicated his belief in sorcery and the power of religious leaders. The youth's older brother had a young girl come to his house to sleep with him one evening. She stayed all night and the next day. The following sunset she set off for her village. The brother called for an age-mate to accompany him and the girl to her village. They went as far as the large tree on one side of the village (the *kurahi* described earlier) when the girl told them to turn around and go home. The two men, however, stood and chatted while the girl went on her way. After having walked a little further the girl crouched behind some bushes to relieve herself. Two shooting stars came out.[18] The two men ran home afraid.

When someone plans a trip, whether long or short, he goes to a religious leader (*karamoko*) to find out what would be a good day to set out. If he is going for a long time, very often he will ask to know his future. When my friend was planning to go to Conakry, he sought advice from a *karamoko*. Prior to giving

18. Shooting stars are thought to be sorcerers.

advice the *karamoko* asked that he offer a sacrifice of *tyobbal* (mixture of rice, corn, and honey). To demonstrate his power, the *karamoko* also specified to his client the conditions under which the sacrifice should be completed. My friend was to walk east at dawn about ten kilometers from the village, where he would meet a light skinned woman with a boy baby on her back. It was to her that he should give the sacrifice. He claimed that this is exactly what occurred.

Despite questioning and skepticism, incidents such as these confirm belief in the existence of sorcerers and the powers of *karamoko*. Even when an individual personally refuses to accept them (and these cases are rare, generally involving university students), he learns through his friends and family of many incidents that cannot be explained any other way.

The merging of spirits and sorcerers is of great importance. Without such a union the contradiction between belief in the all-powerfulness of Allah and the powers of some human beings to kill others by supernatural means would stand out in high relief. The admission that such a contradiction exists would result in great difficulties. If human beings are truly responsible for such harmful actions, then action must be taken against them. But the political situation proscribes such action. Political constraints and ideological difficulties are leading to the unification of sorcery and the spirit world. No longer do men blame illness and death on the action of a sorcerer, for it is only Allah who can take the life of a human being.

Seven

Conclusions

This study has attempted to describe and analyze two interrelated phenomena: the changing nature of Fulbe-serf relations during three periods of history—indigenous, colonial, and independent; and the restructuring of the internal organization of a serf village as a result of the abolishment of serfdom. The most important aspect of precolonial Fulbe-serf relations was economic. Specifically, this took the form of labor obligations of the serfs to their masters, and the exclusive ownership of land—both fields and women's gardens—by the Fulbe. The breakdown and ultimate demise of labor obligations was initiated during the colonial period, and has been reinforced by the present state.

Although the emphasis of this study has been the role of the serfs and the transformation of their lives, the Fulbe society has greatly changed and continues to do so. The same factors that have led to the end of serfdom have also led to the restructuring of Fulbe society as a whole. No longer is access to political power based on maximal lineages, nor is the wealth of the Fulbe any longer dependent on the labor of their serfs. It is in the context of the new lines of development of the Fouta-Djallon that both Fulbe and serfs have been characterized as peasants.

Certain land relations between Fulbe and former serf continue, however, deriving their form in part from the earlier pattern of organization. Most significantly, former serfs still do not own their own fields unless they were bought during the colonial era.

Even those who do own land usually borrow fields during the years their own must lie fallow. It thus continues to be normal behavior for former serfs to borrow land from the Fulbe.

In general, former serfs now may borrow land from any land proprietor, irrespective of whether he is their former master. However, in a crisis such as the one during my last year in the village, former masters can be asked for assistance in obtaining land, and such a request still creates an obligation for the master to which other Fulbe would not respond. A former serf woman is especially likely to seek such help, because she usually retains much closer ties to her former master than does her husband. This is because of the traditional way in which serfs were inherited; the owner of the woman inherited her children. Thus a former master is still likely to accept the request of a woman that he help her obtain the means to feed her children.

The *farilla,* the traditional ten-percent payment of the field crop, is taking on a significance more economic than religious and political. Although giving the *farilla* was and is obligatory for Fulbe and serfs, there are no specific rules with regard to how a person should dispose of the *farilla* he receives. The political significance of a Fulbe's freedom in choosing to whom to give the *farilla* should be underlined. In contrast, the serf's obligation to give the *farilla* to a particular individual validated his subordinate status. The Fulbe, in general, used the *farilla* to demonstrate their greater religiosity, in accord with their belief that eating the *farilla* they received jeopardized the possibility of having many descendants, and that eating the *farilla* of their own fields was to risk going straight to Hell.

With the termination of labor obligations the *farilla* has taken on a much greater economic importance. Land-rich Fulbe are now more likely to use the *farilla* they receive to feed their families or to build up cattle herds from its sale.[1] Another indication of the growing economic significance of individual land

1. Fulbe claim they still always give away the *farilla* from their own fields. I do not have sufficient data to verify this.

proprietorship is the stretching of the meaning of *farilla,* by asking for money from a former serf who wants to borrow land, in addition to ten percent of the harvest. Although this practice is still quite limited, it is possible it will spread in those areas where cultivable land is most scarce.

Ownership of the fields has retained much of its earlier form, but this is not true for the compound. Through a combination of the notion of usufruct and the ideology of the Guinean state that the land where a man lives belongs to him, the former serfs now regard the land on which they live and which their wives cultivate as their own. Whereas traditionally *farilla* on the corn harvest was demanded by the proprietor of the compound land, he can no longer expect it as a matter of course. Both Fulbe and former serfs are cognizant of the changing situation, but both exaggerate it. The Fulbe say they no longer receive anything from their former serfs. (This particular statement was made at the same time that one of the former serfs of the informant was bringing his *farilla.*) The former serfs claim that the Fulbe own all the land. The Fulbe's estimation of the present situation is inaccurate but may very well indicate the direction in which land tenure is evolving. The former serfs seem to be expressing grievances about their lack of full land proprietorship.

In the countryside the former serfs continue to carry out many of the same tasks that they performed when they were still serfs. Whereas in the past these labor services were rendered to the Fulbe without any payment, former serfs are now quite aware that they no longer have to work for the Fulbe except for money at relatively fixed rates. The only exception to this is "work" done in a ceremonial context.

The traditional division of craft specialties persists, but most goods and services are exchanged for money. Both Fulbe and former serfs are engaged in the new occupations—as tailors (at first primarily Fulbe but now increasingly former serfs), butchers (more likely to be former serfs), merchants, and transporters. State supported professions such as teaching and nursing tend to be dominated by Fulbe: this came about mainly during the colonial period and is now being rectified. Earlier differences in status are no longer of key importance within the new occupations and professions as the demands of making a living override social distinctions. Thus, within the area of Popodara kerosene merchants cooperated with each other during times of scarcity regardless of their origin.

The former serfs' acquisition of economic independence is nowhere more clearly marked than in the area of inheritance. Formerly a master had rights to almost all of his serf's property upon the serf's death. Although there was a great deal of variation depending on both region and an individual's relation to his master, it seems clear that this practice did not end entirely until independence. The property of former serfs is now inherited according to Islamic law, which is carried out by the major lineage of the dead person. This has further reinforced kin relationships among the serfs, giving kin groups functions and importance they lacked previously.

We have noted earlier the importance of money and the market in transforming the economic status of the former serf population. This process took place during the colonial era. The result has been that buying and selling in the market place in no way reflects the former status of serfs or Fulbe. Rather, one now finds Fulbe and former serfs competing on equal terms. Further, the national and regional authorities, in their dealings with the population, do not recognize the older distinctions.

In sum, Fulbe economic domination of their former serfs has ended, with the exception that very few former serfs own land. However, the problem of landlessness does not concern only former serfs. Cultivable land is becoming more difficult to find because of an increase in population, and an absence of change in agricultural techniques. In the area around Hollaande finding cultivable land was becoming a problem for all segments of the population, and there were several Fulbe who, because of the exhaustion of some of their fields, had to borrow land from nonkinsmen.[2] Nevertheless, the generalization that former serfs remain a landless group is true, and this fact perpetuates some of the aspects of their former subordinate status.

Dramatic changes have occurred in the political domain. Under the reign of the Fulbe chiefs prior to French colonial rule, serf villages were atomized because the ties of the serfs led outward, toward the various villages of their masters. The political realm centered around the mosque and the chief. Denied access to chieftainship and the offices of the mosque, the serfs retained responsibility for only minor affairs of their village.

Under colonial rule villages became relatively more important as a result of the various kinds of conscription imposed by the French. The French never considered making use of the social organization of the Fulbe in their administration; rather, they insisted on using villages even though these were not the functioning political units. In each serf village a *manga* was appointed by the *chef de canton* whose responsibilities were to see that the orders of the *chef de canton* and French administrators were carried out. In turn he was freed from any labor obligations to the French. The *manga* became both internally and externally the head of the village.

Since independence the political relations between Fulbe and former serfs have been transformed. This transformation has two aspects: first, with the end of colonial rule there now exists political equality of all citizens by state law. Second, the former serf villages now have control over their internal affairs. Both of these aspects are reflected in a new political institution, the committee, which is the main political unit of the Guinean state. The committee system has provided the village with the opportunity to elect officials of their own choosing to deal with their affairs. The committee has also replaced the mosque as the key local political institution.

New attitudes toward the problem posed by traditional political status differences between Fulbe and former serfs are high-

2. In this situation the Fulbe gives the *farilla* to the owner of the field.

lighted by an event that occurred during the yearly "renewal" of the committee. It was necessary to vote for a new president. There was a sharp dispute within the committee provoked by the Fulbe, who wanted a Fulbe to replace the president, a former serf. A letter was sent to the regional authorities stating that the former serfs were interested only in having one of their own become president. In stating the Fulbe position, the writer cited his lineage and village as part of his identity. The response of the officials was that those who use *gorol* (patrilineage), *lenyol* (maximal lineage), and *hodo* (village) were "racists." The writer of the letter was removed from the ten-member executive of the committee by the political officials in charge of the renewal, and another from his village was selected in his place.

It is true that in the eyes of the regional and national authorities earlier status is no longer of any importance, but it remains of some importance in the interrelations of villages and committees. To a great extent this is due to the persistence of Islam and the control of the mosque and its affairs by the Fulbe. To a lesser extent it is due to the difference in access to power between the Fulbe and former serfs during the colonial period, which remains of some importance in the countryside.

The political freeing of the serf villages has been the precondition for a restructuring of the social organization of the *runde*. The greatest social changes have not created new institutions so much as they have given former serfs greater autonomy and control over their lives. The serfs did not have functioning maximal patrilineages, but were said to belong to their masters' maximal patrilineages. The serfs' major patrilineages lacked generational depth in comparison to those of the Fulbe. The only category of serfs to know an ancestor more than seven generations back were the indigenous (*ndima*) serfs.

Today a myth of genealogical common ancestry has been developing. With the end of Fulbe domination and interposition the serfs have been freer to create and sustain their own myths of ancestry. These myths have primarily taken the form of demonstrating that their ancestors were indigenous to the area, and that they were neither war captives nor brought as serfs from other areas. It should be noted that these new genealogical myths will not serve the former serfs as the Fulbe myths served them, because political leadership, authority, and social status are no longer obtained primarily through descent. The myths serve instead to provide a new ideological charter for the new statuses of former serfs, a charter that masks their serf origins. There are two major patrilineages in the Hollaande, neither one of which has a "real" genealogical basis, i.e., a common ancestor for all or most of the members. However, through genealogical fictions there is a greater appearance of genealogical closeness than the village members themselves know to be true. Within two generations the new members might not be cognizant that the genealogical myths are "fictions."

We have also seen that one of the major functions of the major patrilineage in a Fulbe village is to regulate the marriage of its members. The Fulbe formerly had an important voice in the selection of the marriage partners of their serfs. The interest of the Fulbe in having their own serfs intermarry is clear: to insure the proper marriage partner for female serfs, and to maintain their serfs' close proximity for purposes of work. The Fulbe also received a considerable part of the bridewealth from the patrilineage of the groom. The virtual removal of the Fulbe from any decision-making in the choice of marriage partners for former serfs has strengthened the role of the major patrilineages among former serfs. Currently the patrilineage of a man is responsible both for the selection of an appropriate spouse and the wedding arrangements.

The present independence of the serfs from Fulbe control over their marriages can also be observed in the current infrequency of intermarriage between the two groups. At present there are only two former serf women from Hollaande who are married to Fulbe men. The reasons for the decline bear repeating. Formerly, no advantages from intermarriage accrued to the serfs. They did not want their daughters to marry Fulbe because it meant, in essence, losing their grandchildren. When Fulbe-serf marriage did take place, they received only minimal consent or no consent at all from the serf parents. The earlier advantages to the Fulbe of marrying a serf—little or no bridewealth, minimal kin obligations, and the political reasons for which the chiefly lineages chose to marry their serfs—have all come to an end.

There is now virtually no intermarriage between Fulbe men and former serf women in the countryside. In the towns and cities, however, former serfs who have obtained great wealth attempt to marry Fulbe women. There were two individuals from Hollaande who had married Fulbe women. They lived in cities, and did not expect to return to the village. Fulbe men commonly took serf women as lovers and concubines. The former practice continues, but concubinage no longer exists. In a revealing reversal, former serf men now very often attempt to find their lovers among Fulbe women and taunt Fulbe men by saying that they take only Fulbe women as their lovers.

Since my departure from Guinea there have been further changes in the status of women. These changes reached their culmination in the first national congress of Guinean women held on January 28, 1968. At this congress decisions were made to end the practice of polygamy, to limit the reasons for divorce, to increase the literacy of all women, and to increase and expand further the role and importance of women in the P.D.G. Unfortunately, I do not have any indication as to how the women or men of Hollaande responded to these dramatic changes in national law and policy. I am, however, skeptical about their immediate application in villages such as Hollaande. But as guides for the future, and for raising the hopes of women, such actions are of great importance, even though they will probably not affect Fulbe–former serf patterns of intermarriage.

When we turned to a consideration of ideology and religion, we reviewed many practices and beliefs that were part of traditional Fulbe society but that continue after its end. The continuing Fulbe predominance in the area of religion and ceremonies partakes more of the earlier organization of the Fouta than the other areas of life already described. This predominance continues despite the efforts of the government to end all such ideological distinctions rooted in the precolonial past.

Until the independence of Guinea, education of Fulbe children was coterminous with learning the Koran. Serfs and former serf children until recently were systematically denied such education. Ninety-five percent of the boys in Hollaande now go to Koranic school, and of the four boys circumcised during the period 1966 to 1967 all had read the Koran completely. Even when the parents are not particularly religious, they insist that their children have the Koranic education they did not have when they were children. Nevertheless, the vast majority of the children of former serfs still go to Fulbe teachers.

Not only the children have increasing access to Koranic education. Following the end of some of the labor obligations after World War I and the beginning of the commercialization of the Fulbe economy, former serfs with a religious bent could, if they had time and financial means, pursue higher Islamic studies. Some Fulbe *tiernos* became amenable to teaching former serfs. Former serfs who obtained financial means through military service in the French army were particularly able to begin the study of the Koran and its translation into Fulfulde.

A few former serfs have obtained the title of *tierno* and serve within their own villages as muezzins, but they do not assume such positions of leadership at the mosque or when in a mixed gathering of Fulbe and former serfs. The Fulbe are quite conscious of the change of status of their former serfs, but retain their Islamic "right" to dominate in sacred matters. They express this in a statement they believe comes from Islam; namely, that neither serfs nor their descendants can lead free men in prayer.

Former serfs have had one option by which to escape from this form of ideological domination by their former masters. A few former serf villages (not in the immediate area of Hollaande, however) have constructed their own mosques and have provided their own *almamy* and elders. Whether this practice will spread I do not know.

The ideological predominance of the Fulbe over their former serfs also remains significant in life-cycle ceremonies. The Fulbe still play a crucial role in the naming ceremony of a new-born child, circumcision, marriage, and death. In these situations in which the Fulbe interpose themselves between former serfs and Allah, the dominance of the Fulbe reflects their superior religious status.

In the precolonial society serfs, denied religious instruction under the political domination of the Fulbe and augmented in number through the continuing influx of new captives from the east, were regarded by the Fulbe as ignorant in the ways of Islam. However, they were practicing Muslims. With the change in political rule from the Fulbe to the French, the serfs began to look for means to change their status, but within their existing ideological system. Therefore, as the serfs found their social status improving they became better practitioners of Islam. While it is theoretically possible to ask why the serfs did not adopt the Catholicism of the French the answer is not difficult to find. Catholicism was not acceptable due to three factors: the exploitative role of the French; the difficulty, if not impossibility, of living in one's natal village as an adult without being at least a nominally practicing Muslim; and the traditional integration of the serfs into the general Fulbe way of life.

The former serfs' efforts to become more religious Muslims is nowhere more marked than in their changing attitudes toward sorcery. Sorcerers are still believed to exist, and most individuals, including the religious leaders, believe they will exist until the end of the earth. However, according to both Fulbe and former serf informants, there is a decline in the practice of sorcery in former serf villages. This is expressed in terms of numbers, that there are now fewer sorcerers than there used to be. The greater number of children now in the former serf villages is cited as clear evidence of the decreasing activity of the sorcerers.

Women, who receive a minimal religious education, have a belief system different in certain respects from that of the men. Both Fulbe and former serf women continue to believe more than do men in the existence of sorcerers, and they attribute most deaths, except for those of the very elderly, to their actions. Many Fulbe informants remarked on the irreligiosity of their wives and spoke disdainfully of their beliefs about sorcerers. While there is no definite answer as to why sorcery has declined, it is clear that it is sex-related, Fulbe women and former serf women having more in common with each other than they do with their men, and that it is related to the change in the status of the former serf men and their greater concern with Islam.

The continuation of Fulbe dominance in ideological areas is problematical. The older generation, when questioned on the role of the Fulbe, maintained traditional attitudes. The former serfs have many phrases for expressing the superiority of the Fulbe and the belief that their superiority did not come from man but from Allah. For example, they say, "Whoever says a Fulbe and a serf are equal, it's true for the blood. But for the law, that which Allah has made, they are not equal. Don't insult or under-estimate a Fulbe, no matter how poor he may be." The young be-lieve this much less than their elders, but it is difficult to predict how they will act when they become elders for two reasons. First, it is hard to predict how youths will behave when they become adults. Second, the government might intervene more directly in peasant practices that do not fit the ideology of Guinea and the P.D.G. For example, national laws have been passed recently regu-lating the possible age difference between a husband and his wife and outlawing polygyny. If enforced, these laws will produce an even greater social revolution than has yet taken place in the countryside.

The issue of social identity remains a difficult one for the former serfs at this point. In this transition period between an earlier identity and a not-yet-complete national identification, the former serfs literally do not have any clear way of referring to themselves.

The Guinean government has not only abolished the status of serfdom but has declared illegal the terms used for serfs. The terminology of address now used between Fulbe and former serfs is one reflection of the present changing, although still contradictory, state of social relationships between men of formerly unequal status.

Before and during French colonial rule the serfs were referred to as *mattyudo,* or *kaado.* However, with the *de facto* and *de jure* abolishment of serfdom these terms cannot be and are not used (except in certain circumstances). Kin terms are now often employed. This is especially true of the term *kau* (which denotes mother's brother, a relationship of love and support). Used between Fulbe and former serfs it expresses a feigned closeness, a feigned genealogical relationship. Although *kau* may be used reciprocally, it is more often than not employed only by the Fulbe in addressing former serfs. The emotional content is not much different from what Powdermaker describes for the term uncle when used by whites to address blacks in Indianola, Mississippi (1966: 151).

A former serf still refers to the Fulbe who in former times would have been his master as "my Fulbe" (*pullo ang*) and to his wife as "my Fulbe's wife" (*fulamusa*). A Fulbe man is usually addressed by prefacing his name by *modi* or *modibo,* now roughly equivalent to our *mister* or *sir.* Fulbe do not use these terms with former serfs, nor do the latter use them when addressing one another.

Religious titles are always applied to Fulbe who achieve them, but only with reluctance to former serfs. There were two former serfs in Hollaande who had obtained the title of *tierno,* but the Fulbe in the area referred to them by the lesser title of *karamoko;* the former serfs employed the full title. Former serfs who served in the French army and who achieved any position at all—usually sergeant or corporal—are referred to by their former army ranks. In the case of those who have achieved the status of *karamoko* or *tierno,* it is a slight to call them by their army titles.

The way former serfs refer to themselves is in a state of flux, The traditional term *mattyudo* is clearly unsatisfactory, and the earlier status differences do not permit the former serfs to refer to themselves as Fulbe.[3] The most frequently employed usage is simply the word for an occupant of a serf village, *rundedyo*. The alternative is *baledyo* (someone who is black), which has a connotation of inferiority when referring to someone of serf ancestry.[4]

As one might expect, there are differences in the usage of terms of identity depending on the age of the individual concerned. Older former serfs use *mattyudo* in describing themselves and their relative position in the world given to them by Allah. They also employ the term as a compliment to younger children who are particularly hard-working, strong, and relatively uneducated, characteristics formerly associated with the serfs. Younger former serfs are ashamed, if not angry, about their background and refer to themselves most often as *baledyo*. They are searching for an identity independent of the Fulbe. Older Fulbe men still use *mattyudo*, generally in an insulting way, toward former serfs and their children. Younger Fulbe are embarrassed to employ the term.

The Guinean state has taken the position that within the Republic of Guinea there are no longer any "tribal" differences or status distinctions, but only the Guinean people. The P.D.G. has formulated a detailed and advanced program to eliminate the remnants of traditionalism or colonialism in the new society. The attitude of the Guinean political leaders in the face of invidious distinctions between Fulbe and former serfs has been to deny them any semblance of legality and to term those who raise them as "racists" or "tribalists."

An important step taken by the government in the creation of a

3. In the cities former serfs refer to themselves as Fulbe and attempt to hide their origin.

4. The word is also used to refer to other peoples whom the Fulbe think are darker than themselves. It is not known to what extent the Fulbe were influenced by the French, who considered them less dark and less "negroid" than other African peoples.

national identity has been the establishment of schools in the countryside. The Guineans have already developed some of their own textbooks which emphasize Guinean history and culture and the equality of all the peoples of Guinea. Moreover, close supervision is given to the teachers to see that they do not lapse into earlier Fulbe beliefs about the negative qualities of the former serfs. As more children go to school, many of the attitudes of the Fulbe about former serfs, and of the former serfs about Fulbe, should change still further.

The different languages and traditions within the country, however, are given recognition and support. These differences are being used to help create a national identity by means of the current alphabetization program. In this program it is planned that Guineans will learn the other major languages of Guinea aside from their own and French. The major languages of Guinea (Fulfulde, Malinke, Soussou, and Kissi) will have the status of national languages. An alphabet has been developed which is being used to create a literature accessible to everyone in the various national tongues. Other institutions have been created to support the cultural traditions. The best example is the biannual national dance competition in which performers from all over Guinea develop and perform art forms that reflect both their own heritage and their experiences within the new Guinean nation.

The forces acting on the Fouta-Djallon as a whole irreversibly changed the basis of the economic wealth and political position of the Fulbe. This has led to convergence of the formerly stratified society. The termination of legitimate Fulbe chieftainship and the decline of serfdom during the colonial period weakened the strata differences among the Fulbe themselves. Thus the earlier social and political distinctions based on descent group and rank have lost most of their significance. With the legal abolition of serfdom and its political and social privileges, the process of convergence of the Fulbe and former serfs has been accelerated. Further, the introduction of money and markets emmeshed all segments of Fulbe society in a money economy. Thus a peasantry has been created whose economy remains geared to self-subsistence while it serves as a major supplier of labor.

In the ideological sphere a different kind of convergence is taking place. The former serfs are adopting the ideology and life-style of the Fulbe which were denied to them as serfs. Those features of serf life that epitomized their inferior postion, such as sorcery and the lack of Islamic education, are being consciously changed. This is leading to a growing similarity in life-style between the Fulbe and former serfs.

The *Parti Démocratique de Guinée* is attempting to create a national identity for all the people of Guinea. This identity is based on the historic role that each people has played and on what each can further contribute to the building of the Guinean nation. At the same time, the common aspirations and goals of all Guineans, as an African nation, are emphasized. As of now it appears that the present trend in the Fouta-Djallon will continue until there is commercialization of agriculture or until the introduction of industry. What will happen in the future depends a great deal on what further economic and ideological changes the Guinean government can bring about in the Fouta-Djallon. In my view, the transformation of peasants into socialists will be far more difficult than the transformation of serfs into peasants or the transformation of Guinea from colony to independent nation.

Appendix I

FULBE KINSHIP TERMINOLOGY

A. Descent on Ego's father's lines
 I. The generation of ego's father
  Fa—baaba or beng
  FaBr—usually bappa, sometimes baaba or beng
  FaSi—yaiye
  FaFaBrSo—bappa
  FaFaBrDa—yaiye
  FaFaFaBrSoSo—bappa
  FaFaFaBrSoDa—yaiye
 II. The generation of ego's grandfather
  FaFa—soro or baaba—or soroang ka baaba
  FaFaBr—soro
  FaFaSi—paati
  FaFaFaBrSo—soro
  FaFaFaBrDa—paati
 III. The generation of ego's great-grandfather
  FaFaFa—mama
  FaFaFaBr—mama
  FaFaFaSi—mama
 IV. Other generations above
  Ancestor—mama
 V. Ego's generation
  Brother—none
  Elder brother (same or different mothers, same or different fathers if mother the same.) koto, mownyiraawo
  Younger brother—minyiraawo
  Sister—younger—minyiraawo, older—dyaya (The word bandiraawo can be used by one to refer to his [or her] siblings of the opposite sex.)
  FaBrSo—younger—minyiraawo, older—koto or mownyiraawo (for both men and women)

FaBrDa—younger—minyiraawo, older—dyaya
FaFaBrSoSo—same terms as for FaBrSo
FaFaBrSoDa—same terms as for FaBrDa
VI. The generation of ego's son
Son—biddo (child), gorko (male)
Da—biddo (child), dyiwo (female)
BrSo—biddo
BrSo—f.s.—yaiye or his name (Reciprocal terminology for
generation—must call FaBr bappa. He in turn calls you by
your name, or bappa.
BrDa—biddo
BrDa—f.s.—yaiye
FaBrSoSo—m.s.—biddo
FaBrSoSo—f.s.—yaiye or his name
FaBrSoDa—m.s.—biddo
FaBrSoDa—f.s.—biddo
FaFaBrSoSoSo—biddo
FaFaBrSoSoSo—f.s.—yaiye or his name
FaFaBroSoDa—biddo
FaFaBrSoSoDa—f.s.—biddo
VII. The generation of ego's grandchildren
SoSo—tanyiraawo or his name
SoDa—tanyiraawo
BrSoSo—tanyiraawo
BrSoDa—tanyiraawo
FaBrSoSoSo—tanyiraawo
FaBrSoSoDa—tanyiraawo
VIII. The generation of ego's great grandchildren
SoSoSo—dyatiraawo
SoSoDa—dyatiraawo
IX. The other generations under—great great grandchildren
SoSoSoSo—kukku
B. Descent of ego's mother's lines
I. The generation of ego's mother
Mo—neene, yumma (polite form)
MoBr—kau or badiraawo
MoSi—neene
MoFaBrSo—kau or badiraawo

MoFaBrDa—neene

MoFaFaBrSoSo—kau

MoFaFaBrSoDa—neene

II. The generation of ego's maternal grandfather

MoFa—soro (ka neene)

MoFaBr—soro

MoFaSi—paati

III. The generation of ego's maternal great-grandfather

MoFaFa—mama (usually said mama soro)

MoFaFaBr—mama

MoFaFaSi—mama

IV. Ego's generation

MoBrSo—dendang

MoBrDa—dendang

MoSiSo—m.s. reemiraawo or terms for siblings

MoSiSo—f.s.—reemiraawo

MoSiDa—reemiraawo

MoFaBrSoSo—dendang

MoFaFaBrSoSoSo—dendang

C. Ego's kinfolk by affinity

I. The Generation of ego's father

FaWi—neene or yumma

FaBrWi—neene

FaSiHu—bappa

MoSiHu—kau

II. The generation of ego's grandfather

FaFaWi—paati

MoFaWi—soro

III. Ego's generation

BrWi—dyekiraawo or beingu (wife)

BrWi—f.s.—younger—esiraawo, older—kenang

SiHu—m.s.—younger—esiraawo, older—kenang

SiHu—f.s.—younger—esiraawo, older—kenang

FaBrDaHu—esiraawo or kenang (depends on age)

FaBrSoWi—same as BrWi

FaSiSoWi—for wife of cross cousins—if the cousin is older
than ego, ego calls the wife, "my wife"; if cousin is
younger than ego, ego calls her esiraawo

FaSiDaHu—f.s. beingu or esiraawo
MoSiSoWi—m.s.—kenang or esiraawo
MoSiDaHu—f.s.—esiraawo or beingu
MoBrDaHu—f.s.—kenang or esiraawo
MoBrSoWi—m.s.—esiraawo or beingu
FaFaBrSoSoWi—m.s.—dyekiraawo or beingu

IV. The Generation of ego's son
SoWi—esiraawo
DaHu—esiraawo
BrSoWi—esiraawo
SiSoWi—esiraawo
BrDaHu—esiraawo
SiDaHu—kau
FaBrSoSoWi—esiraawo
FaBrSoDaHu—esiraawo

V. The generation of ego's grandchildren
SoSoWi—soro
SoDaHu—soro
DaDaHu—soro
DaSoWi—soro
BrSoSoWi—soro
SiSoSoWi—soro

D. Ego's Wife's Kin
I. Wife's parents' generation
WiFa—esiraawo
WiMo—esiraawo
WiFaBr—esiraawo
WiFaSi—esiraawo
WiMoBr—esiraawo
WiFaFaBrSoSo—esiraawo
HuFa—esiraawo
HuMo—esiraawo
HuFaBr—esiraawo
HuFaSi—esiraawo
HuMoBr—esiraawo
HuFaFaBrSoSo—dyatiraawo

II. The second generation above ego
WiFaFa—soro

255

WiFaFaBr—soro
WiFaMo—paati
WiMoFa—soro
HuFaFa—soro
HuFaFaBr—soro
HuMoFa—soro
HuFaMo—paati

III. Ego's generation

WiSi—younger than wife—kenang, older than wife—esiraawo

WiFaBrDa—younger than wife—kenang older than wife—esiraawo

WiMoSiDa—esiraawo or beingu

WiSiHu—name or esiraawo or kenang

WiFaBrDaHu—name

WiMoSiDaHu—name

WiBr—younger than wife—kenang, older than wife—esiraawo

WiBrWi—name

WiFaBrSo—same as WiBr

WiMoSiSo—kenang or esiraawo

WiFaSiSo—kenang or esiraawo

WiFaSiDa—esiraawo or beingu

WiMoBrDa—esiraawo or beingu

HuBr—Hu—dyekiraawo ang (my husband)

HuSi—younger than husband—kenang, older than husband—esiraawo

HuFaBrSo—same as HuBr

HuMoSiSo—younger than ego—kenang, older—esiraawo

HuFaSiSo—younger—esiraawo, older—beingu

HuMoBrDa—younger—esiraawo, older—beingu

HuMoSiDa—younger than ego—kenang, older—esiraawo

HuFaBrDa—younger than ego—kenang, older—esiraawo

HuWi—nauliraawo (co-wives of same husband)

HuBrWi—petyiraawo (wives of two brothers)

Appendix II

A NOTE ON THE FIELDWORK

One might ask why a former serf village was chosen for this study. I wanted a Fulbe village. A former serf village was chosen by chance. There are no obvious physical or visible signs to distinguish former serf from Fulbe villages. Only much later in my stay did I come to perceive the differences between the two. The differences were more the carriage of the body, dress, and bearing than actual physical differences. The government officials who took me to visit villages were not willing to discuss social distinctions which are no longer supposed to exist. Thus when I asked those accompanying me whether Hollaande was a Fulbe village, the answer was an unhesitating yes.

Fieldwork always includes various elements of chance. In this case living in a former-serf village gave me access to a population I would not have had if I had been in a Fulbe village. The former serfs suffered most from French colonial rule, so they are much more suspicious and reserved with whites than are their former masters. If I had been living in a Fulbe village, they would have classed me with all the other whites who hobnobbed with the chiefs and would have assumed I would adopt the attitude of the Fulbe toward them. By living in a former serf village I avoided these problems. However, it did not close off the world of the Fulbe to me. Exactly why this was I am not sure. It was due, at least in part, to the Fulbe's desire (particularly on the part of the elders) to indicate that they knew more about the history and religion of the Fouta-Djallon than did their former serfs. They were also anxious to let me know their views in order to balance the opinions of the former serfs.

Information was obtained through informants, participant-observation, and research in the National Archives of Guinea and Senegal. Most of my informants were inhabitants of the village of Hollaande, and were of every age and sex category—children, young men and women, adults, and elders. In addition, I interviewed some former

257

serfs of neighboring villages. I also had several Fulbe informants. Most Fulbe informants were elders from nearby villages. This was necessary because I was most interested in gathering information on the history and social organization of the area prior to and during the early part of French rule. The two young men who worked with me as assistants and translators were Fulbe. I also did an economic survey of Hollaande to obtain basic information on the amount of seed planted, the extent of marketing, the extent of labor employment, and the number of animals. The survey was taken of every male household head in the village.

Participant-observation made up the most extensive—the time-con-suming—part of the fieldwork. This catch-all category includes many hours spent with friends, and attendance at all ceremonies, occasions marked by cooperative labor, markets, and so forth. I found that to ask questions during ceremonies was impolite and disruptive; to ask questions during work prevented the work from being completed. Participant-observation meant observation to verify predictions about expected behavior (for example, between father and son at public occasions), or raising further questions (why did X behave to Y in such a manner, or why did X bring so much food and Y none at all).

The former serfs and their village could not be studied in isolation. The relation of both individuals and groups to the dominant social group had to be studied, because there were, and are, many essential ties and relations with the Fulbe. Therefore, some time was spent in the surrounding villages where the former masters of the villagers of Hollaande lived.

In order to obtain the needed historical information I read most of the archives available for Labe catalogued in the Institut Nationale de Recherches et Documentation de la République de la Guinée at Conakry. The most valuable of the archives were the monthly reports of the French regional governors. These reports were written spe-cifically for other administrators and, in their candor, were the most interesting. Of the various administrators Gilbert Vieillard stands out for his interest in all aspects of the life of the Fulbe. His most valuable collection of manuscripts is available at the Institut Fonda-mental D'Afrique Noire at Dakar. Although it would have been preferable to have travelled more in other areas of the Fouta-Djallon, this was not possible. However, for additional comparative data I have used the work of Gilbert Vieillard from the region of Timbo (where the head of the entire Fouta-Djallon formerly resided), the 1954 French Demographic Study for the region of Pita, and the work of the geographer Jacques Richard-Molard, who travelled widely in the Fouta.

in Dantari (?).

Glossary of Fulbe Words

AFO—the oldest son

AINDE (NDE), *pl.* AYƊE (ƊE)—valley

ALLUWAL (NGAL) *pl.* ALLUUDYE (ƊE)—a small plank of wood on which one writes; ceremony making completion of Koran

ALMAMY—ALMAAMI (O), *pl.* ALMUƁƁE (ƁE)—political and religious head of the Fouta-Djallon; the leader of a mosque. (I have used the French spelling in the text, although I have listed the correct spelling here.)

ARDOOWO, (O), *pl.* ARDOOƁE (ƁE)—those who were brought as captives, in contrast to those who were born as serfs in the Fouta

ARTIRGOL DYOMBA—part of the steps involved in marriage; the return of the bride to her natal village to celebrate the consummation of the marriage

BA—first stage of religious education

BAABA/BENG (O)—father, papa

BAILLO (O), *pl.* WAILUƁE (ƁE)—blacksmith

BALEDYO (O)—someone who is black

BANDIRAAWO (O) *pl.* BANDIRAAƁE (ƁE)—sibling(s) of the opposite sex

BAREDYELI (O)—the circumciser, or the clitoridectomist

ƁEINGUURE (NDE)—translated by Sow as *family;* I use *household*

BOLONDA (O)—neighborhood, with implication of kin connections

BONƊO (O)—someone who is rotten

BOOBO (O), *pl.* BOOBOOƁE (ƁE)—a baby, babyhood

DABA (O)—the all-purpose hoe

DEBEERE(NDE)—a large indigenously made basket

DEEWOL (NGO)—matrilateral kindred, the maternal line

DENABO (O)—the ceremony held one week after the birth of a child to announce its name

DENDANG (O)—cross-cousin

DIA (O)—payment for having spilled the blood of another Fulbe

DIWAL (NGAL), *pl.* DIWE (ɓE)—the indigenous province

DOLOKKE BAABA—literally the robe of the father, but refers to the part of the bridewealth that goes to the father of the bride

DOTITUNGAL (NGAL)—those gifts of household items given to a newly married daughter by her mother

DYAARUGOL—to chant religious chants; DYAAROORE (nde), the religious chants

DYAGAFARA (o)—the kinsmen of the *misside* chief

ɓYAMAL NGAL—the giving and accepting of gifts that marks the acceptance of a coming marriage between two individuals

DYANANO (o)—a nonkinsmen or stranger

DYAYA (o)—older sister

DYELIBA (o)—drummer or, more generally, entertainer

ɓYIIɓYANG GOOTANG—those of one blood, referring to those related on the paternal line. Blood symbolizes paternal relations, milk maternal ones

DYINNA (o), *pl.* DYINNAADYI (ɓI)—devil(s) or spirit(s)

DYIWO (o)—unmarried girl, virgin

DYOKKUDE ENƊANG—literally to follow one's kin ties, refers specifically to the practice of intensive visiting at the start of the new year

DYOM BENTE—the holiday celebrating the new year

DYOM GALLE—household head, and since colonial times he who owns the land of the household

DYOM GOOTO—two serfs in close relation by virtue of belonging to the same master

DYULɓE (ɓE)—members of the Islamic faith

DYULDE DONKING—the holiday of the month of Donking

DYULDI (ɓI)—the Muslim spirits

DYULIIRDE (NDE), *pl.* DYULLIRɓE (ɓE)—mosque

ESIRAAWO (o), ESIRAAɓE (ɓE)—affines

FAATUNDE (NDE)—death, funeral

FANDA (o)—gift; FANDA FUTU—money given to women who accompany the bride to her marriage

FARRILLA (o)—obligatory religious duties; the ten-percent payment on all grain crops

FIDYO (NGO), *pl.* FIDYOODYI (ɗI)—circumcision

FIRUGOL (OR TIMINGOL TAFSIR)—to translate the Koran from Arabic into Fulfulde

FOYONG (O)—leaves gathered for a woman's garden to be used as mulch

FULAMUSA (O)—almost slang for a serf's master's wife, "my Fulbe's wife"

FULASSO (O)—a Fulbe village without a mosque

FURE (NDE)—corpse

GALLE (DE)—compound; has both a physical and social referent

GARANKEDYO (O), *pl.* GARANKƁE (ƁE)—leatherworker

GOREE/GOREEDYO (O) *pl.* GOREEƁE (ƁE)—age-mates

GOROL (NGOL), *pl.* GORI (ɗI)—patrilineage

GUDDYO (O)—thief

HAIRE (NDE), *pl.* KAAƊYE (ƊE)—stone; cultivable mountain land

HOƊO (NGO), KOƊEELI (ɗI)—hamlet, village

HOORE (NDE)—head

HUMPITOOƁE (ƁE)—those who "seek news" from the bride's family

IIDI (O)—prayers held on special occasions when many people attend

INTERE—weaning period of a child

JIHAD/DYIHAD (O)—holy war against pagan peoples (Common Arabic spelling has been used rather than phonetic Fulbe pronunciation).

KAAƊO (O), *pl.* HAAƁE (BE)—serf

KARAMOKO (O)—religious leader

KASANGE—the robe used to dress a corpse

KAU (O)—mother's brother

KAUTAL (NGAL), *pl.* KAUTE (ƊE)—neighborhood

KAUTITAL (NGAL) *pl.* KAUTITE (ƊE)—meeting or assembly

KEEFEERO (O), *pl.* HEEFERƁE (ƁE)—pagan, infidel

KEEFEERI (ɗI)—heathen spirits

KENANG—younger siblings of one's spouse

KHALDUYAAƁE (KHALDUYANKE)—chiefly lineage of Labe

KHALIYAAƁE—patrilineage at Popodara

KILE—to have kinsmen and friends assist one in the fields

KILASAKKE—major gift formerly given to the serfs of the father of a new bride

KORƊO(O), *pl.* HORƁE (ƁE)—female serf

KORTUGOL—the saying of select verses to take vengeance and cause harm to any enemy

KORUNG—small basket

KOSANG (NDANG)—sour milk

KUMMABITE (O) *pl.* KUMMABITEEDYI (ƊI)—wealth paid to the chief of a *misside* upon the death of a Fulbe

KUMPITAL (NGAL)—news-seeking, part of the marriage steps

KURAHI (NGI)—a large tree; bears eatable fruit; the abode of spirits

KURKAADE—to serve, work as a domestic

KURKAADU (NDU)—domesticity, generally female

LAAMU (NGU), *pl.* LAAMUUDYI (ƊI)—sovereignty, chieftainship, political power

LAMƊO/LANƊO (O) *pl.* LAMƁE (ƁE)—chief, sovereign

LANDITAL (NGAL)—the re-asking following the dyamal

LASSILIƁE (ƁE)—free men, members of the free maximal patrilineages. Also pronounced LASLIIƁE. Can have implication of pure, authentic, and noble

LENYOL (NGOL), *pl.* LENYI/LEƊƊYI (ƊI)—singular means geographically dispersed patrilineal agamous named group. In plural can mean people, nation, or ethnic groups

LOUNDU (NDU)—marriage within the patrilineage

MAAKAGOL—to speak, using the polite and respectful form

MAAMAARE (NDE), *pl.* MAAMAADYE (ƁE)—an older woman; an older woman who has not had children, and, by virtue of that, is often thought to be a sorceress.

MANGA (O)—political leader of a serf village

MARGA (O)—same meaning as *fulasso*

MATTYAGAAKU (NGU)—servitude

MATTYUƊO (O), *pl.* MATTYUƁE (ƁE)—serf

MBATULA (O)—courtier of a chief

MBILEDYO (O)—sorcerer; someone who cures illness, or discovers other sorcerers

MINYIRAAWO (O), *pl.* MINYIRAAƁE (ƁE)—younger sibling

MISSIDE (O)—village that has a mosque; parish; villages having a common mosque; or a common political chief

MODI/MODIBO—term of polite address equivalent to *sir* or *master*

MOKOBAR (O)—male adulthood

MOWƊO GOROL—eldest active man who serves as head of a major patri-lineage

MOWNYIRAAWO—older brother

MUSIƊƊO (O), *pl.* MUSIƁƁE (ƁE)—kinsman

MUSIDAL (NGAL)—kinship

NAAMU (O)—custom, tradition

NAƁUGOL INDE—to bring the name of the new born to the mother's kinsmen

NASI (O)—washing off religious words to ward off danger or to cure illness

NDANTARI (NDI)—plains

NDIMA—indigenous, usually in reference to serfs

NEENE (O)—mother, mama

NGERIANKE, *pl.* NGERIAAƁE—a maximal free Fulbe patrilineage

NGERU (NDU)—prayer site usually marked by stones; stone courtyard by the side of or in front of Fulbe homes

NGESA (MBANG)—field

NYAAMUGOL—to eat; or to eat someone as in sorcery

NYAAWOORE (O)—judge

NYAMAKALA—someone who entertains through verbal skill in telling funny stories or mocking

NYANEDYO/NYANE (O)—sorcerer

PEERA (O)—marriage ceremony

PULLO (O), *pl.* FULƁE (ƁE)—how Fulfulde speakers refer to themselves

RABBINGOL—to sing traditional Fulbe New Year's song

RAGNAADYO (O) *pl.* RAGNAAƁE (ƁE)—a maximal patrilineage at Popo-dara and Labe

REEMIRAAWO (O), *pl.* REEMIRAAƁE (ƁE)—female parallel cousins

RIMDINGOL/RINDINGOL—to liberate, to emancipate; also the name of the ceremony at which a serf became Fulbe

RUNDE/RUMDE (NDE), *pl.* DUNE (ƁE)—serf village

SAARE (NDE), *pl.* TYA'E (ɓE)—large town or city

SADAKA (O) *pl.* SADAKAADYI (ɗI)—sacrifice

SAGATAA (O), *pl.* SAGATAAɓE (ɓE)—young man

SALA (O)—head, or top of a house

SALAATU (O)—prayer

SALADYANG (NDANG)—sack of salt involved in marriage exchange

SALLI (O)—muezzin

SANNYOWO (O), *pl.* SANNYOɓE (ɓE)—cloth-weaver

SANYOWO (O)—basket-weaver

SELEYAAɓE—a patrilineage at Popodara

SEEDIGAL (NGAL)—separation, divorce

SEEDUGOL—to separate, to divorce from someone

SEEWOɓE (ɓE)—those who sit on the side

SHAIKU/SAIXU—sheikh, scholar, descendant of Muhammad

SIGI—second stage of religious education

SOODUGOL—to buy

SOOGE—those gifts given by the father to his daughter at her marriage

SUKA (U)—young men, but circumcised; younger than *sagataa*

SUNNA—religious practices recommended but not required; the sacrifice of the goat or sheep at Tabaski

SUNTURE (O)—woman's garden

SUUDU (NDU), *pl.* TYUUƊI (ƊI)—house/home; minimal lineage

SUUFA/SUUFADYO, *pl.* SUUFAAɓE (ɓE)—serf soldiers of the chief

SUUMAYEE—Fulbe month and word for Ramadan

TALKURU (NDU), *pl.* TALKI (ƊI)—amulettes

TANDE (NDE)—courtyard

TARIKA—written history

TEDDUNGAL (NGAL)—respect

TEFUGOL—to inquire

TENGE—the part of the bridewealth that becomes the property of the bride

TIERNO—religious title of respect and accomplishment

TORAGOL—to ask, to solicit, to ask specifically for marriage

TUUBUGOL—to repent, in the sense of assuming religious obligations

TYOBBAL—ritual food eaten on many religious occasions, made of rice, honey (or sugar), and corn

WARUGOL—to kill

WORTOWAL (NGAL)—sickle

WOULUGOL—to speak, to tell

WUDERE NEENE—literally mother's skirt; but in the context of marriage, the bride's mother's share of the bridewealth

YEEYUGOL—to sell

YETTORE—the "particlans" according to Cantrelle and Dupire; the names of the Fulbe

YUMMA (o)—mother

A Note on Orthography:

I have used the international phonetic alphabet with the following exceptions: where words have become common in French (e.g., *almamy* or *tierno*) I have kept their French spelling. I have not employed "ŋ" since it is not phonemic with "ng", I have utilized "ny" rather than "ñ". I have indicated long and short vowels and consonants which are phonemic in Fulfulde. The parenthesized words after the Fulbe indicate the noun class (e.g., *musidal* (*ngal*)).

Bibliography

Abun-Nasr, J. M. 1965. *The Tijaniyya: A Sufi Order in the Modern World.* London: Oxford University Press.

Almeida, D. 1962. *Premier Répertoire des Archives Nationales de Guinée, Série A–Série N* (1720–1935). Berlin: Academie Verlag.

Ameillon, B. 1964. *La Guinée: Bilan d'une Indépendance.* Paris: François Maspero.

Anonymous. 1966. "A Propos de l'Impôt." In A.I. Sow (ed.), *La Femme, La Vache, La Foi: Ecrivains et Poètes du Fouta Djallon.* Paris: Julliard Press.

Arçin, A. 1911. *Histoire de la Guinée Française.* Paris: Challamel Press.

Attwood, W. 1967. *The Reds and the Blacks: A Personal Adventure.* New York: Harper & Row.

Bascom, W. R. 1962. "Tribalism, Nationalism and Pan-Africanism." *Annals of the American Academy of Political and Social Science* 342: 22–29.

Bénot, Y. 1968. *Les Idéologies des Indépendances Africaines.* Paris: François Maspero.

Boutillier, P., P. Cantrelle, J. Causse, C. Laurent, and R. N'Doyle. 1962. *La Moyenne Vallée de Sénégal.* Paris: Presses Universitaires de France.

Brokensha, D. and C. Erasmus. 1969. "African 'Peasants' and Community Development." In D. Brokensha and M. Pearsall (eds.), *The Anthropology of Development in Sub-Saharan Africa.* Society for Applied Anthropology, Monograph 10.

Butcher, D. A. P. 1964. "The Role of the Fulbe in the Urban Life and Economy of Lunsar, Sierre Leone: Being a Study of the Adaptation of an Immigrant Group." (Ph.D. dissertation, University of Edinburgh.)

Caillié, R. 1830. *Travels through Central Africa to Timbuctoo and across the Great Desert to Morocco. Performed in the Years 1824–1828.* Vols. I–II. London: Henry Colburn.

Cantrelle, P. and M. Dupire. 1964. "L'Endogamie des Peuls du Fouta-Djallon." *Recherches Africaines: Etudes Guinéennes N.S.* Conakry.

Cohen, R. and J. Middleton. 1970. "Introduction." In R. Cohen and J. Middleton (eds.), *From Tribe to Nation in Africa: Studies in Incorporation Processes.* Scranton, Pennsylvania: Chandler.

Crowder, M. 1968. *West Africa Under Colonial Rule.* Evanston, Illinois: Northwestern University Press.

Dalton, G. 1962. "Traditional Production in Primitive African Economies." *Quarterly Journal of Economics* 76: 360–378.

1964. "The Development of Subsistence and Peasant Economies in

Africa. *International Social Science Journal* 16: 378–389.

1969. "Theorectical Issues in Economic Anthropology." *Current Anthropology* 10(1): 63–80.

1972. "Peasantries in Anthropology and History." *Current Anthropology* 13 (3–4): 385–416.

De Decker, H. 1967. *Nation et Développement Communautaire en Guinée et au Sénégal.* The Hague: Mouton Press.

Demougeot, A. 1964. *Notes sur l'Organisation Politique et Administrative du Labé avant et depuis l'Occupation Française.* Dakar: Institut Fondamental d'Afrique Noire, Mémoire VI.

Derman, William. 1972. "Peasants: The African Exception?" *American Anthropologist* 74 (3) 779–782.

Diallo, O. P. 1961. "Evolution Sociale chez les Peuls du Fouta-Djallon." *Recherches Africaines: Etudes Guinéennes N.S.* Conakry.

Dobert, M. 1970. "Liberation and the Women of Guinea." *Africa Report* 15: 7.

Donald, L. 1968. "Changes in Yalunka Social Organization: A Study of Adaptation to a Changing Cultural Environment." (Ph.D. dissertation, University of Oregon) Ann Arbor: University Microfilms.

Doutressoulle, G. 1947. *L'Elévage en Afrique Occidentale Française.* Paris: Larose.

Dupire, M. 1962 *Peuls Nomades. Etude Descriptive des Wodaabe du Sahel Nigérien.* Paris: Institut d'Ethnologie.

1963. "Matériaux pour l'Etude de l'endogamie des Peuls du Cercle de Kédougou (Sénégal oriental)." *Bulletin d'Anthropologie de la Société de Paris,* Vol. 5, 11th s.

Fallers, L. 1961. "Are African Cultivators to be Called Peasants?" *Current Anthropology* 2: 108–110.

Firth, R. 1963. *Elements of Social Organization.* Boston: Beacon Press.

1964. "Capital, Saving, and Credit in Peasant Societies." In R. Firth and B. S. Yamey (eds.), *Capital, Saving, and Credit in Peasant Societies.*
1969. "Social Structure and Peasant Economy: The Influence of Social Structure Upon Peasant Economies." In C. Wharton, Jr. (ed.), *Subsistence Agriculture and Economic Development.* Chicago: Aldine.

Forde, D. 1964. *Yako Studies.* London: Oxford University Press.

Fortes, M. 1949. *The Web of Kinship Among the Tallensi.* London: Oxford University Press.

Fried, M. 1968. *The Political Evolution of Society.* New York: Random House.

Froelich, J. C. 1954. "Le Commandement et l'Organisation Sociale chez les Fulbe de l'Adamoua (Cameroun)." *Etudes Camerounaises* Numbers 45–46: 5–91.

Gluckman, M. 1965. *Politics, Law, and Ritual in Tribal Society.* Chicago: Aldine.

Goldschmidt, W. and E. Kunkel. 1971. "The Structure of the Peasant Family." *American Anthropologist* 73: 1058–1076.

Hallett, R. (ed.). 1965. *The Penetration of Africa*. Vol. II New York: Praeger

Halpern, J. and J. Broode. 1968. "Peasant Society: Economic Changes and Revolutionary Transformation." In B. J. Siegel (ed.), *Biennial Review of Anthropolgy: 1967*.

Harris, J. E. 1968. "The Kingdom of Fouta Diallon." (Ph.D. dissertation, Northwestern University.) Ann Arbor: University Microfilms.

Hopen, C. E. 1958. *The Pastoral Fulbe Family in Gwandu*. London: Oxford University Press.

Johnson, R. W. 1970. "Sékou Touré and the Guinean Revolution." *African Affairs* 69: 350–365.

Joshi, N. R., E. A. McLaughlin, and R. W. Phillips 1957. *Types and Breeds of Cattle*. Rome: F.A.O.

Laing, A. G., 1825. *Travels in the Timanneee, Kooranko, and Soolima Countries*. London: J. Murray.

Lestringant, J. 1969. *Les Pays de Guider au Cameroun: Essai d'Histoire Régionale*. Cameroon: Government of the Republic of Cameroon.

Levy, R. 1957. *The Social Structure of Islam*. Cambridge: Cambridge University Press.

Lombard, J. 1967. *Autorités Traditionnelles et Pouvoirs Européens en Afrique Noire*. Paris: Armand Colin.

Marshall, G. 1964. "Women, Trade and the Yoruba Family." (Ph.D. dissertation, Columbia University.) Ann Arbor: University Microfilms.

Marty, P. 1921. *Islam en Guinée*. Paris: Leroux.

Mercier, P. 1965. "On The Meaning of 'Tribalism' in Black Africa." In P. Van den Berghe (ed.), *Africa: Social Problems in Change and Conflict*. San Francisco: Chandler Press.

Mission Démographique de Guinée. 1955. *Etudes Agricoles et Economiques de Quatre Villages de Guinée Française 1. Futa-Djalon, Hameaux de Dantari*. Haut Commissariat de l'Afrique Occidentale Française.

Mollien, G. 1820. *Travels in the Interior of Africa to the Sources of the Senegal and Gambia*. London: Henry Colburn.

Morgenthau, R. S. 1964. *Political Parties in French-Speaking West Africa*. London: Oxford University Press.

Muhammed. 1956. *The Koran*. Hammondsworth: Penguin.

Murdock, G. P. 1967. *The Ethnographic Atlas*. Pittsburgh: University of Pittsburgh Press.

Nadel, S. F. 1942. *A Black Byzantium: The Kingdom of Nupe in Nigeria*. London: Oxford University Press.

———. 1954. *Nupe Religion*. London: Oxford University Press.

Newbury, C. W. (ed.). 1965. *British Policy Towards West Africa: Select Documents 1786–1874*. London: Oxford University Press.

Neiboer, R. 1900. *Slavery as an Industrial System*. The Hague: Martinus Nijhoff.

Noirot, E. 1882. *A Travers le Fouta-Djallon et la Bambouc*. Paris: Flammarion.

Portères, R. 1964. "Notes de Toponymie Rurale au Fouta-Djallon." *Recherches Africaines: Etudes Guinéennes N.S.* I–IV. Conakry.

Powdermaker, H. 1966. *Stranger and Friend*. New York: Norton.

Rahman, R. 1968. *Islam*. Garden City, N.Y.: Anchor-Doubleday.

Révolution Démocratique Africaine, No. 22 (Organ of the Parti Démocratique de Guinée). Conakry, 1968.

Reining, P. 1970. "Social Factors and Food Production in an East African Peasant Society: The Haya." In P. McLoughlin (ed.), *African Food Production Systems: Cases and Theory*. Baltimore: Johns Hopkins Press.

Ribeiro, D. 1968. *The Civilizational Process*. Washington D.C.: Smithsonian Institute Press.

Richard-Molard, J. 1944. "Essai sur la vie paysanne au Fouta-Djallon." In P. Pélissier (ed.), *Hommage à Jacques Richard-Molard (1913–1951)*. Special Issue of *Présence Africaine* 15: 155–251.

———. 1949. "Notes Démographiques sur la Région de Labé." In P. Pélissier (ed.), *Hommage à Jacques Richard-Molard* (1913–1951). Special Issue of *Présence Africaine* 15: 83–94.

———. 1951. "Les Densités de Population au Fouta-Djallon." In P. Pélissier (ed.), *Hommage à Jacques Richard-Molard* (1913–1951). Special Issue of *Présence Africaine* 15: 95–106.

Rodney, W. 1968. *"Jihad* and Social Revolution in the Fouta Djallon in the Eighteenth Century." *Journal of the Historical Society of Nigeria* IV: 269–284.

Saul, J. and R. Woods. 1971. "African Peasantries." In A. Shanin (ed.), *Peasants and Peasant Societies*. Middlesex, England: Penguin.

Skinner, E. 1966. "Group Dynamics in the Politics of Changing Societies." In J. Helm (ed.), *The Problem of Tribe*. Proceedings of the American Ethnological Society, Seattle.

Smith, P. 1965. "Les Diakhanke, Histoire d'une Dispersion." *Bulletins et Mémoires de la Société d'Anthropologie de Paris* 8, 11th s.

Sow, A. I. (ed.). 1966. *La Femme, La Vache, La Foi: Ecrivains et Poètes du Fouta-Djallon*. Paris: Julliard Press.

Stenning, D. J. 1959. *Savannah Nomads: A Study of the Wodaabe Pastoral Fulani of Western Province, Nigeria*. London: Oxford University Press.

Suret-Canale, J. 1959. "La Guinée dans le Système Colonial." *Présence Africaine* 29: 9–44.

———. 1964a. *L'Afrique Noire: L'Ere Coloniale (1900–1945)*. Paris: Editions Sociales.

———. 1964b. "Les Sociétés Traditionelles en Afrique tropical et le Concept de Mode de Production asiatique." *La Pensée* 177: 21–42.

———. 1966. "La Fin de la Chefferie en Guinée." *Journal of African History* 7: 459–493.

1969. "Les Origins Ethniques des Anciens Captifs au Fouta Djalon." *Notes Africaines.* 123: 91–92. Dakar.

n.d. Manuscript

Tauxier, L. 1937. *Moeurs et Histoire des Peuls.* Paris: Payot.

Touré, Sékou. 1964. *Le 8 Novembre 1964.* Conakry: Government of Guinea.

n.d. *Action Politique du P.D.G.* XII. Conakry: Government of Guinea.

n.d. *Le Pouvoir Populaire.* XVI. Conakry: Government of Guinea.

Trimingham, J. S. 1959. *Islam in West Africa.* London: Oxford University Press.

1962. *A History of Islam in West Africa.* London: Oxford University Press.

Tuden, A. and L. Plotnicov. 1970. "Introduction." In A. Tuden & L. Plotnicov (eds.), *Social Stratification in Africa.* New York: Free Press.

Van den Berghe, P. (ed.). 1965. *Africa: Social Problems of Change and Conflict.* San Francisco: Chandler Press.

Vieillard, G. 1939. *Notes sur les Coutumes des Peuls du Fouta-Djallon.* Paris: Larousse.

1940. *Notes sur les Peuls du Fouta-Djallon.* Paris: Institut Fondamental d'Afrique Noire, Bulletin 7.

Weber, M. 1947. *The Theory of Social and Economic Organization.* Glencoe: Free Press.

Wallerstein, I. 1960. "Ethnicity and National Integration in Africa." *Cahiers d'Etudes Africaines* 3: 129–139.

Watson, W. 1958. *Tribal Cohesion in a Money Economy: A Study of the Mambwe People of Northern Rhodesia.* Manchester: Manchester University Press.

Watt, T. and W. Winterbottom. 1803. "Travels in Sierra Leone." In R. Hallett (ed.), *The Penetration of Africa.* Vol. I. New York: Praeger, 1965.

Wolf, E. R. 1966. *Peasants.* Englewood Cliffs, N.J.: Prentice-Hall.

1969. *Peasant Wars of the Twentieth Century.* New York: Harper & Row.

UNPUBLISHED MATERIAL

National Archives of Guinea:
Instructions for a Mission to the Fouta-Djallon. October 16, 1891.
Economic Report for Labe. 1903.
Gauthier, P. Monographs on the Cercle of Labe. 1908

Institut Fondamental d'Afrique Noire:
Fonds Vieillard, Manuscripts at Dakar. Catalogued by T. Diallo, M. M'Backe et al., Dakar.

Index

Adamwa: place, 28n; mythological person, 31

Adultery, 197

Adulthood for males, 198, 214

Affines, 41–42, 67–68, 72, 76, 85, 92–93, 98–100, 104, 118, 142, 210–211, 218, 220

Age-mates (*goree*), 68, 75–78, 85, 107, 194–195, 197, 219, 235

Agriculture, 25, 121; slash-and-burn, 25, 140; primitive, 61–62; Nupe, 122n; on mountainsides, 134–135, 142. *See also* Cash-crop gardens; Fields; Women's gardens

Ahmad al Tijani, 212n

Ahmadu, *Almamy*, 43

Alfayas, 16–17, 22, 43

Alfa Yaya (*chef de canton*), 10

Alfa Yaya (province chief), 26–27, 44–45, 50

Algeria, 212n

Allah: sanctions of, 184, 185; and punishment, 191; and destiny, 192, 215, 232–233; and funeral ceremonies, 211; power of, 236. *See also* Islam

Alluwal: ceremony, 206–207, 223; plank, 222, 231

Almamy: Fouta, 2, 7, 14, 16–17, 19–20, 37n, 43–44, 47, 49, 50; the term, 14; of a *misside* or mosque, 23, 61, 191, 212–213, 215; of Labe, 24, 33; of Popodara, 24, 217–218; of former serf mosques, 246

Alphabet, Guinean, 250

Ameillon, B., 6

Animals: domesticated, 26, 83, 121; sacrifice of, 39, 42, 93–94, 147, 210, 211, 215, 216, 218–219, 223; and the market, 166. *See also* Cattle; Chickens; Goats; Sheep

Anthropologists, social, 58–59

Ardoobe (those who have been brought), 32

Artisans. *See* Basket-makers; Black-

smiths; Cloth, weavers; Crafts; Embroidery; Leather workers; Sandal-makers

Ashanti, 151

Asiatic Mode of Production, 15

Asking, 103, 109; again, 105, 109

Atwood, William, 6

Avoidance, 76, 98–99

Ba, a "family" name, 18, 19

Babyhood, 194. *See also* Childhood; Children

Baga, 13

Baledyo, 249

Bambara, 33

Bantingnel, 8

Baredyeli, 209. *See also* Circumcision

Bari, a "family" name, 18, 19

Barnes, 64

Barter, 26. *See also* Markets; Merchants; Trade

Basket-makers, 38, 157, 159, 164, 165

Bastards, 88

Bayol, 43

Beng Mata, 87

Bénot, Yves, 6

Binde Pellung, 87, 100, 101, 188–190

Blacksmiths, 37–38, 52–53, 145n, 156–158, 164

Bokar Biro, 44

Bolonda, Hollaande as a, 91

Bouria, 14

Bridewealth, 32, 39, 41, 83, 93, 104, 109–112, 115–118, 151, 153, 243, 244

Brode, John, 63

Brokensha, D., 62–63, 64n

Brothers: relations between, 72–73; relations with sisters, 73–74

Bureau Fédéral, 176

Bureau Politique Nationale, 176

Bush: maximal lineage, 48; Fulbe (*see* Fulbe of the bush)

Butchers, 53, 59, 161, 165–166, 170–172, 239

273